I0808139

BRIAN KELLY

THE CUT-UPS 2

More Tattoo Flash from the Third Mind

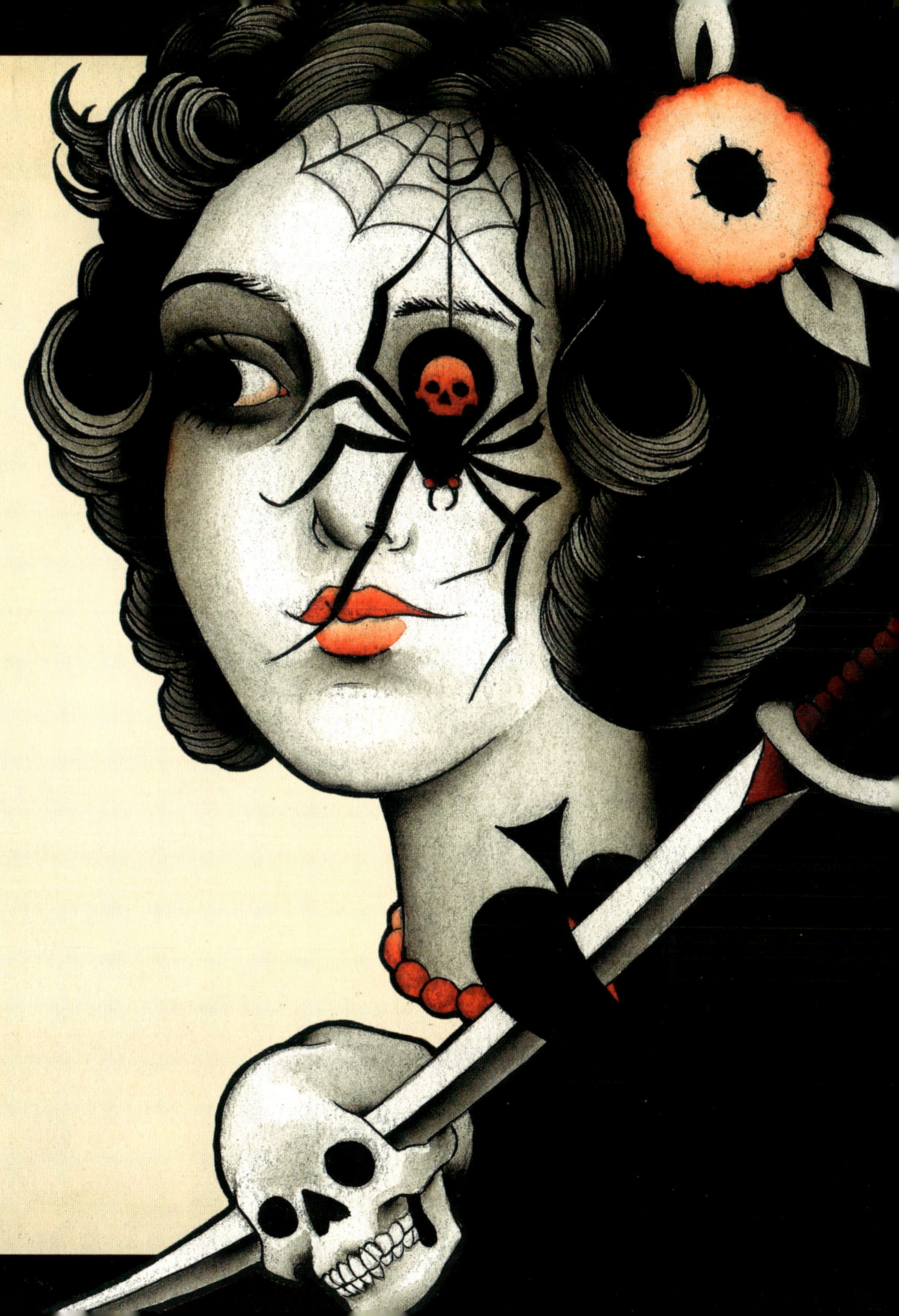

SCHIFFER PUBLISHING

4880 Lower Valley Road • Atglen, PA 19310

Text Copyright © 2025 by Brian Kelly
Photographs Copyright © 2025 by Brian Kelly

All rights reserved. No part of this work may be reproduced or used in any form or by any means—graphic, electronic, or mechanical, including photocopying or information storage and retrieval systems—without written permission from the publisher.

The scanning, uploading, and distribution of this book or any part thereof via the Internet or any other means without the permission of the publisher is illegal and punishable by law. Please purchase only authorized editions and do not participate in or encourage the electronic piracy of copyrighted materials.

"Schiffer," "Schiffer Publishing, Ltd.," and the pen and inkwell logo are registered trademarks of Schiffer Publishing, Ltd.

Designed by Molly Shields
Cover design by Justin Watkinson
Type set in Times LT Std/Cambria

ISBN: 978-0-7643-6937-7
ePub: 978-1-5073-0543-0

Printed in India
Library of Congress Control Number: 2024941572

Published by Schiffer Publishing, Ltd.
4880 Lower Valley Road
Atglen, PA 19310
Phone: (610) 593-1777; Fax: (610) 593-2002
Email: info@schifferbooks.com
Web: www.schifferbooks.com

For our complete selection of fine books on this and related subjects, please visit our website at www.schifferbooks.com. You may also write for a free catalog.

Schiffer Publishing's titles are available at special discounts for bulk purchases for sales promotions or premiums. Special editions, including personalized covers, corporate imprints, and excerpts, can be created in large quantities for special needs. For more information, contact the publisher.

FSC MIX Paper | Supporting responsible forestry FSC™ C016779

This book is dedicated to all the flash painters.

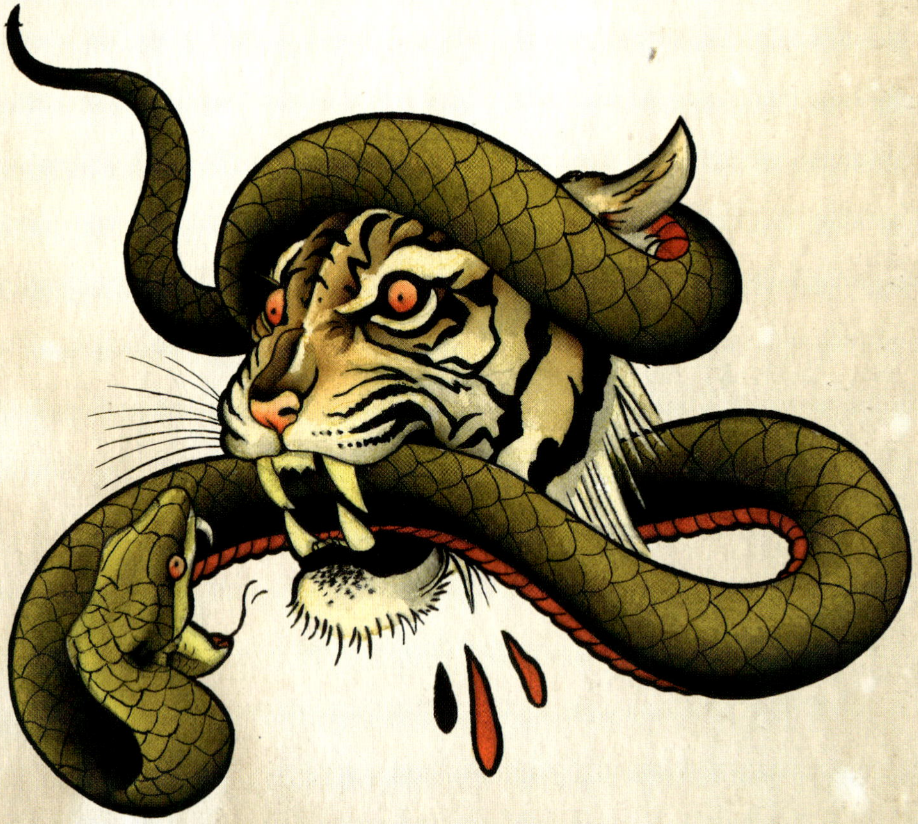

Contents

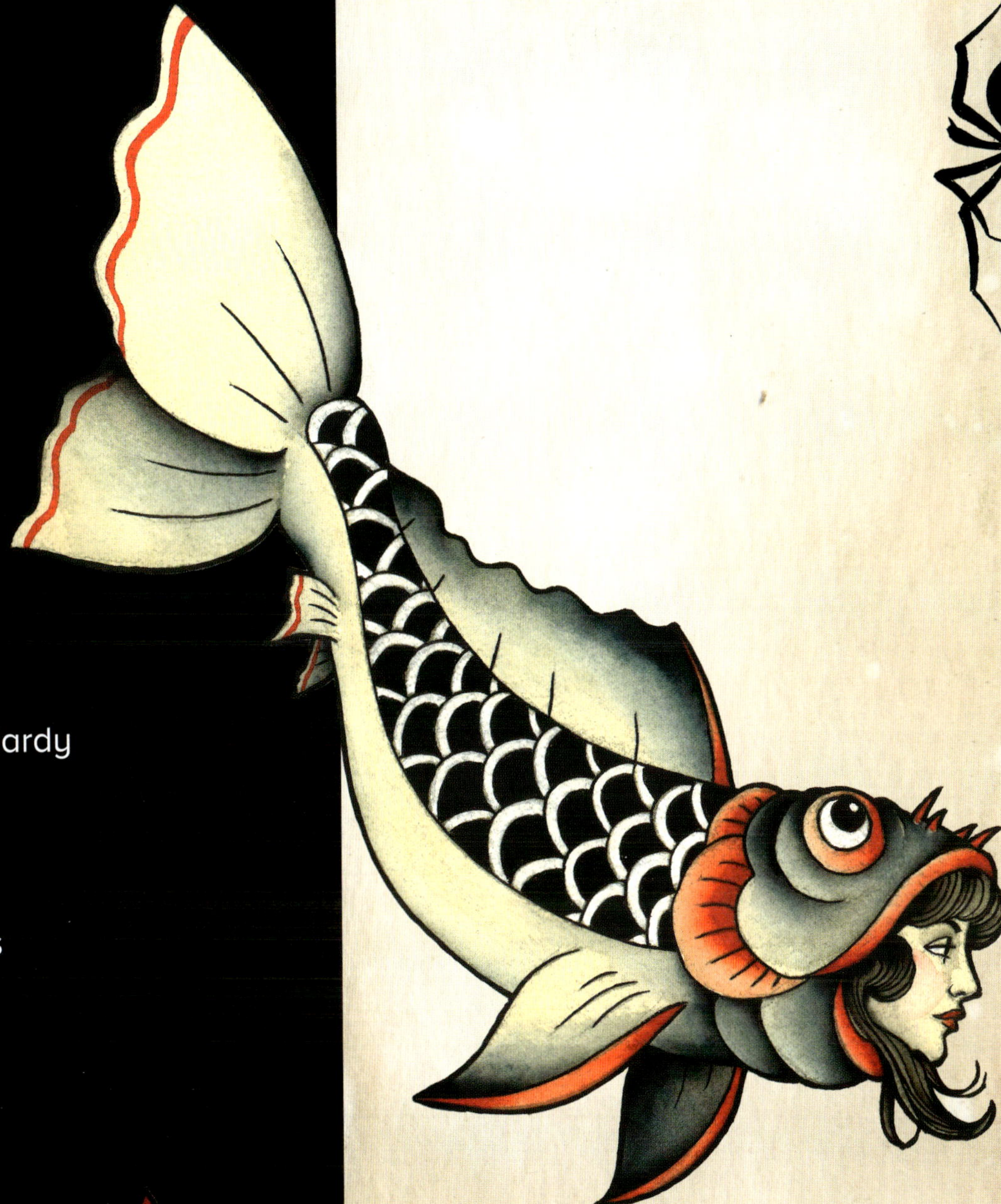

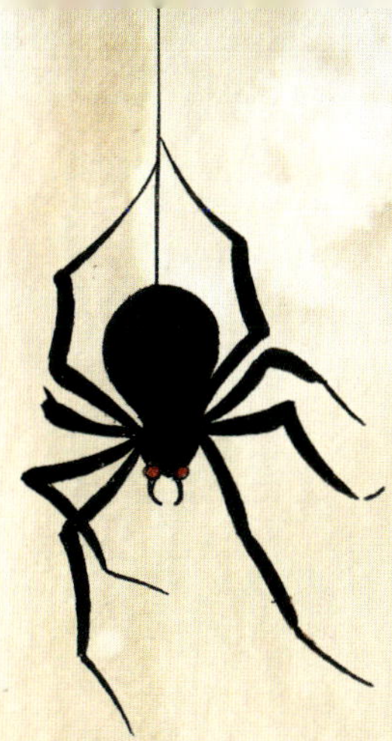

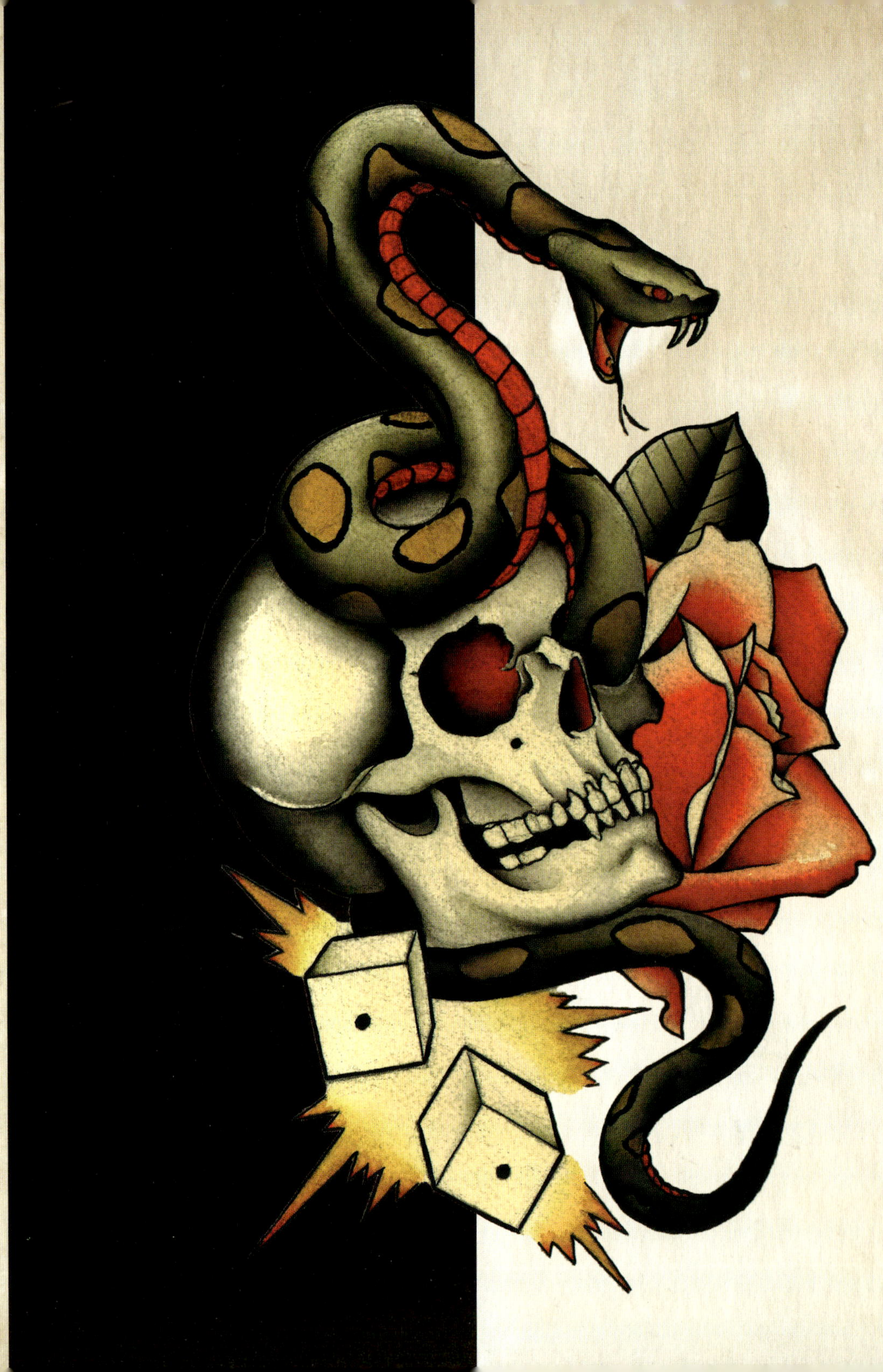

Foreword

As a young child I would look in fascination at the tattoos emblazoned on the arms of my Uncles Peter and Fred, who had sailed with the British Royal Navy, and at the ones my Uncle Bobby had acquired as a young Teddy Boy during the rock 'n' roll heyday of the 1950s.

The full-rigged galleons conjured up images in my mind of pirate ships and swashbuckling adventures on the high seas. The rose with its scroll bearing the words "Mary, my wild Irish rose" reminded me of my Auntie's family's roots in the Emerald Isle.

I loved reading the names of the places my uncles had served in and visited. In an era long before the internet and satellite TV, my young mind was fired up by these inky inscriptions upon the skin.

As I reached my midteenage years, I developed a love for rock 'n' roll music and started to frequent pubs and clubs where this music was found. At these clubs were Teddy Boys, resplendent in their drape suits. Many Teds sported tattoos, and that is when my interest in this ancient art was truly ignited.

In 1976, I went under the tattoo needle for the first time, and my life changed forever. Within the little studio, I stared at all the images we now call tattoo flash. In those days, many old-timers called the sheets of designs show cards, a throwback, no doubt, to the days of carnivals, sideshows, and circuses, where the tattooist and tattooed lady could be found.

As my thirst for knowledge regarding tattooing raged, I drank in as much information as I could regarding images and their origins, inspirations, creators, and meanings.

Early pioneers, such as Lew "the Jew" Alberts, Brooklyn Joe Lieber, Ben Corday, William Grimshaw, Charles Burchett Davis, Cash Cooper, Alexander Gordon, Pinky Yun, and, of course, Sailor Jerry Collins, were names I discovered.

Later, I discovered contemporary flash designers such as Mike "Rollo" Malone with his "The flash that makes you cash" slogan. In the UK, there were Roy Proudlove, Graham Townshend, Ron Ackers, and Tony Clifton, who I believe produced the first full-color flash in the UK. By the mid-1980s, full flash was readily available from the likes of Cherry Creek and J. D. Crowe, with the great art of Lynne Yowell.

Flash, though, seemed to make a bit of a decline as new technology, such as tablets and iPads, became popular. However, many artists still love to paint flash in the time-honored tradition of spit shading and rollerball lining. Many used the old classics as inspiration and started to create new flash with a twist.

I am an avid collector of flash and flash books. Whilst looking through books at a tattoo convention, I discovered the book *The Cut-Ups: Tattoo Flash from the Third Mind* by Brian Kelly. As I flipped through the pages, I was drawn to the eclectic nature of the designs and, upon reading the introduction page, I learned that Kelly had used the inspiration of the cut-up technique to create the designs. This novel approach is refreshing and unique. I found the book inspirational and a great reference source.

Such was the success of the volume that you now hold in your hands volume 2 of *The Cut-Ups*, which I'm sure you will find exceedingly pleasing to the eye, and, like the previous volume, a great source of inspiration.

Brian Kelly truly is a machine when it comes to creating and painting flash, and he most certainly is a major player in promoting and preserving this important form of folk art.

Lal Hardy
London, 2024

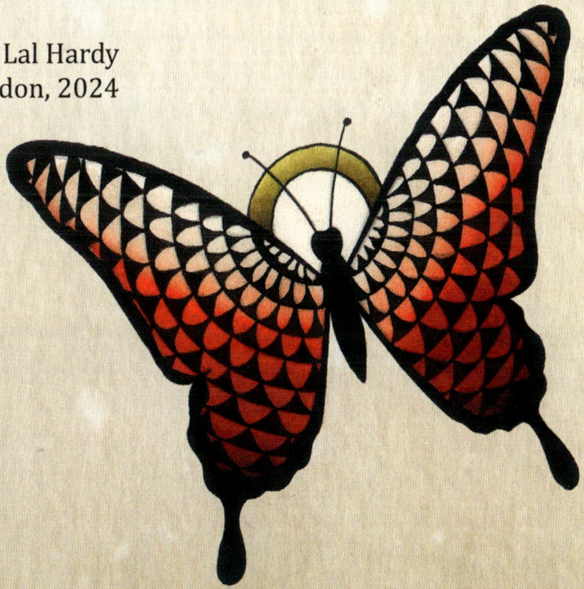

Introduction

This is a continuation of my last book, *The Cut-Ups: Tattoo Flash from the Third Mind.* If you haven't already picked it up, you should. I go into more detail about the cut-up technique in the introduction to that book. Briefly, cut-ups are randomly chosen elements spliced together. Tattoo flash are the design sheets that you see in traditional tattoo shops. When you walk in and are met with a wall of images, generally of skulls and snakes, of daggers and women. Sometimes flash may be displayed in a folder on a table, or in racks on the wall that the customer flips through. My method for creating cut-up tattoo flash is that I have a box. In the box, I have many pages of tattoo flash, photocopied from my vast collection of mostly vintage tattoo flash books, and the images have been cut in half. I usually make photocopies of the flash on used pages of scrap paper: pages that have other pictures of tattoo images drawn on them, or sketches of tattoos for clients. Sometimes the scrap paper has some German contract about something or other, explained in excessive detail. I then cut the photocopies of tattoo flash in half, place them in the box, and shuffle them around. When I make my flash pages, I draw two pieces of cut-up paper out of the box for each image. Sometimes the images come out almost fully formed. One of the two cut-up pieces of paper will have the photocopied image imposed over the images already on the scrap paper, creating a mind-blowing idea. The second piece of cut-up paper may be disregarded or used to add elements to the initially selected piece of paper. Other times, it takes a lot of effort to create something out of the two very disparate pieces of paper that have come out of the cut-up box. It may be the cut-off legs of a woman on one piece of paper and the cut-off handle of a dagger surrounded by contractual German language on the other. Once the ideas are formed, or deciphered, from the cut-up images, I draw directly onto my paper that I will use for the flash page I am creating. I am not too picky about the brand of paper I paint on, as long as it is cotton paper. Smooth grain, rough grain; I like to use them all. After the images are drawn on, I usually coffee-stain the paper and paint with only brushes. Yes: all lines, excluding the borders, are painted with a tiny brush. I have a second, bigger brush that I use for shading the ink with the spit-shading technique. Spit shading is a technique where one brush is used to apply ink to the paper, and a second brush is used to dilute the ink to create a fade. The painter controls the amount of moisture on the brush by sticking it in their mouth and using saliva to control the amount of pigment being blended out; hence the name "spit shading."

I'm writing this in 2024 in Berlin, Germany. I started tattooing in 2002 in Minneapolis, Minnesota, USA. I lived in and tattooed in Ireland before I moved to Berlin, and I've also tattooed in many countries in Europe and several states in the USA. Tattooing has brought so much to my life and taken me on a wild ride. The last few years have been quite strange for tattooing; 2020 and 2021 saw tattooing in Germany closed for a period of time because of the coronavirus pandemic. This gave me a lot of time to paint much of the tattoo flash in this book. As Europe finally emerged from the long lockdowns, the EU decided to ban all available inks on the market for tattooing. The lockdowns had distracted most of us from this impending calamity, and I was caught off guard. I knew the EU would ban pigments that make up blue and green inks, which I had been okay with. I even made some flash with that fact in mind. Limiting my color palette is kind of interesting. When all the colors became illegal, however, I decided to focus on making more black-and-gray tattoo flash. While there are now legal colors available again (though no one can attest to how well they will age), I've grown to like black-and-gray tattooing more and more. It's a lot easier!

Along with the legal challenges facing tattooers in the EU, technological advances have also greatly changed tattooing. More and more tattooers work with electric pens. Most young tattooers find an iPad as important to tattooing as a pencil was to us older tattooers. I, however, have stuck to my coil tattoo machines. The coil tattoo machine is the one that most people think of when they think of a tattoo machine. It makes a buzzing noise, telling you the pain is coming. It looks heavy and unwieldy. When I fly on airplanes with my tattoo machines, I am usually stopped at security after the machines go through the metal detector. Half the time the security people know what they are; the other half let me pass despite their misgivings. I like the noise of the coil machines, and it took me so long to figure out how to use them that I've decided I might as well stick with them. All the tattoo flash in this book was painted on paper. I don't think I stick to using paper only because it took me so long to learn how to paint on it. I like to paint on paper. I like the errors that occur and the corrections needed to fix things. Bob Ross would call them happy accidents. My girlfriend also enjoys coming home and seeing my ink-stained lips from spit shading all day. It makes life more interesting. Of course, I may just be stuck in my ways.

I hope you enjoy this book and that it inspires you to create tattoo flash of your own. All images in this book may be tattooed as is. In fact, I would love to see them if you do!

Brian Kelly
Berlin, 2024

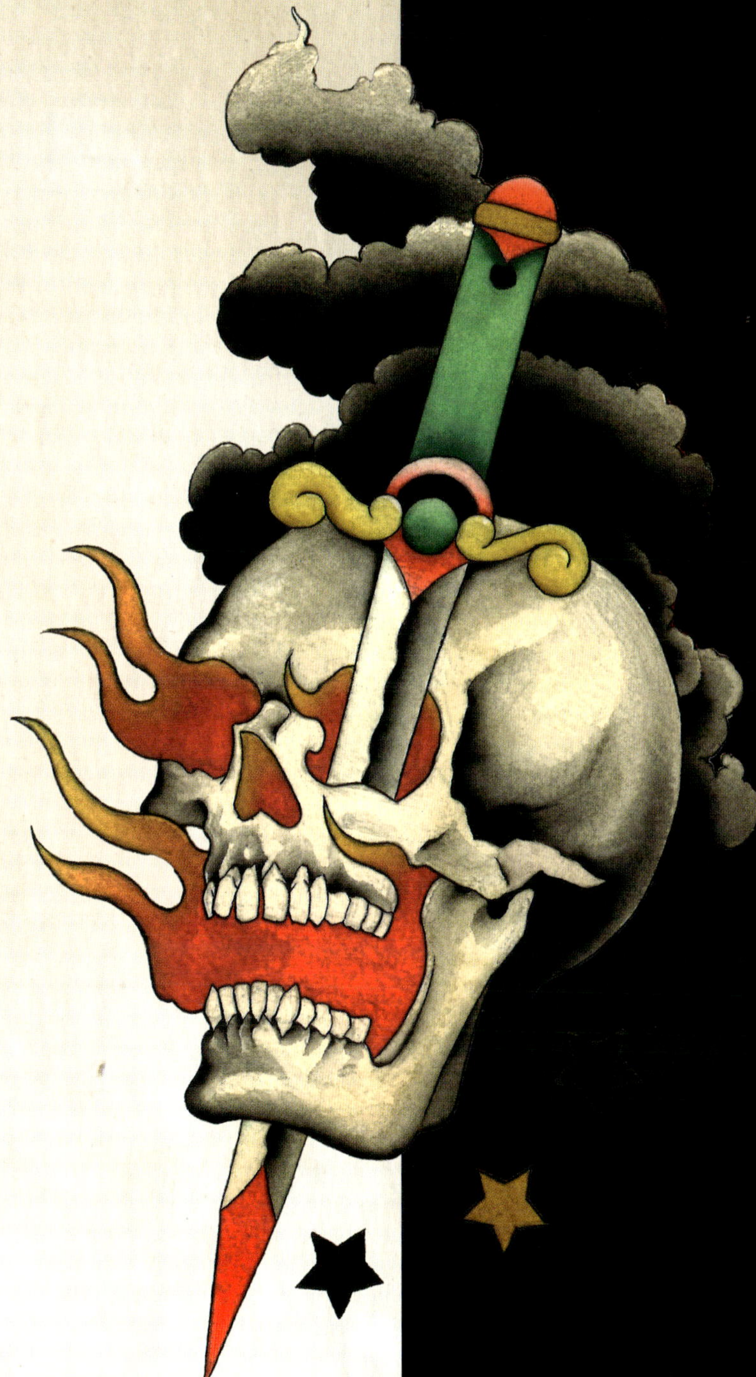

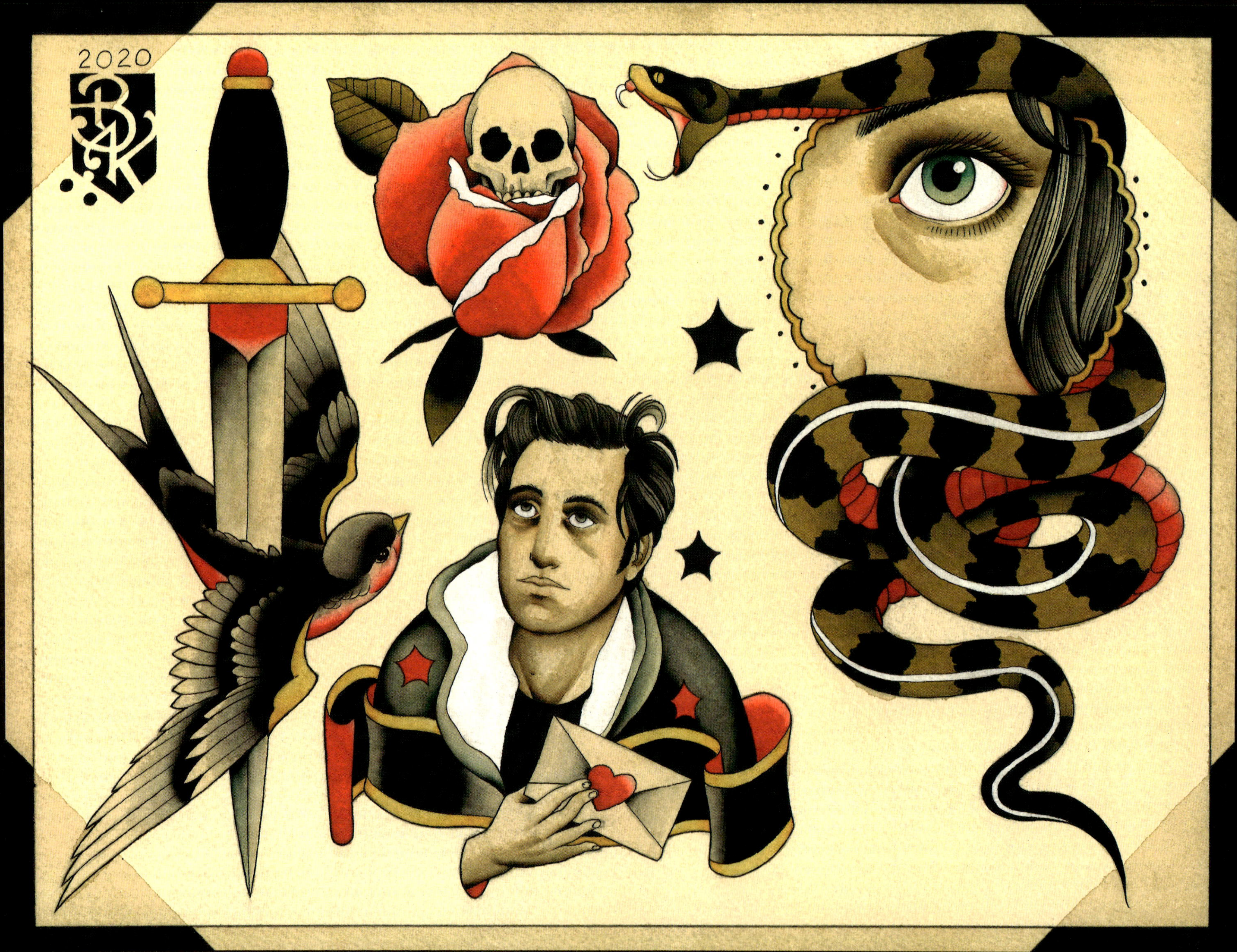
2020

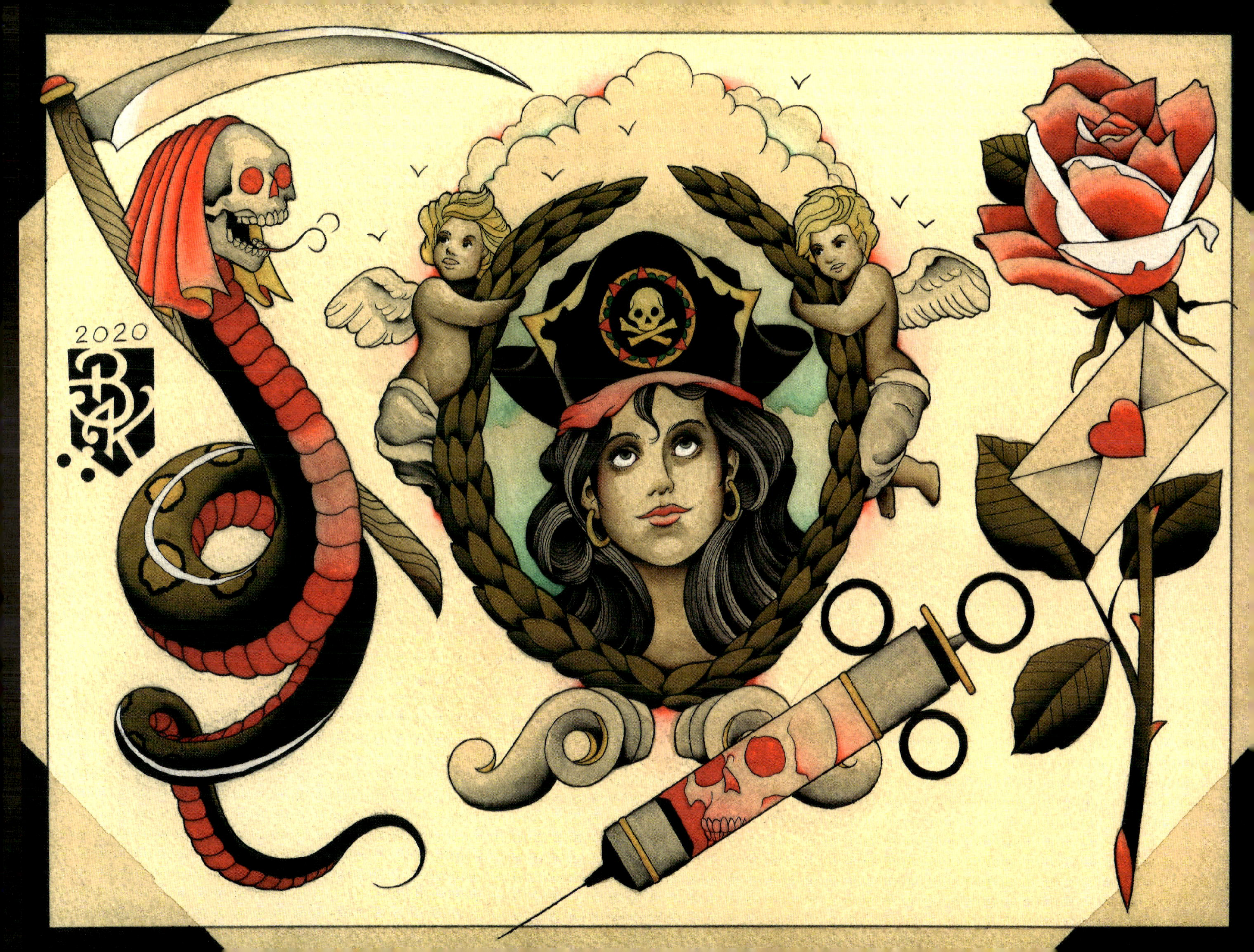
2020

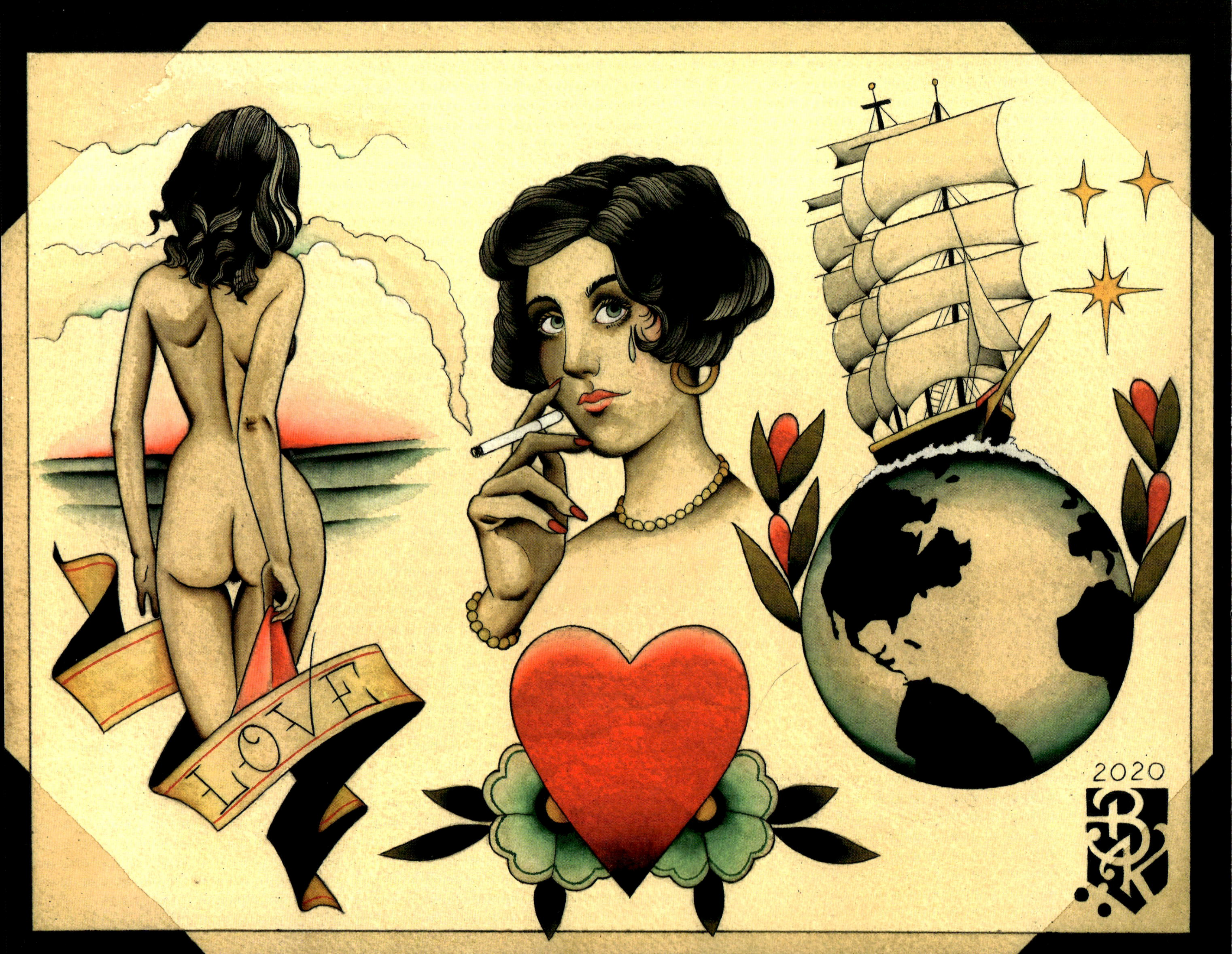
LOVE
2020

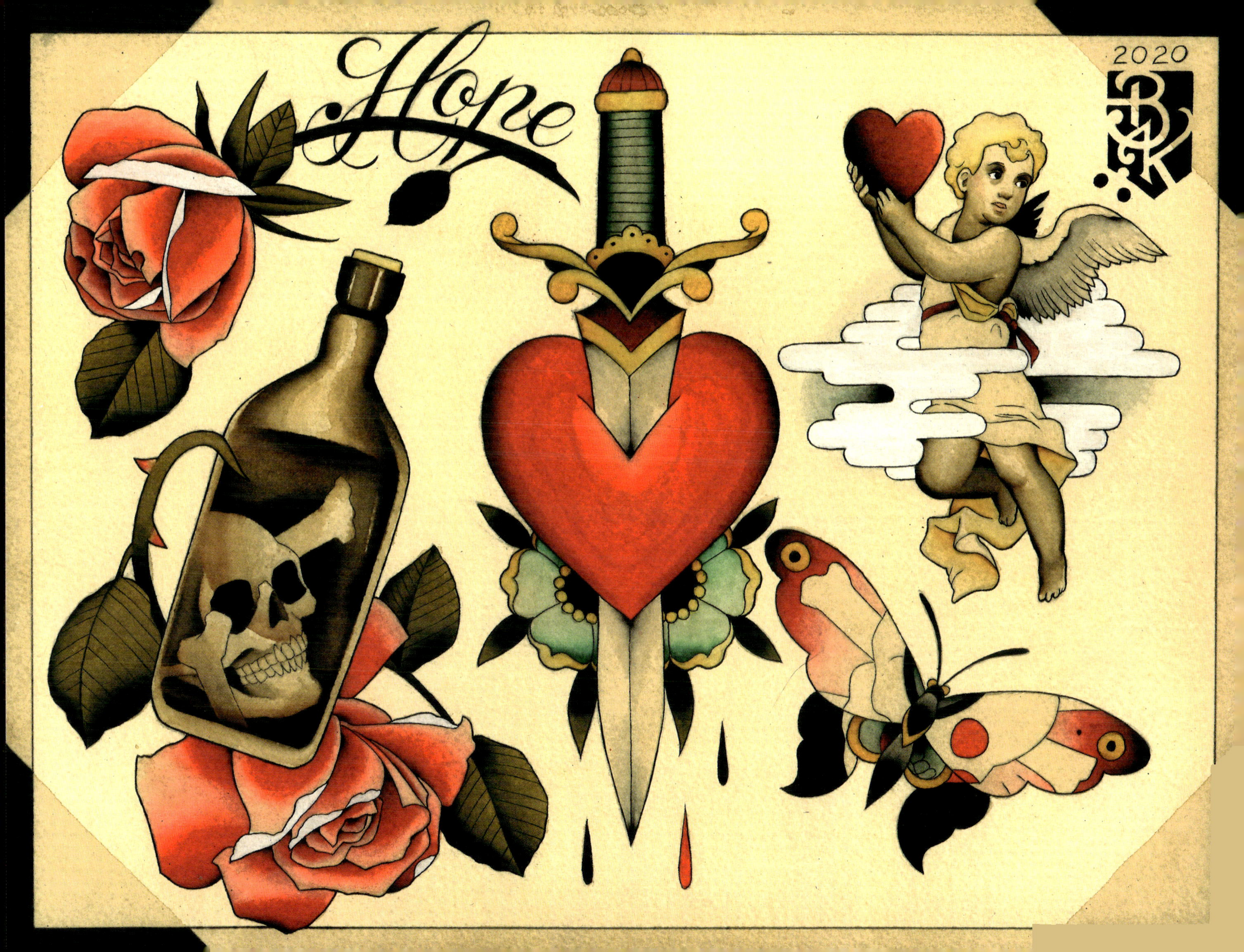
Hope
2020

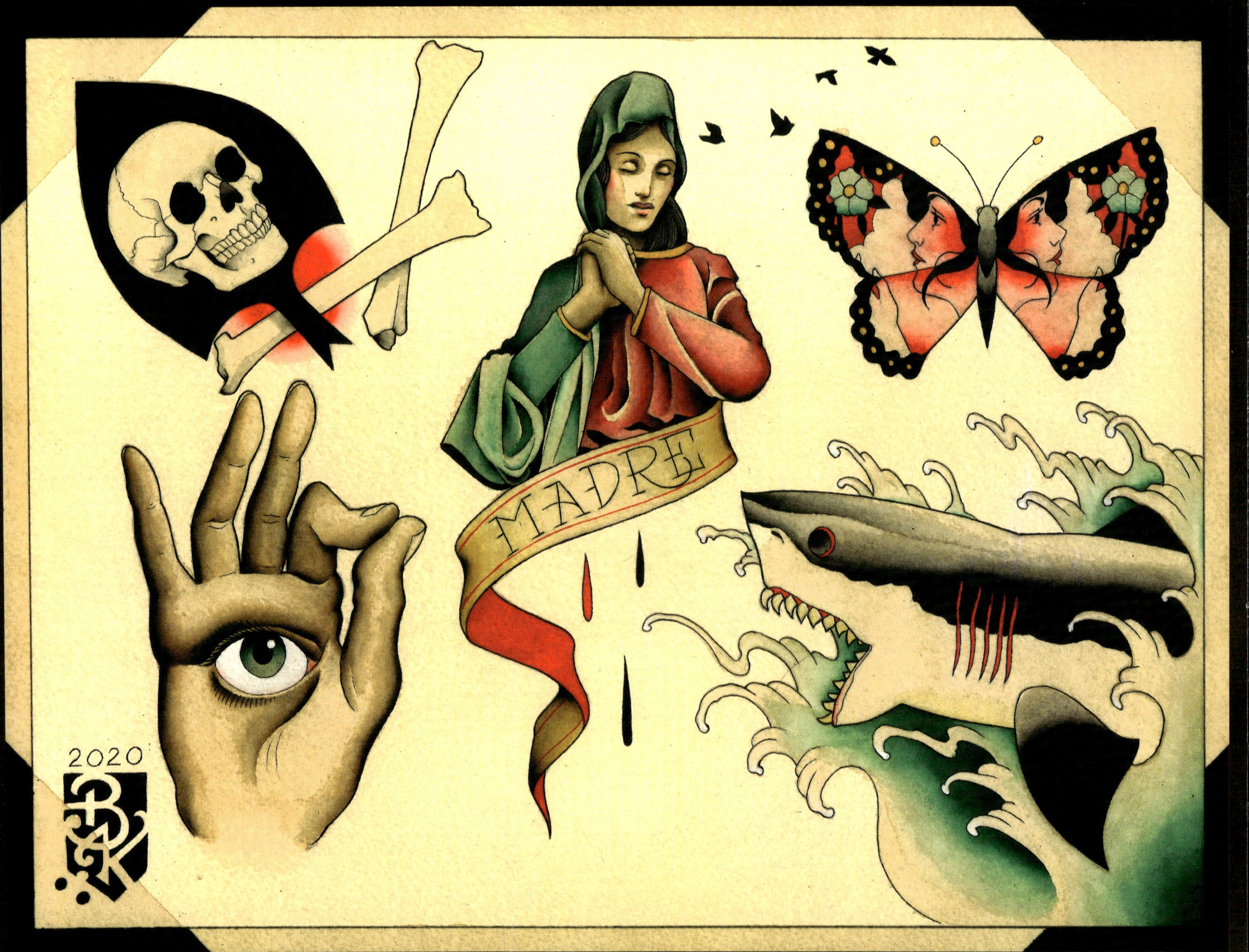
MADRE
2020

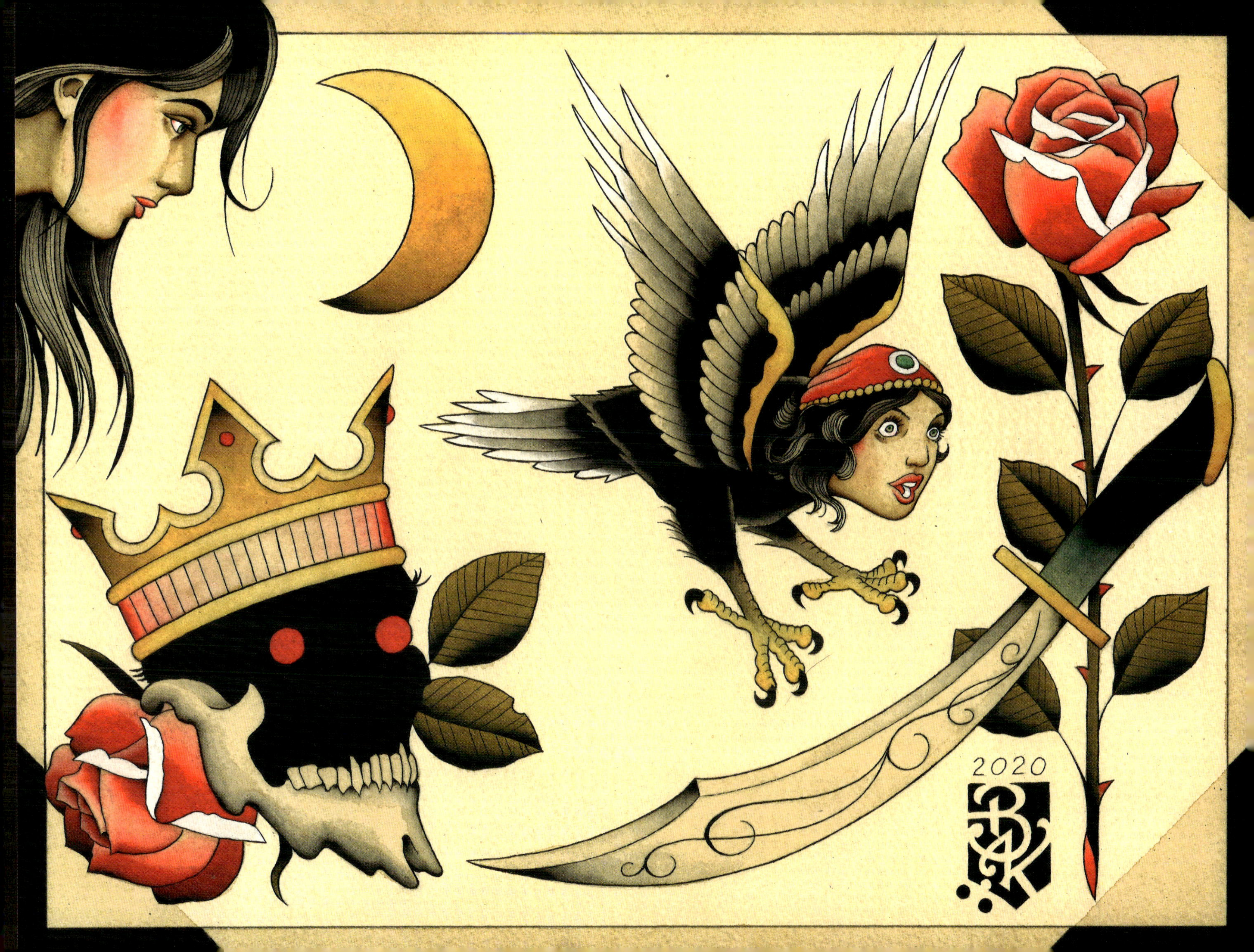
2020

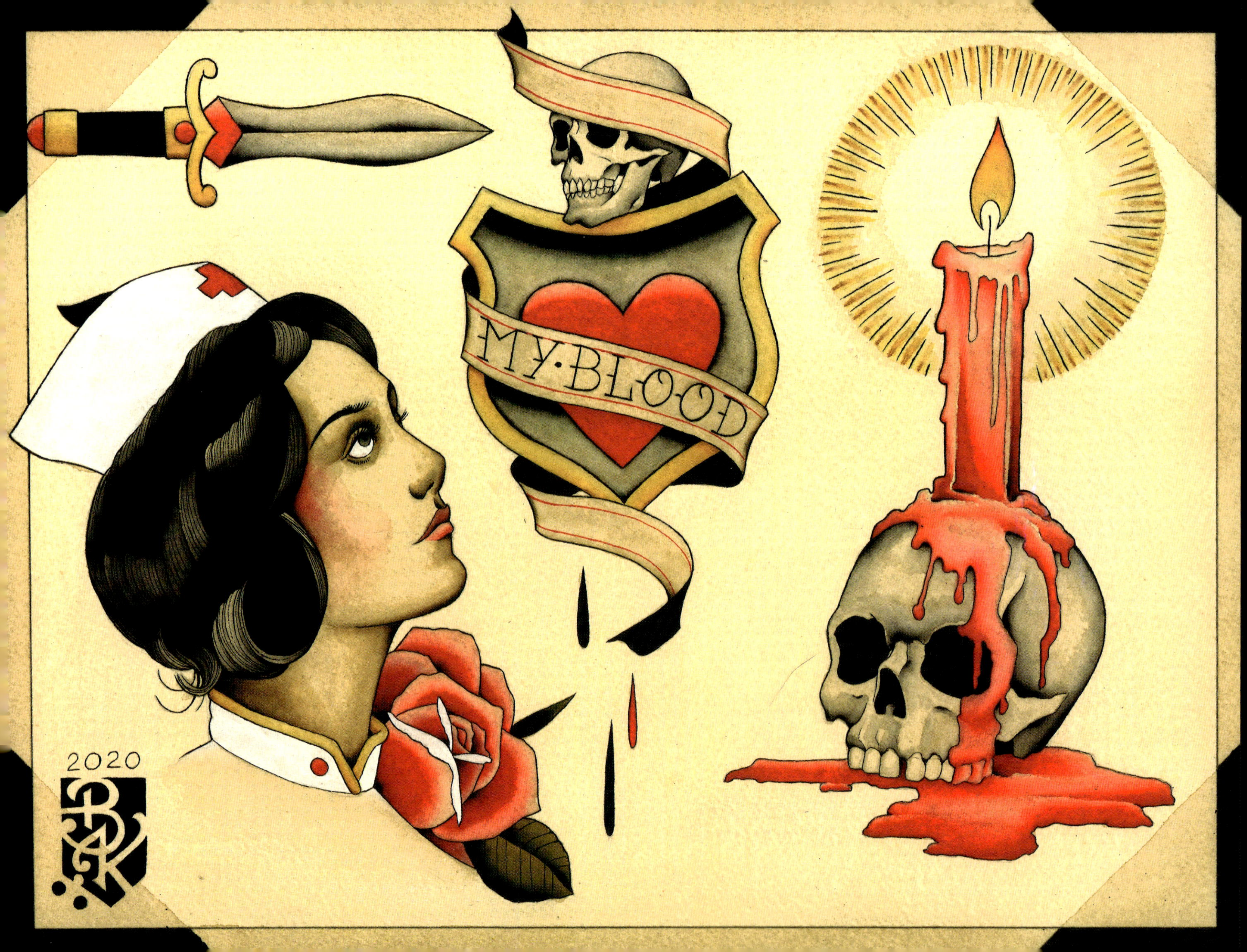
MY·BLOOD
2020

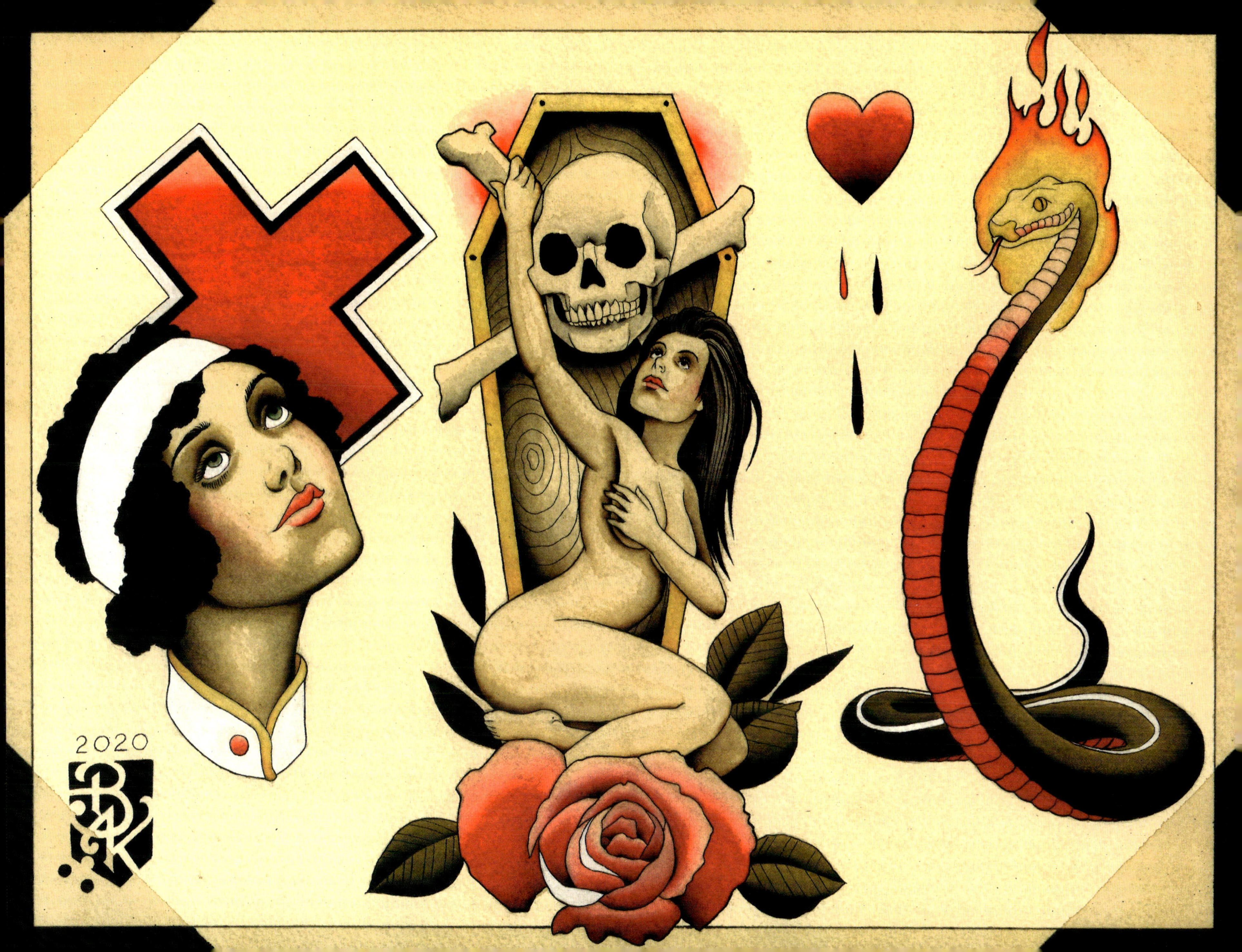
2020

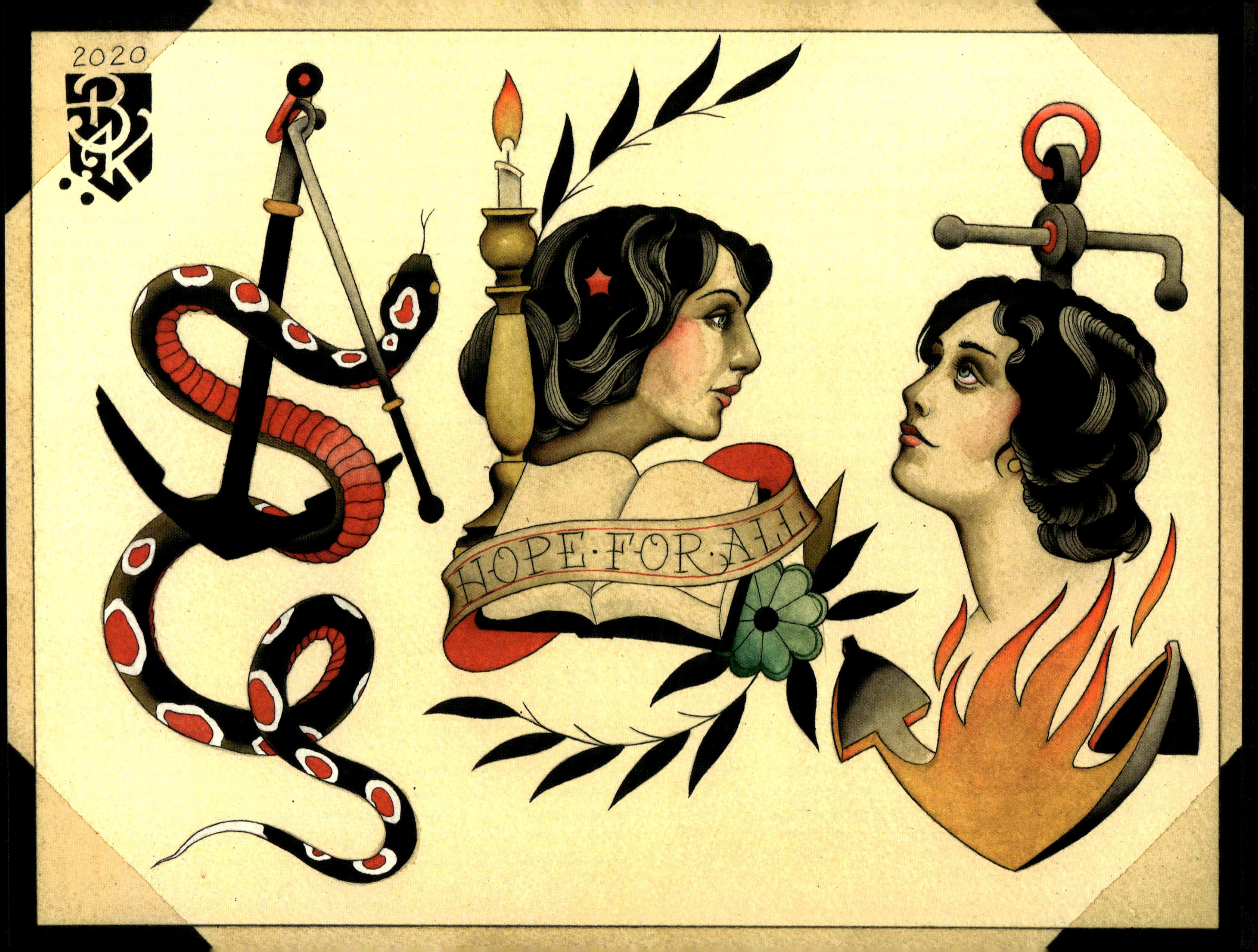
2020
HOPE·FOR·ALL

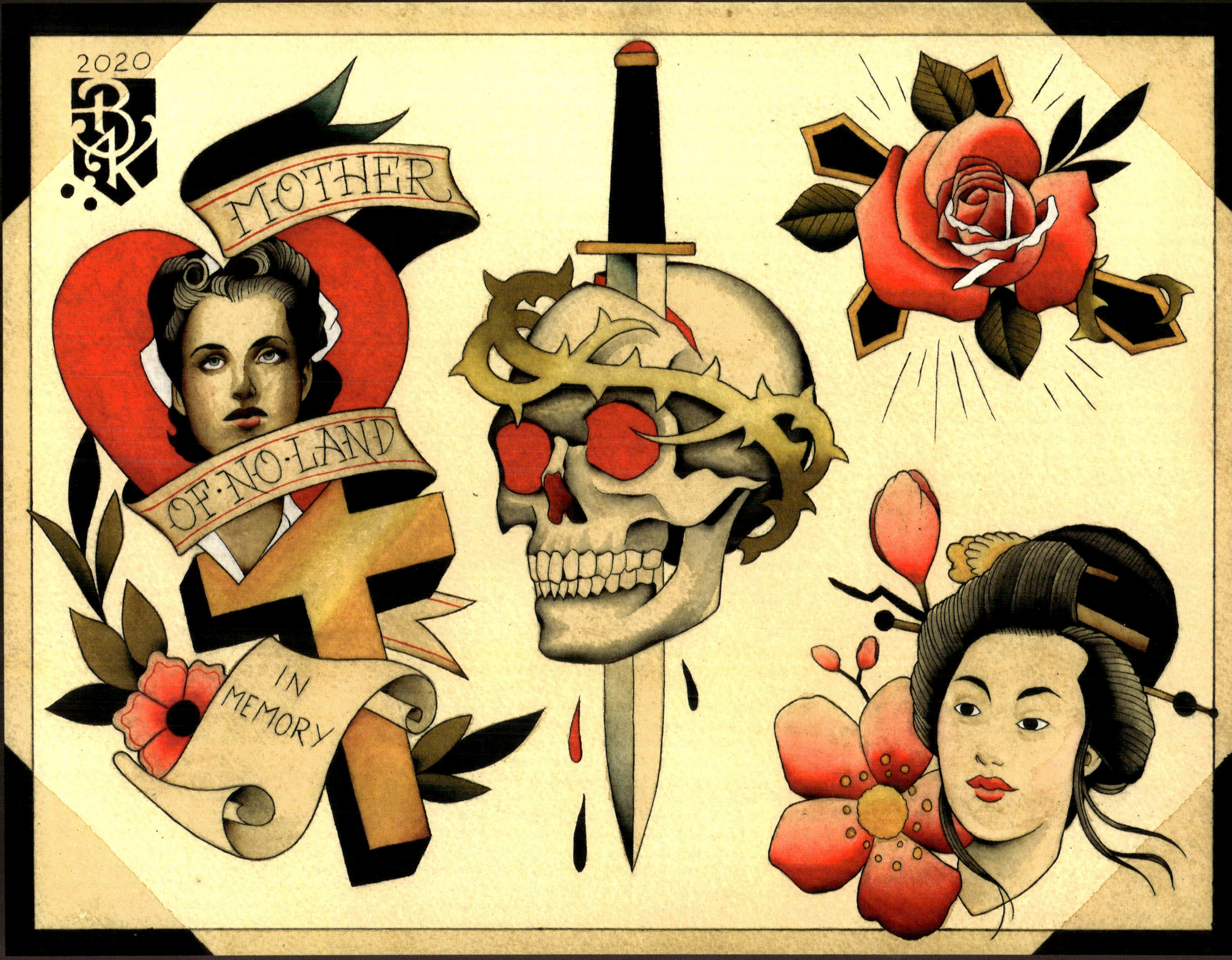
2020
MOTHER
OF·NO·LAND
IN
MEMORY

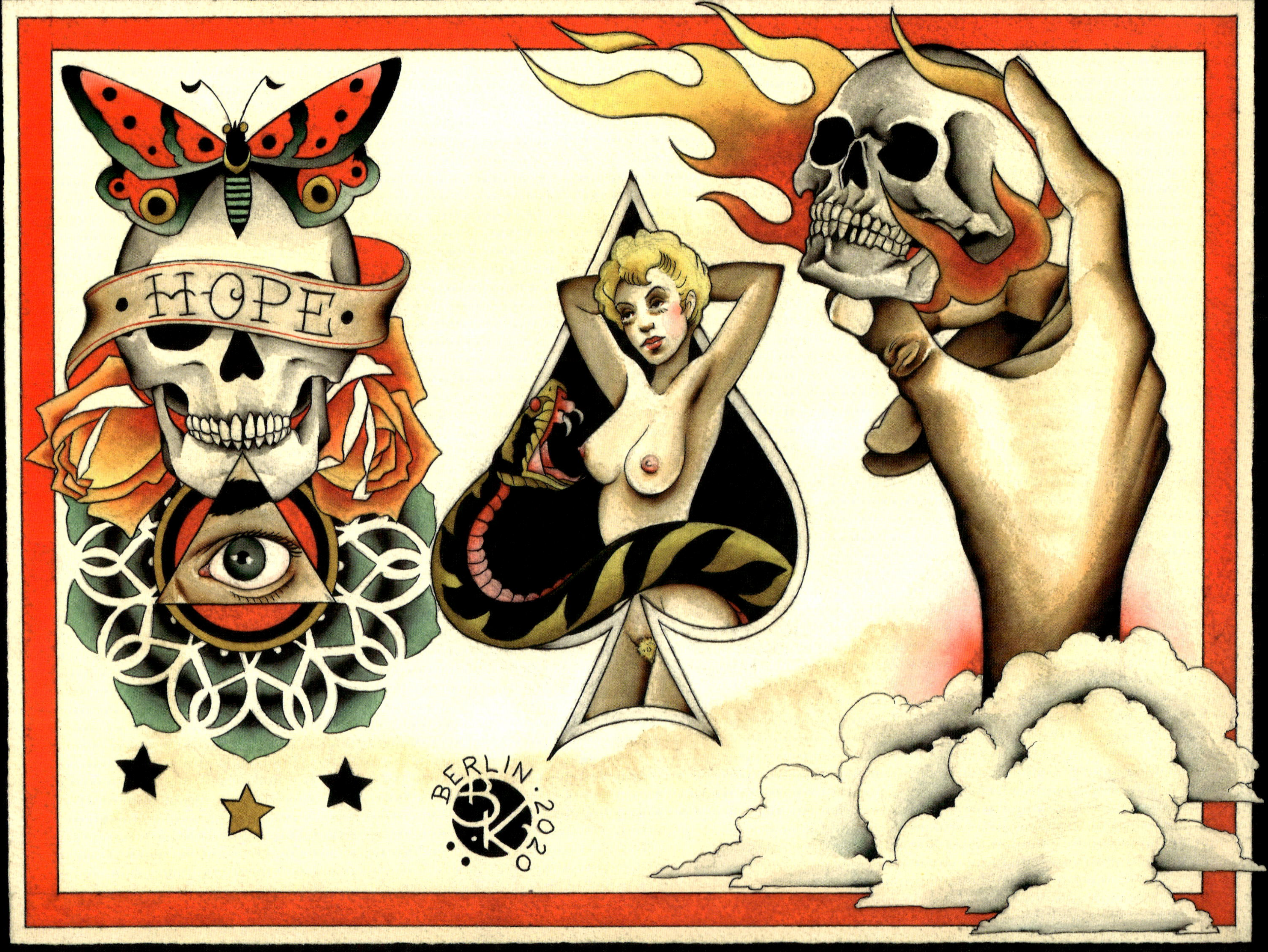
HOPE
BERLIN
2020

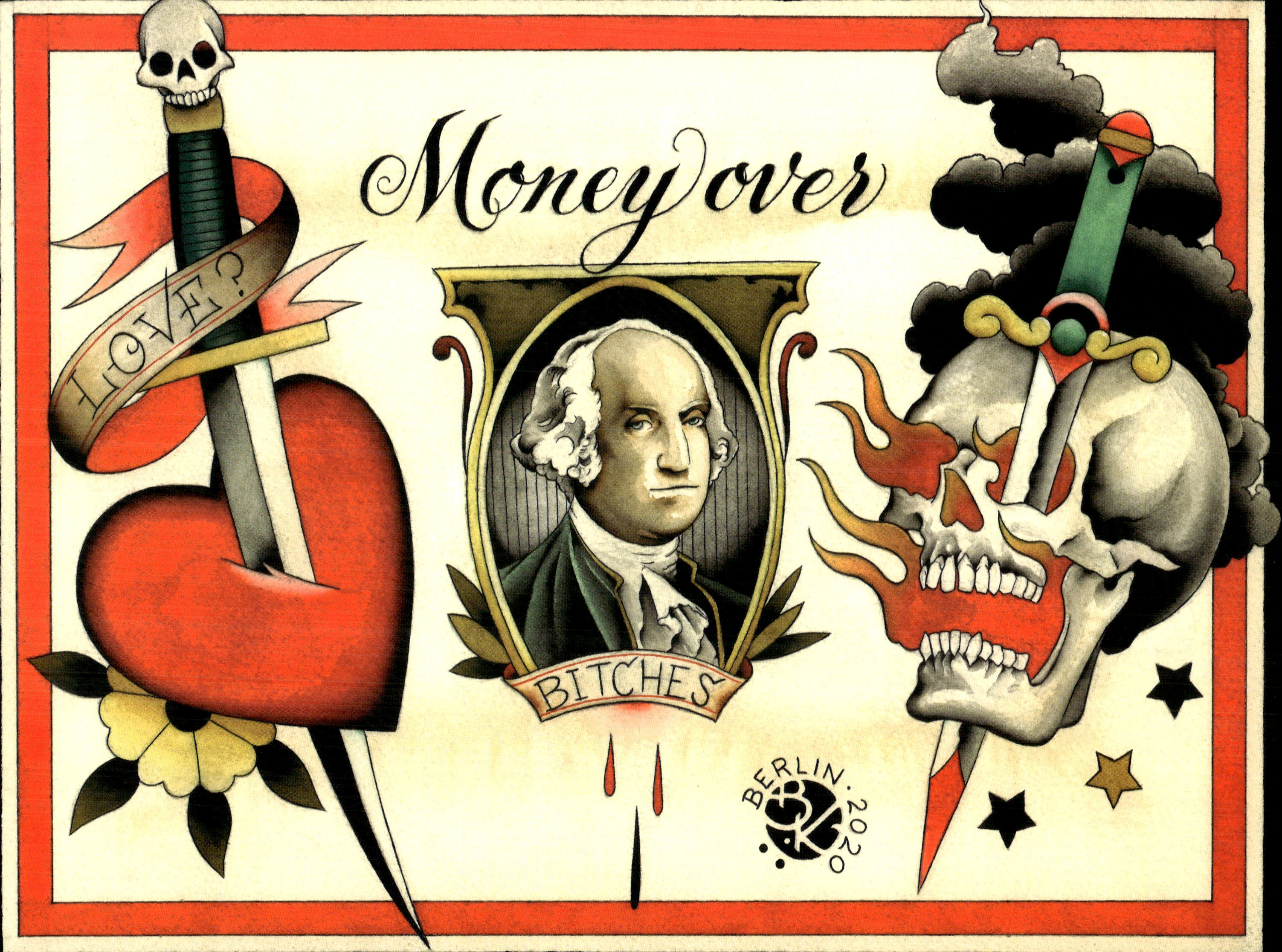
Money over
LOVE?
BITCHES
BERLIN. 2020

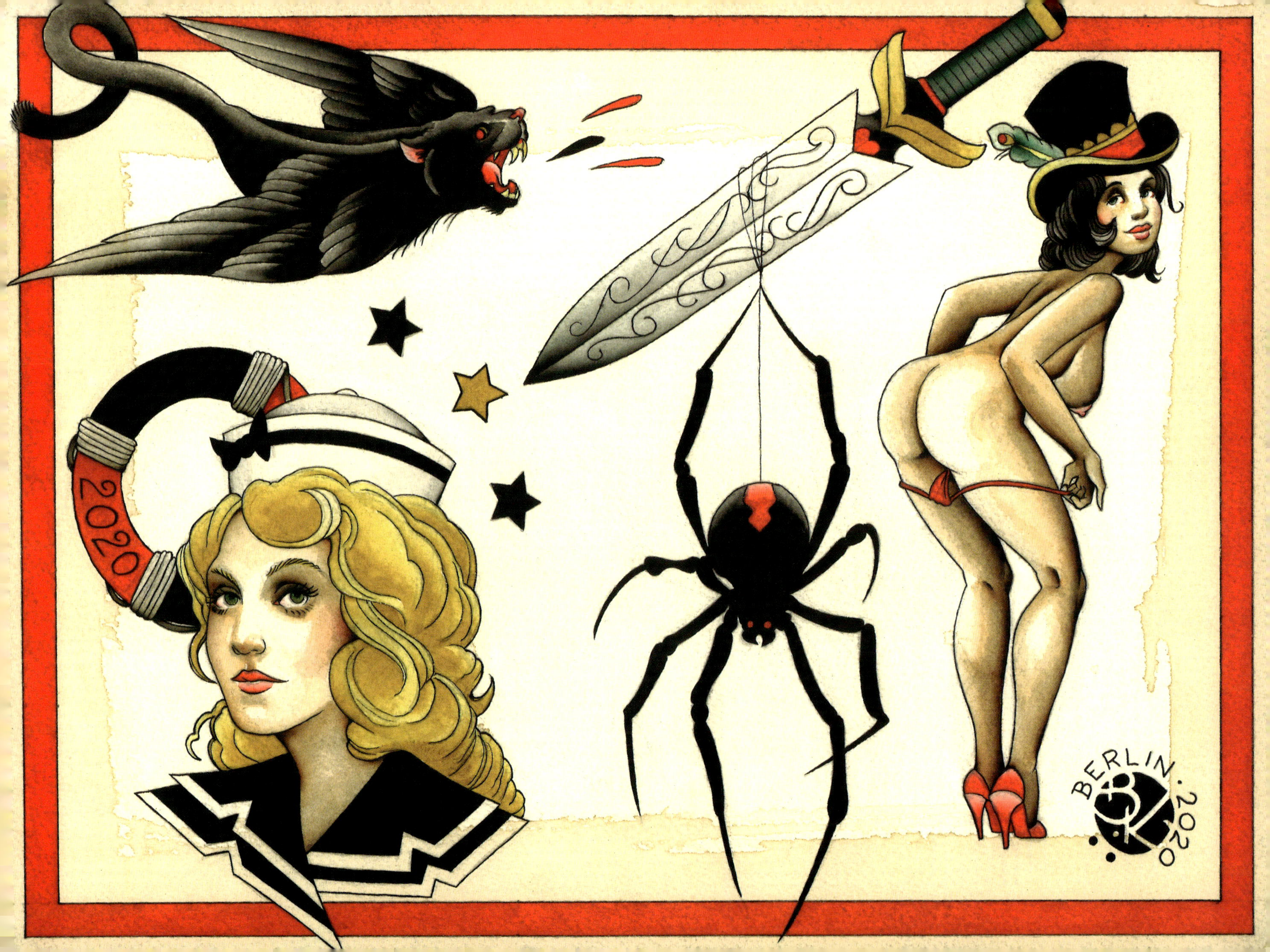
2020
BERLIN
2020

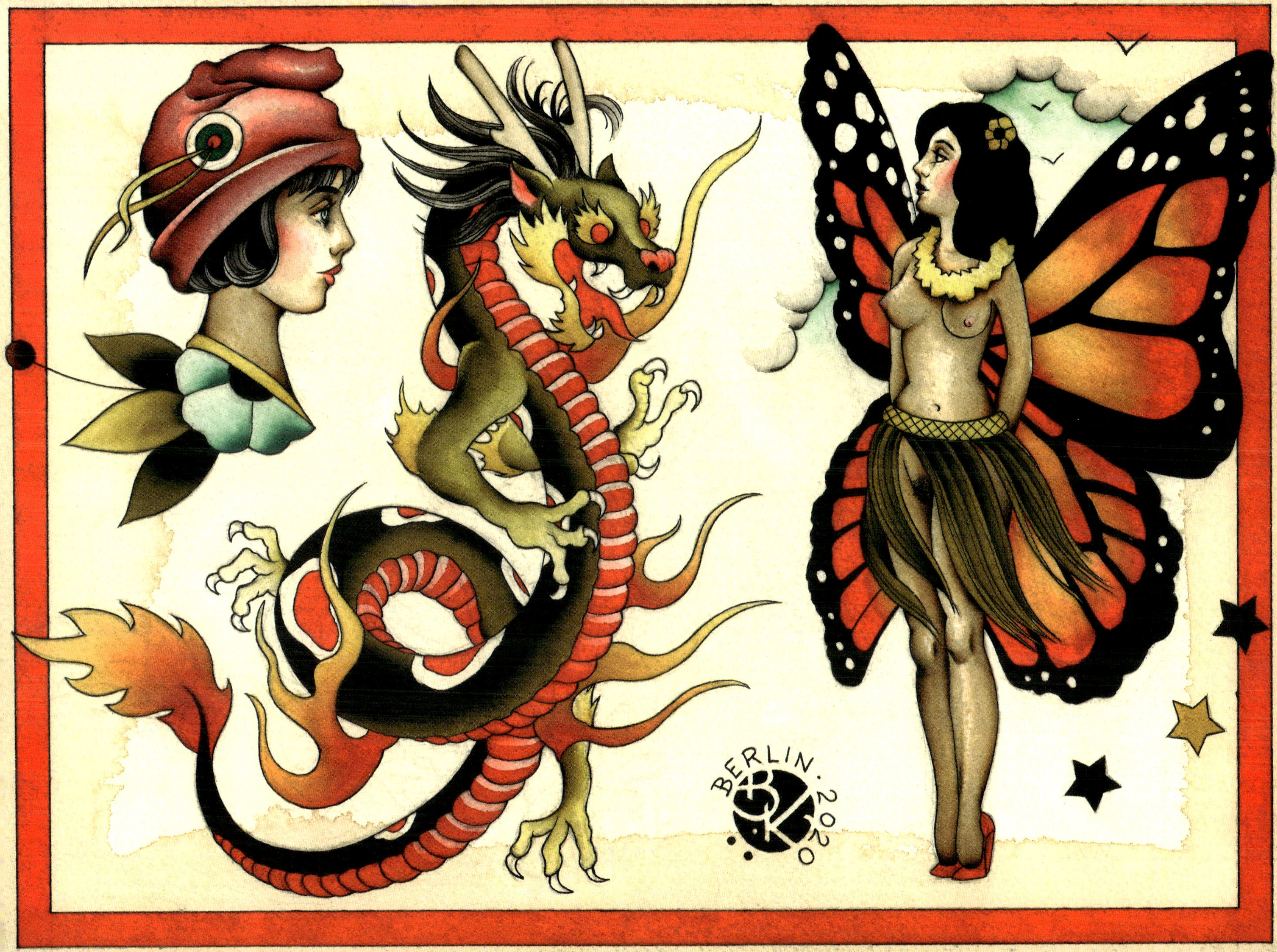
BERLIN. 2020

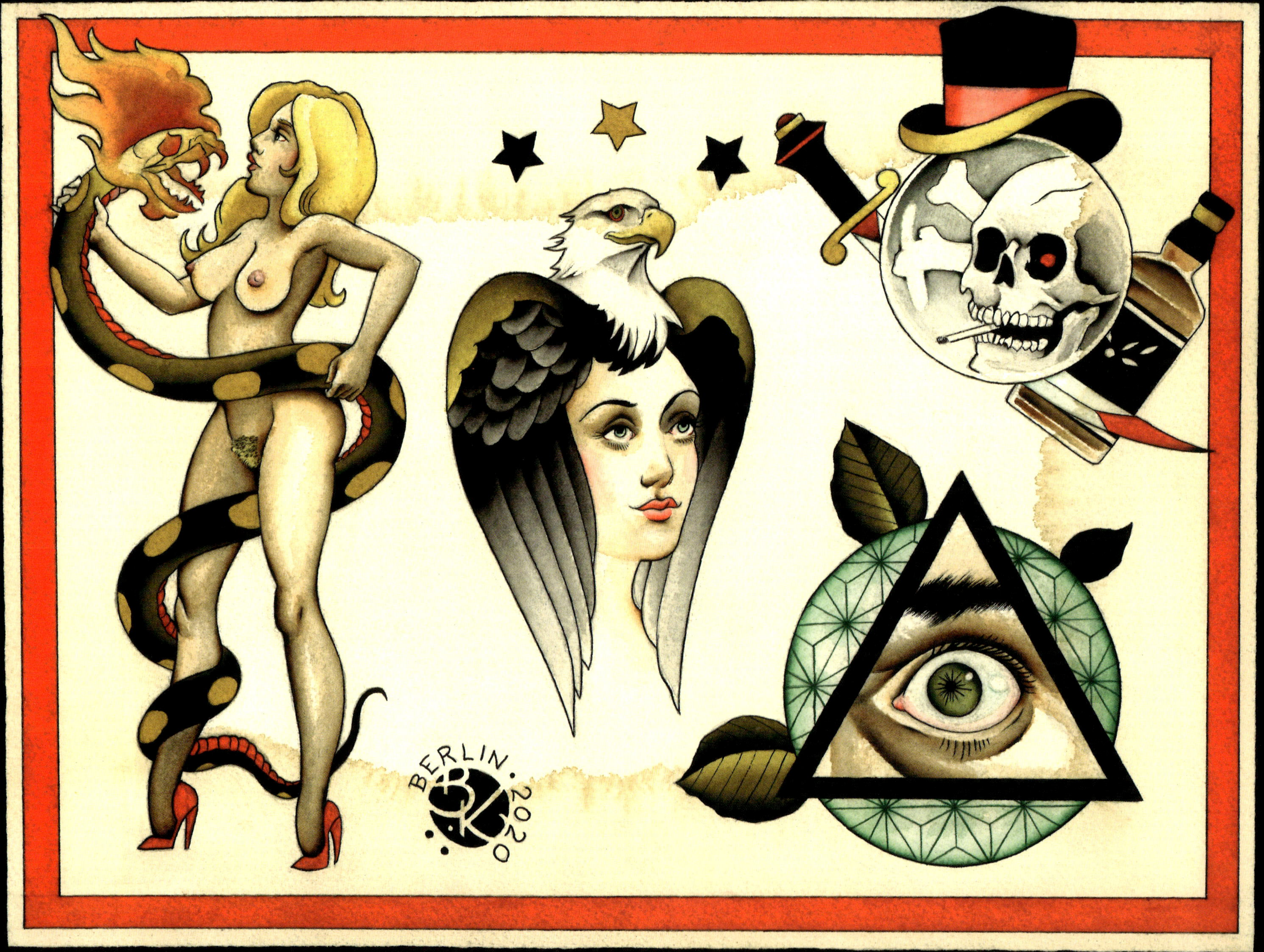
BERLIN
2020

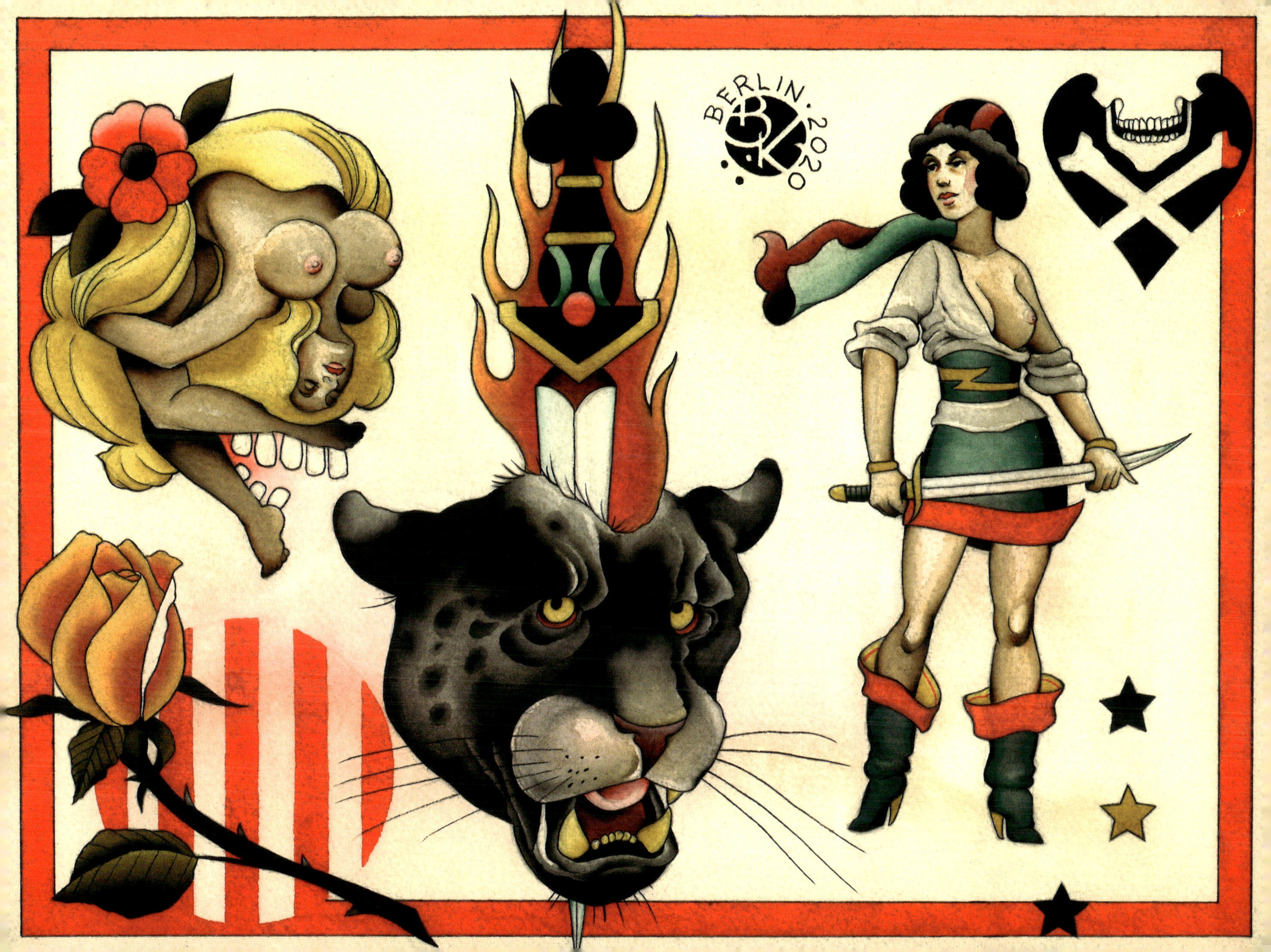
BERLIN.
2020

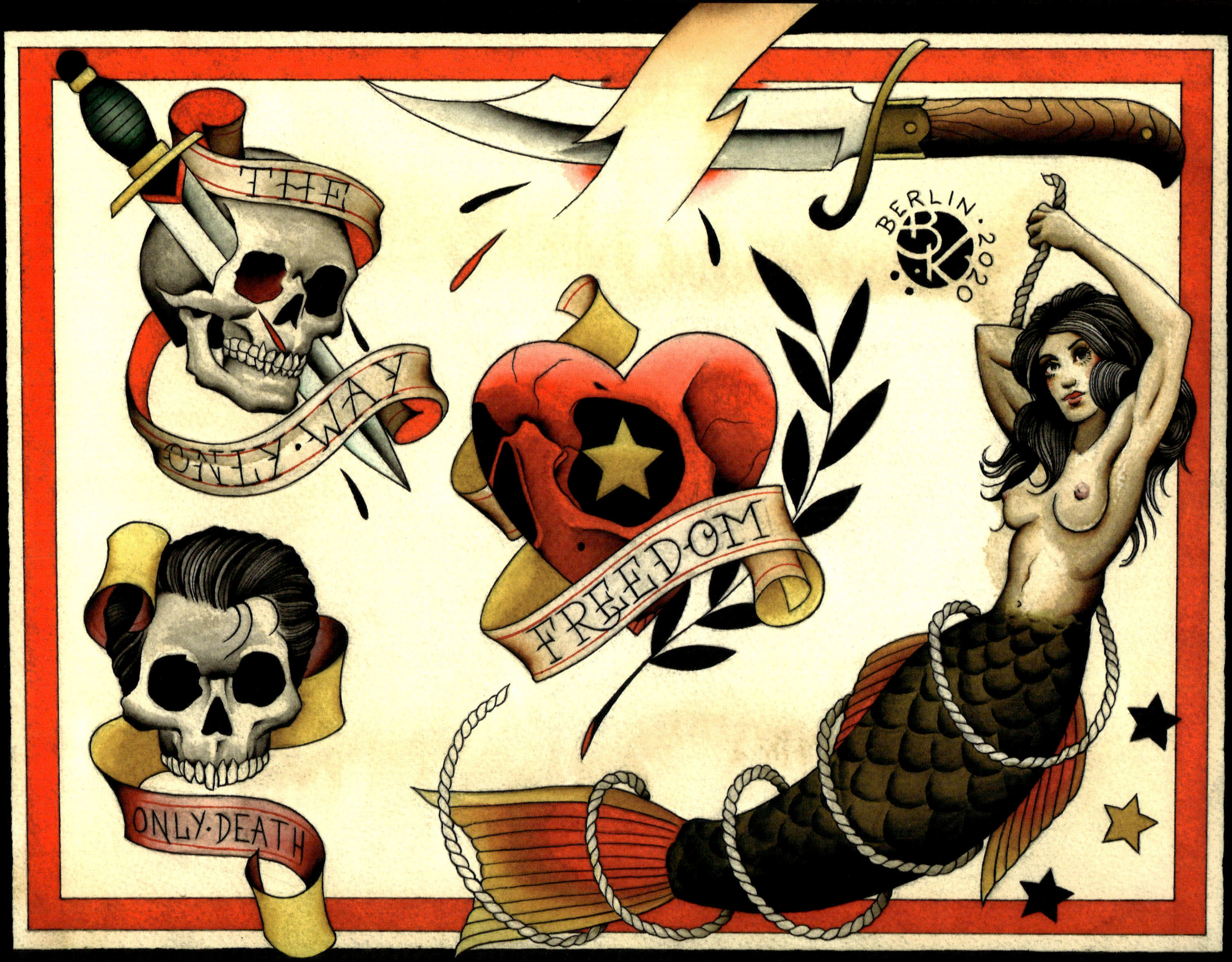
THE
ONLY·WAY
FREEDOM
ONLY·DEATH
BERLIN·2020

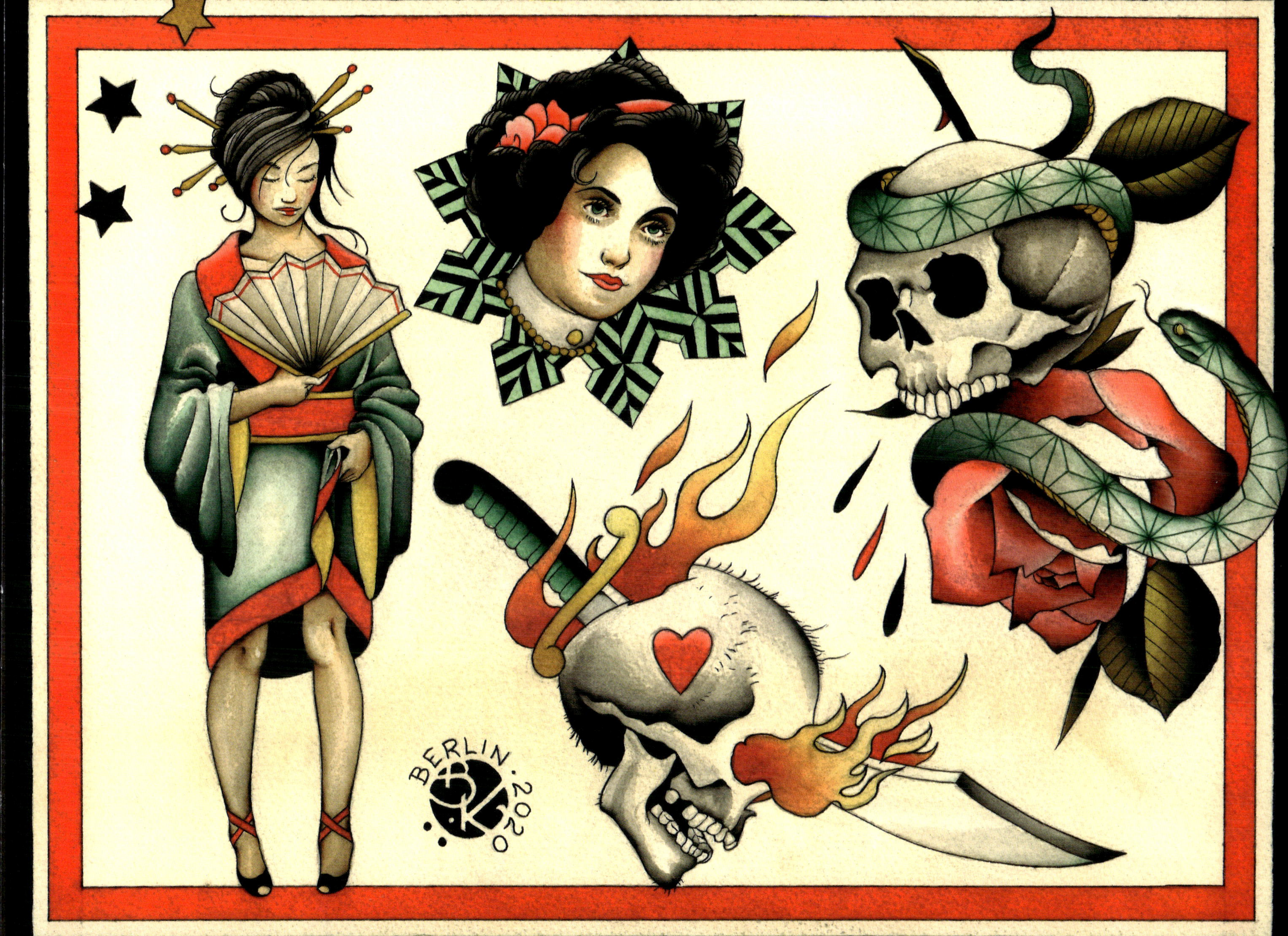
BERLIN
2020

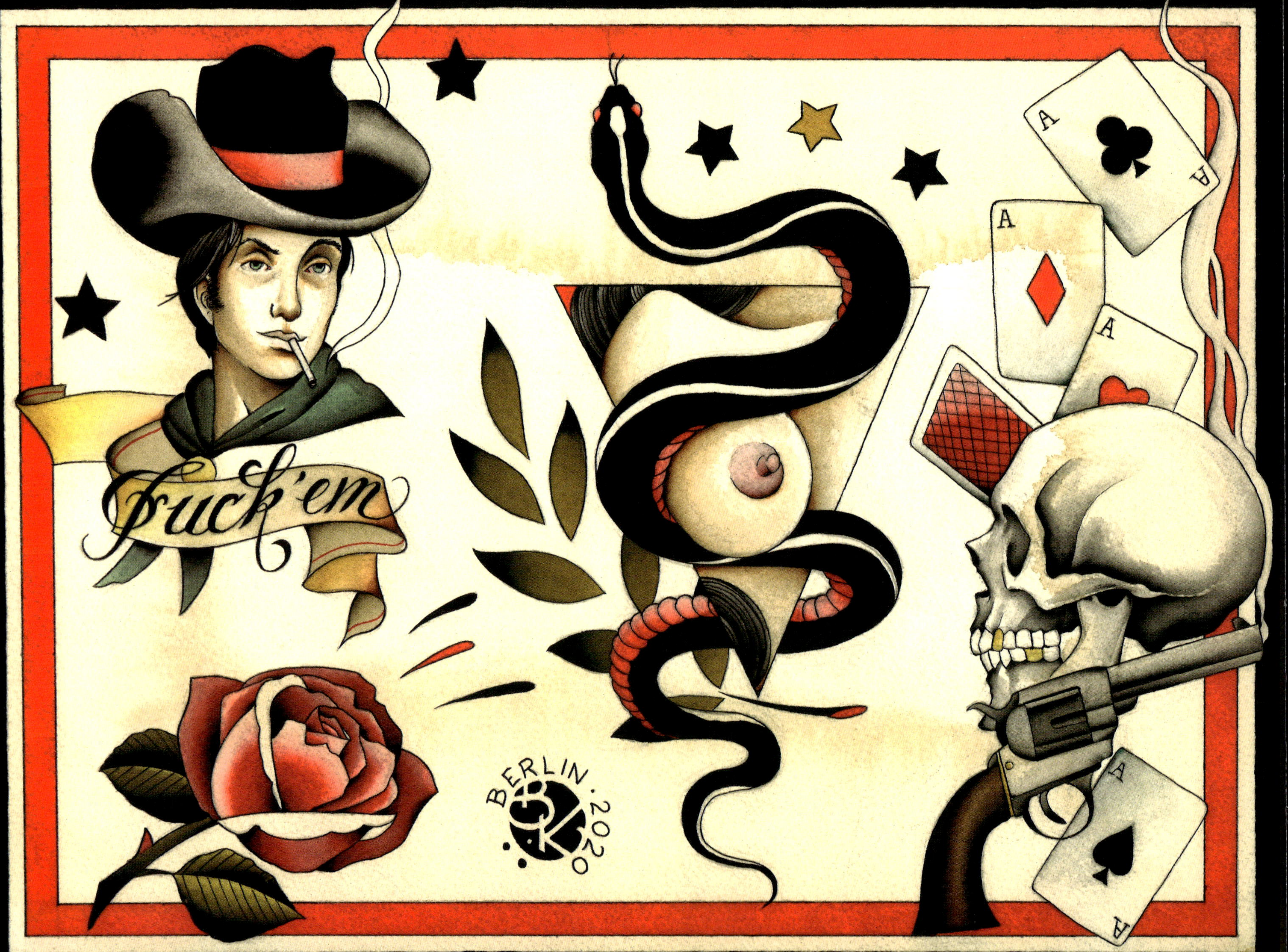
Fuck'em
BERLIN. 2020

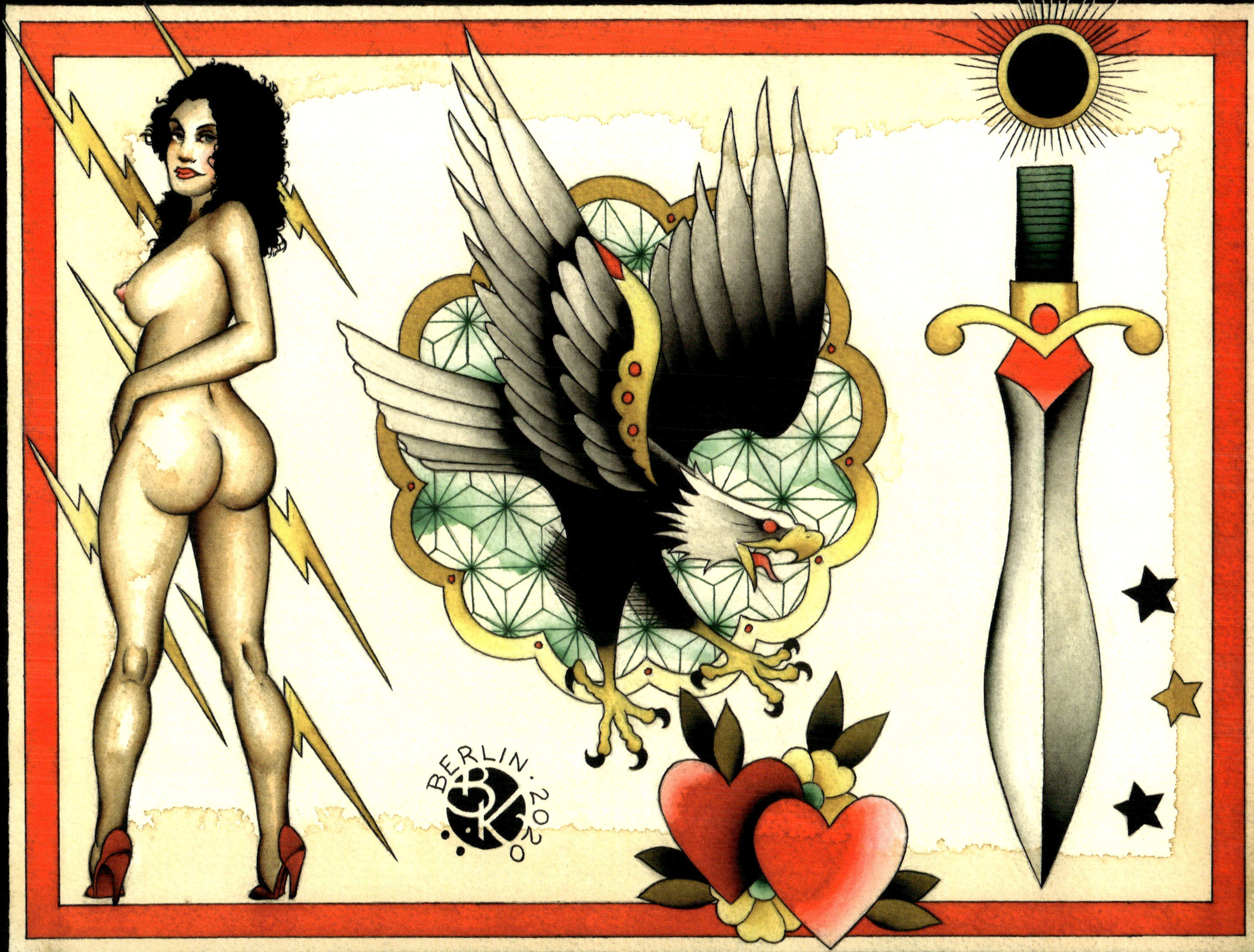
BERLIN · 2020

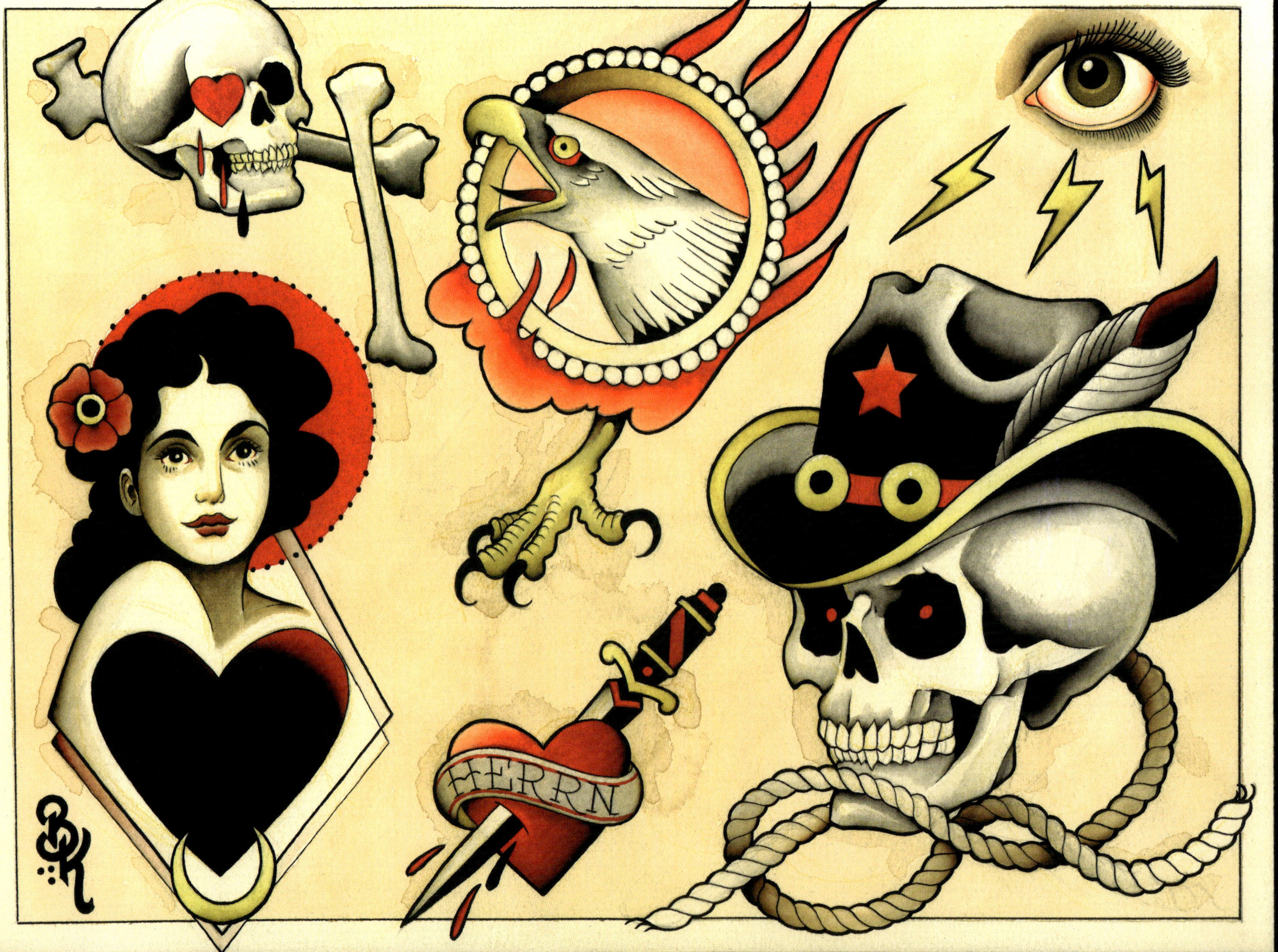
HERRN

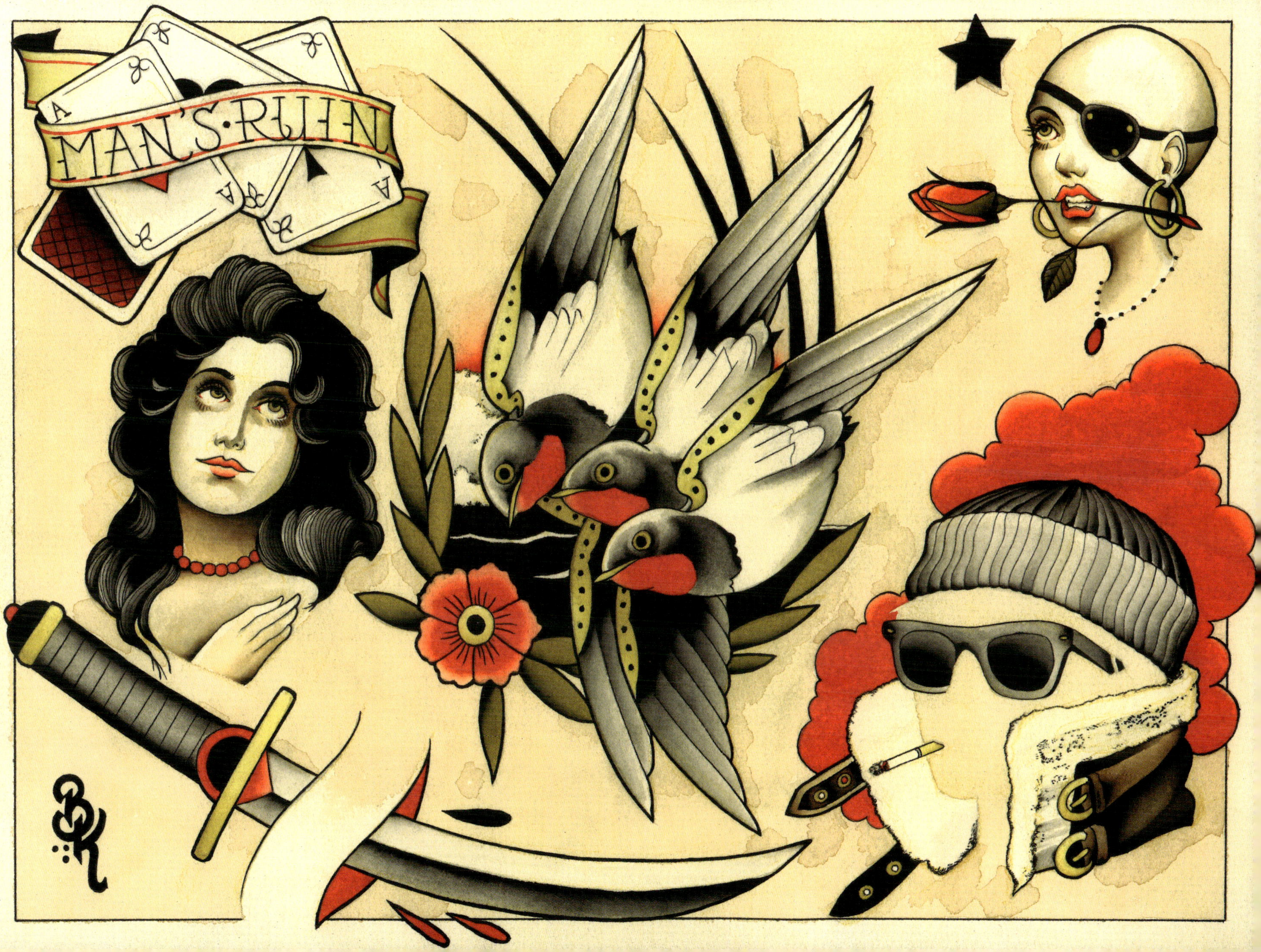
MAN'S·RUIN

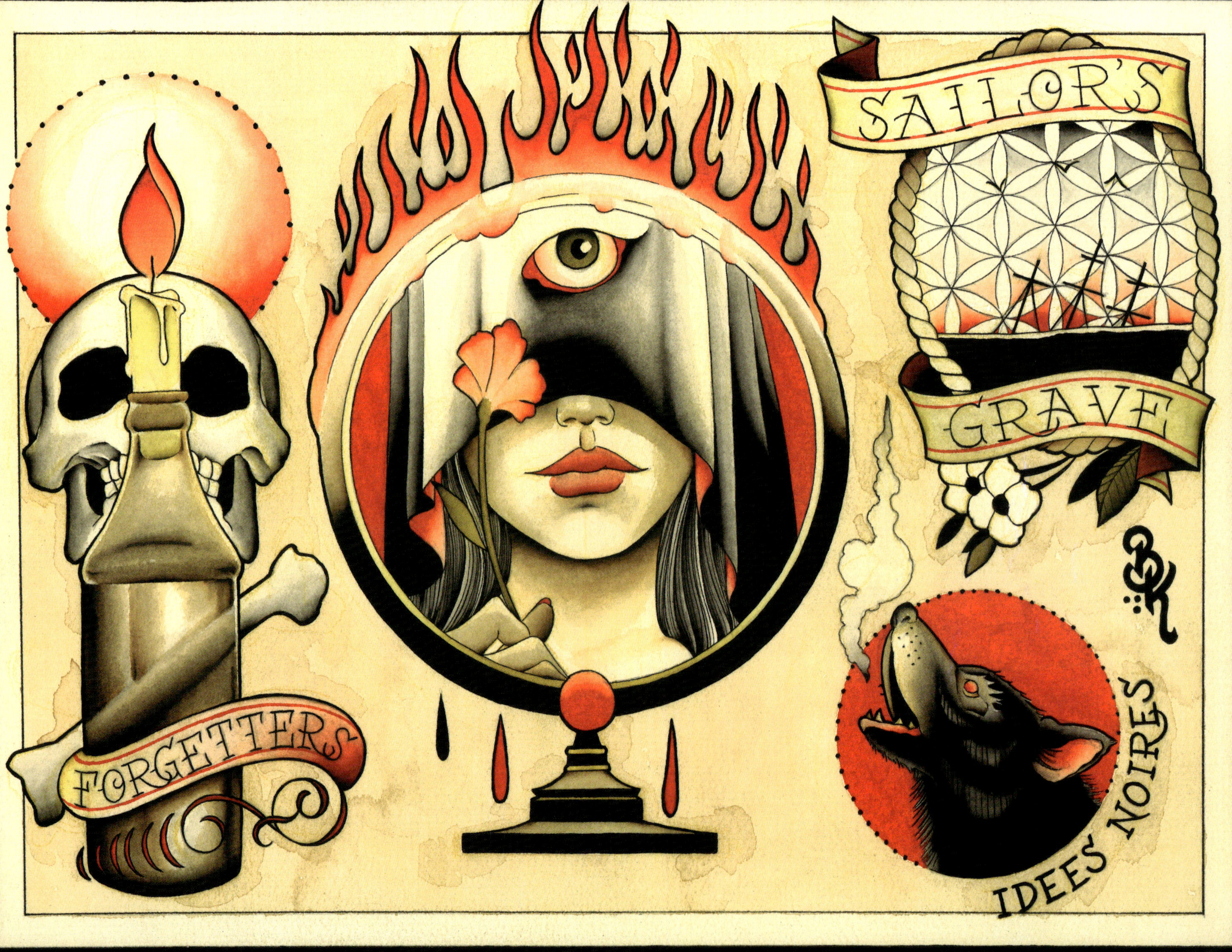
SAILOR'S
GRAVE
FORGETTERS
IDEES NOIRES

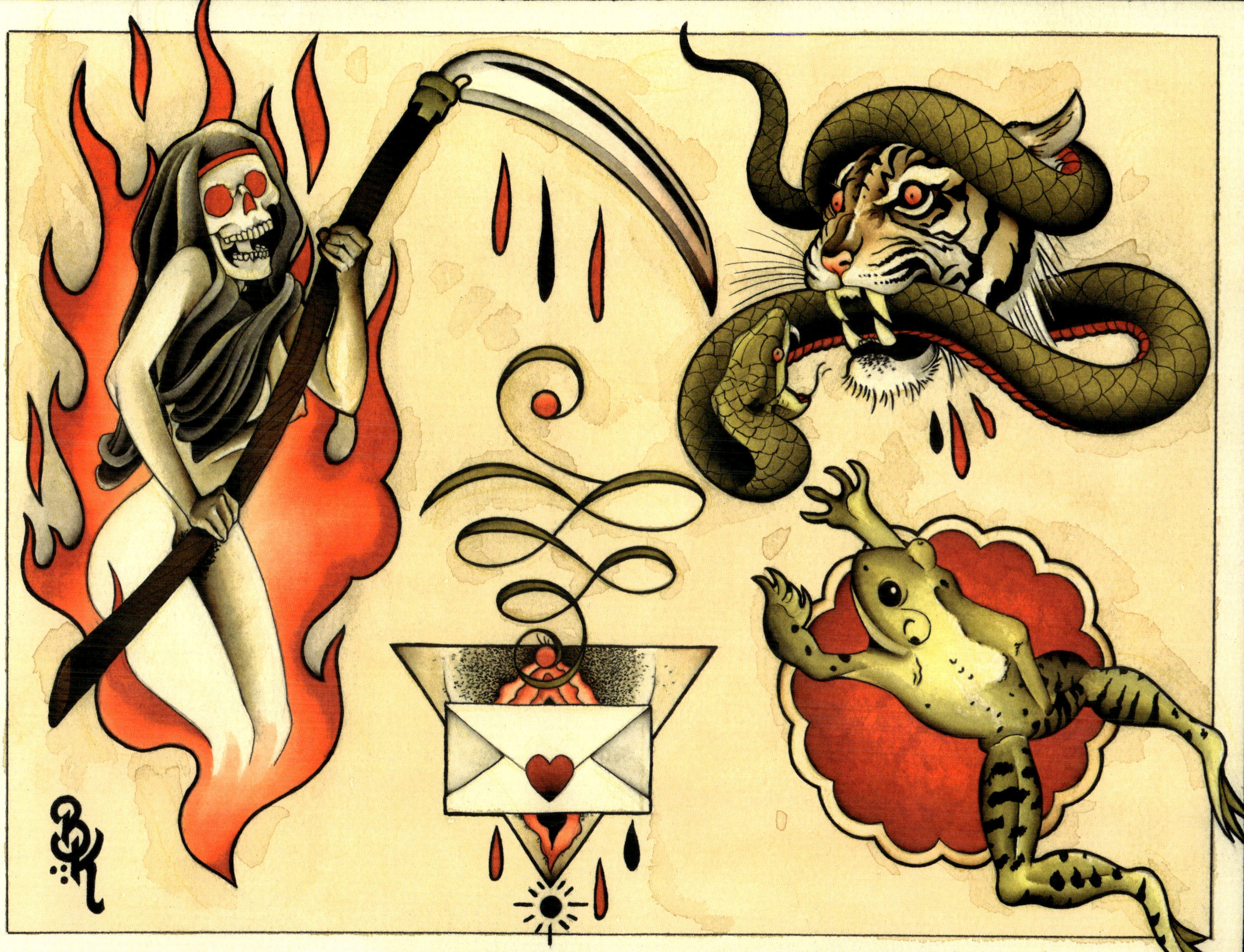

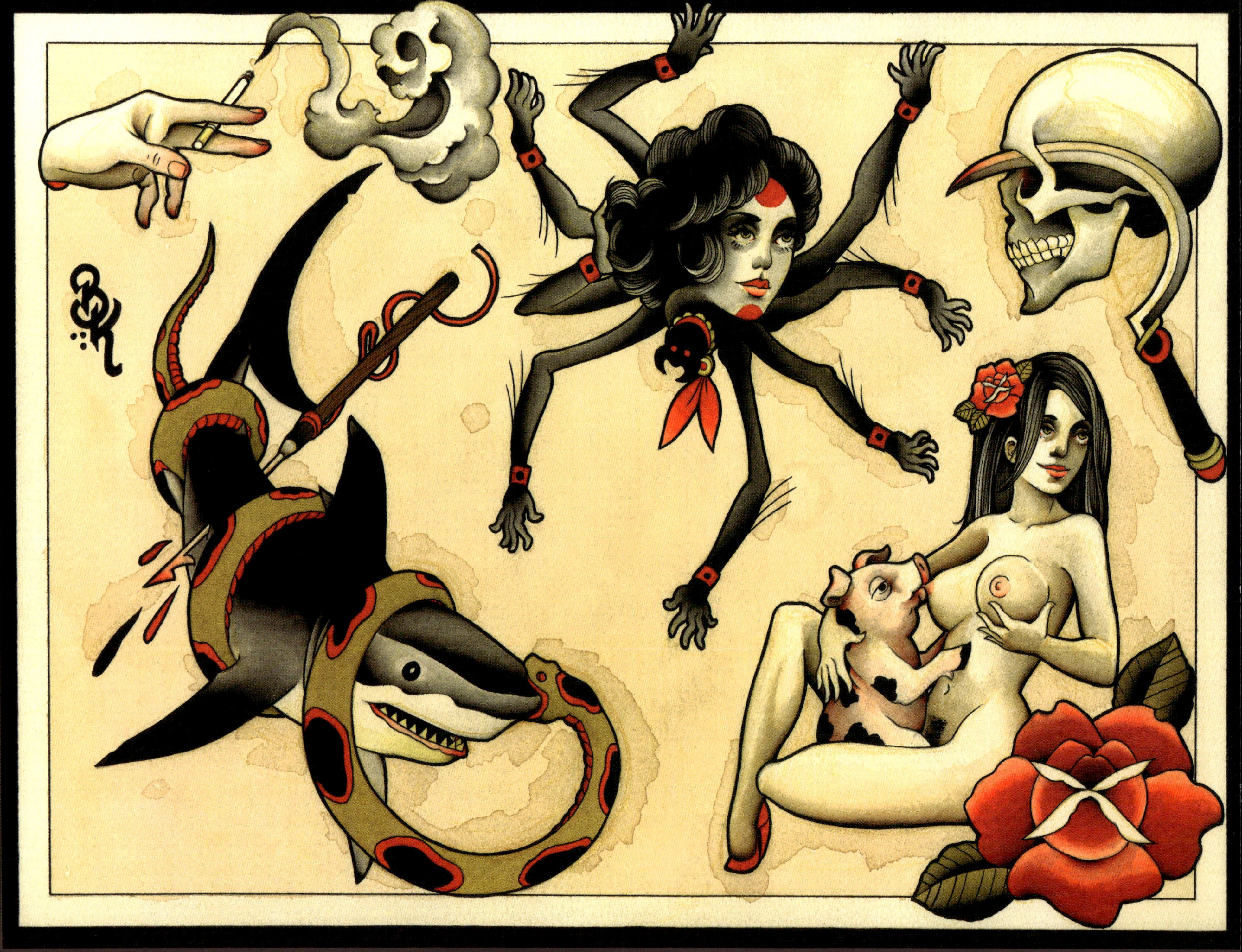

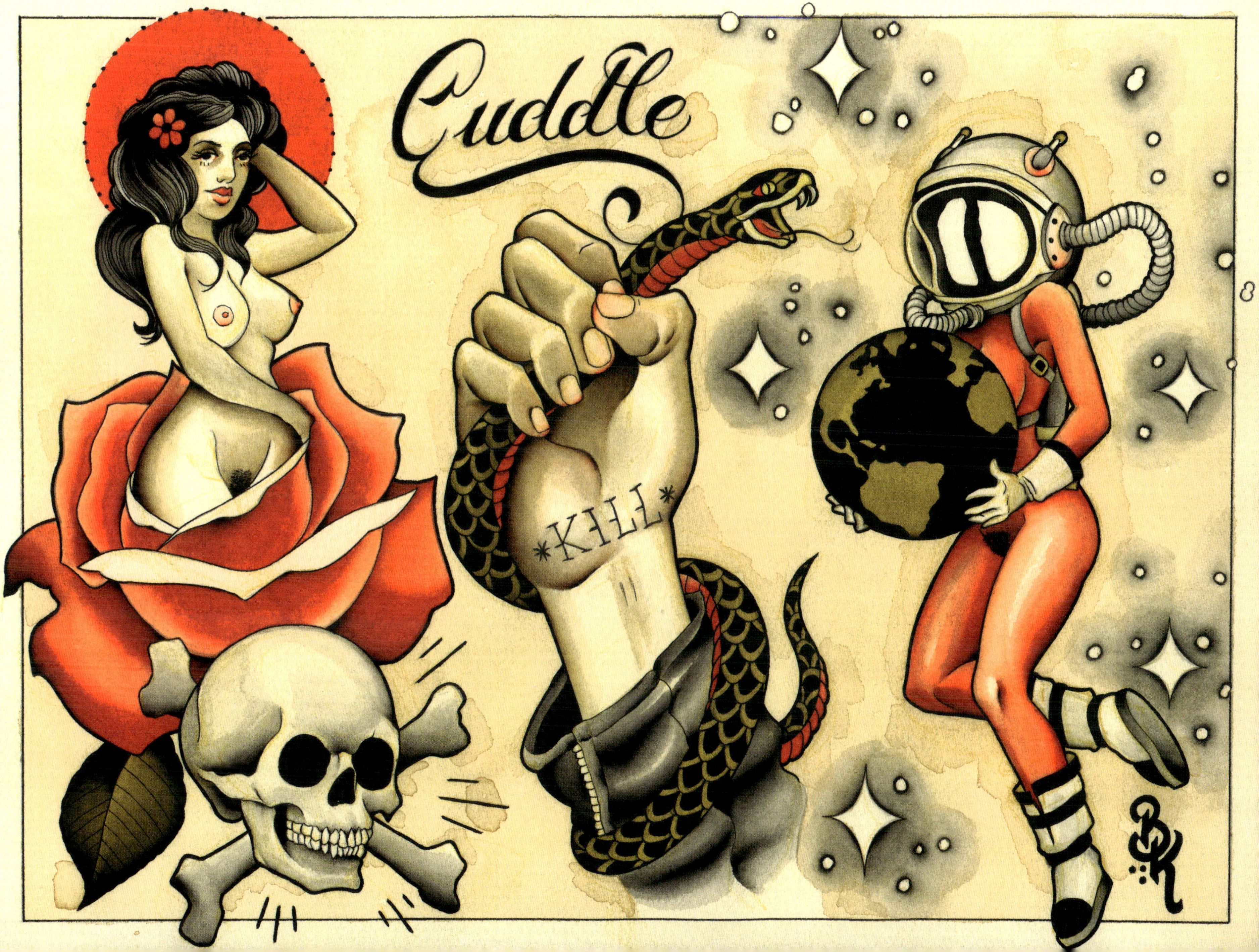
Cuddle
KILL

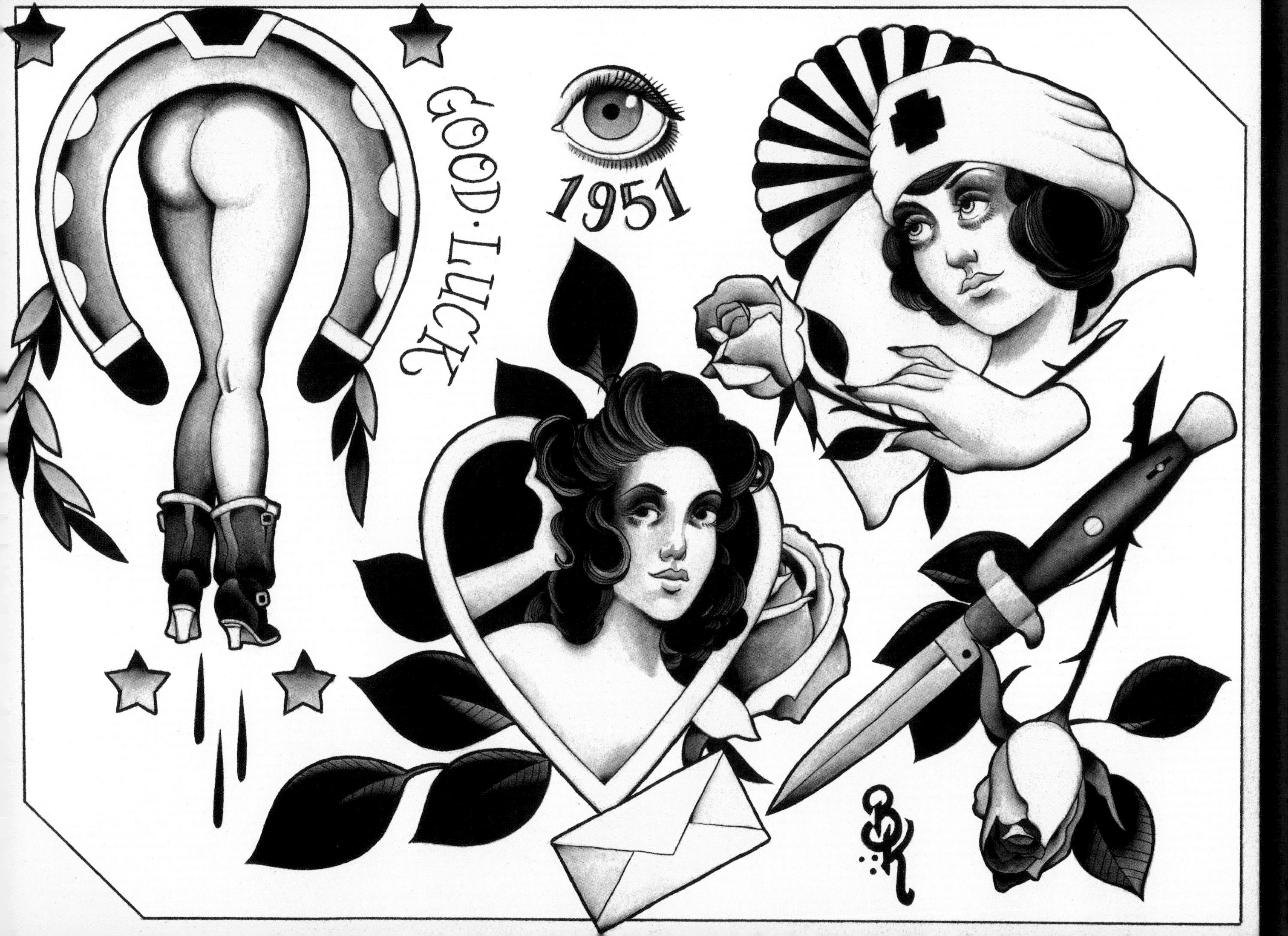
GOOD·LUCK
1951

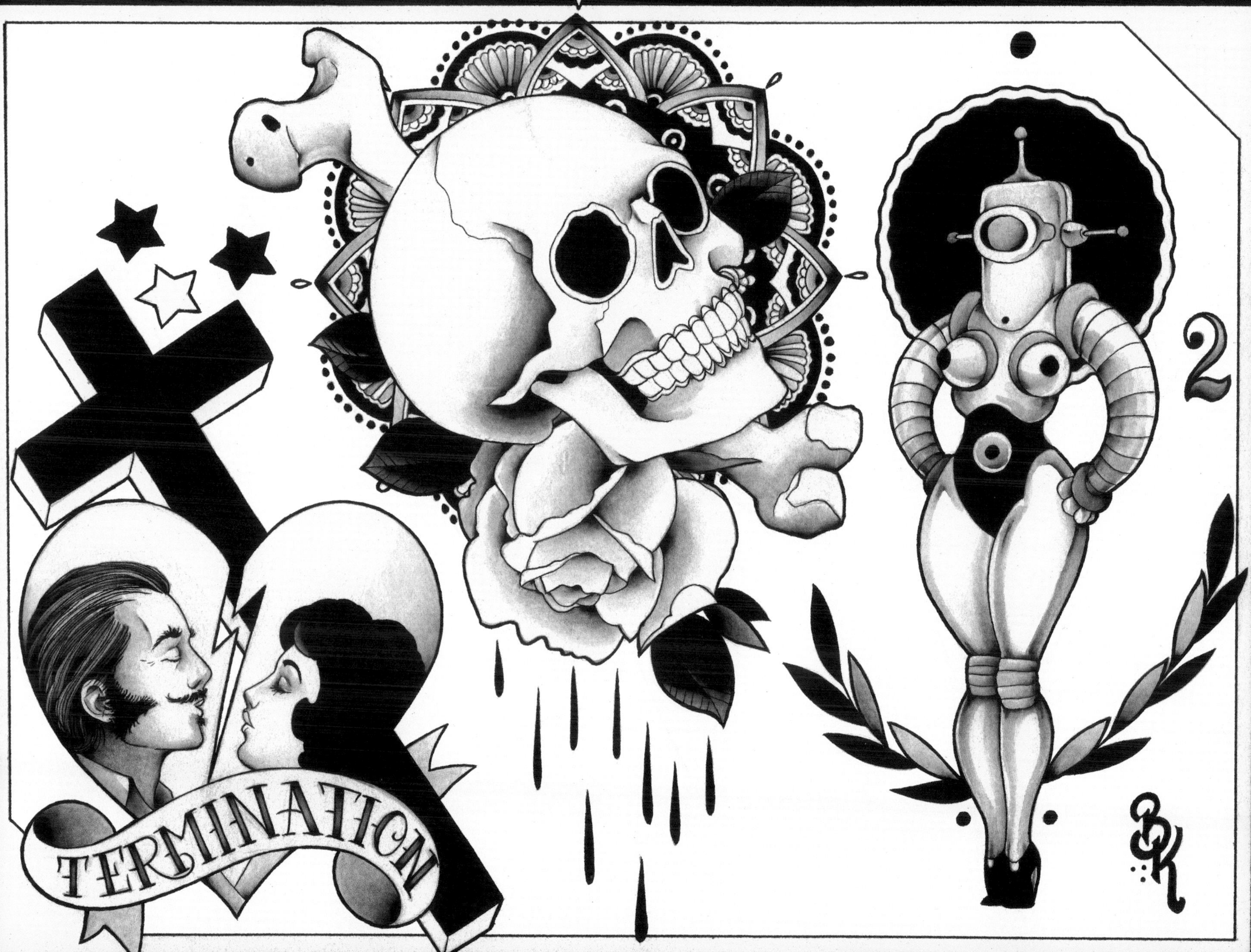
TERMINATION
2
BK

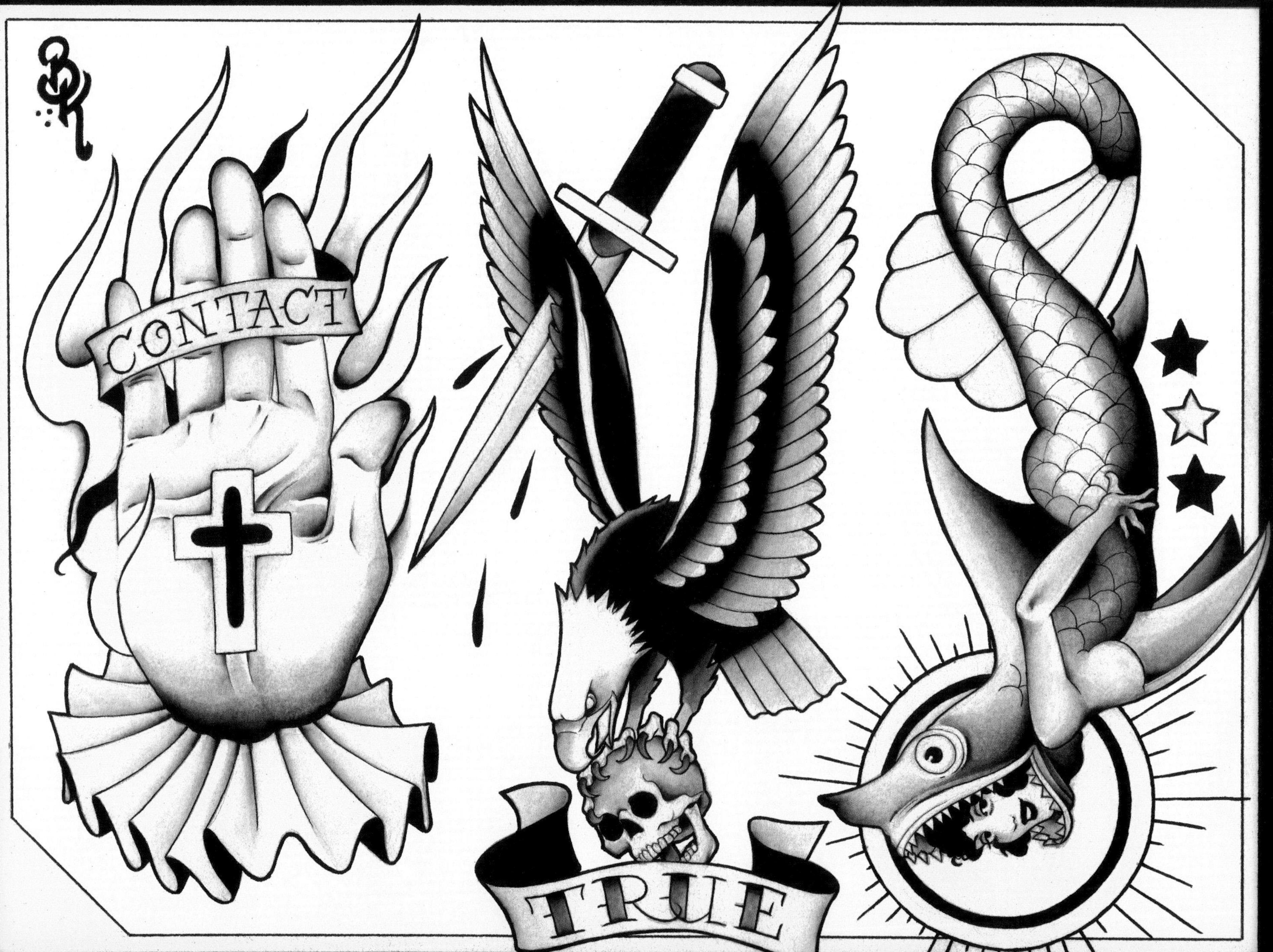

CONTACT
TRUE

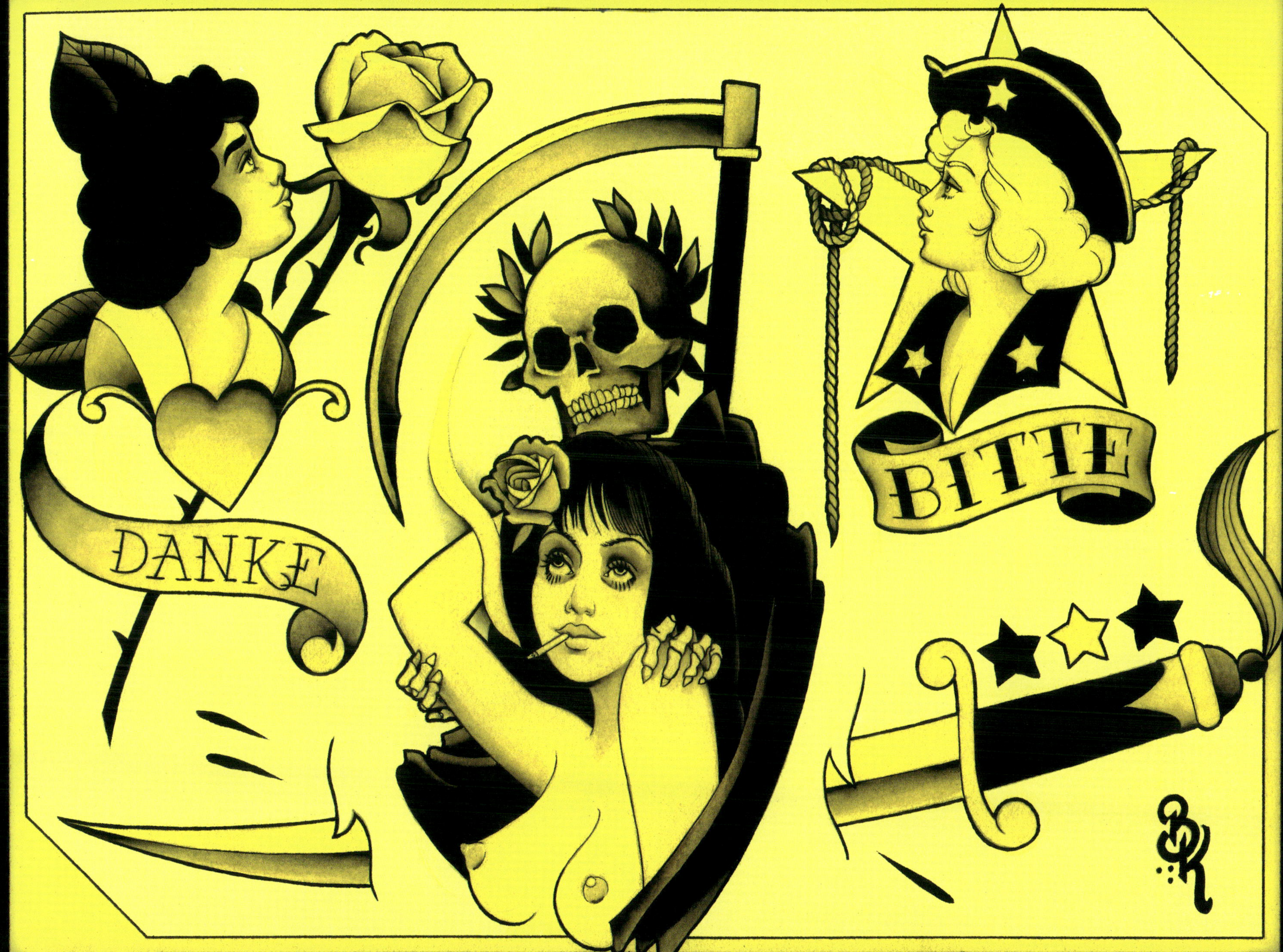
DANKE
BITTE

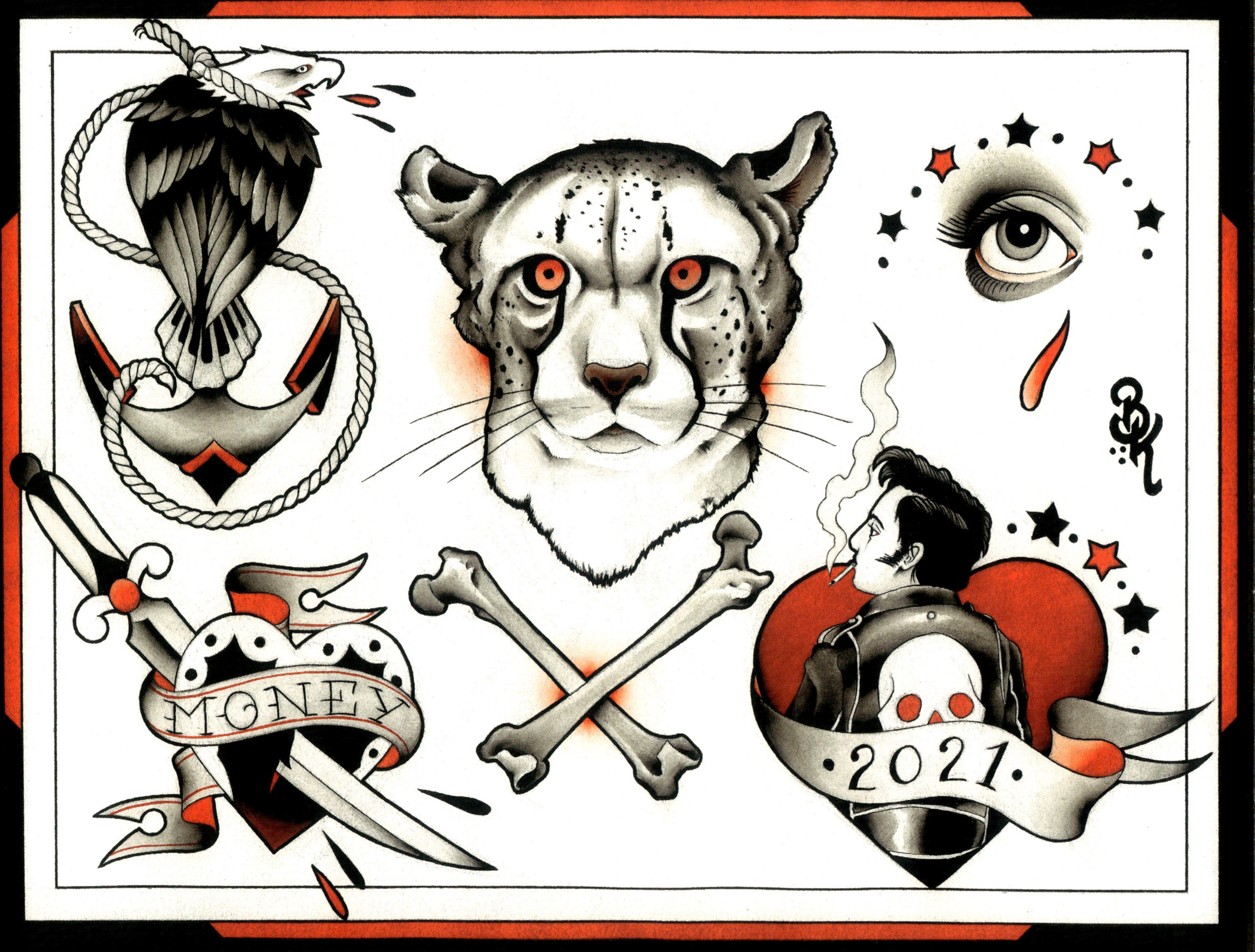

MONEY
2021
BK

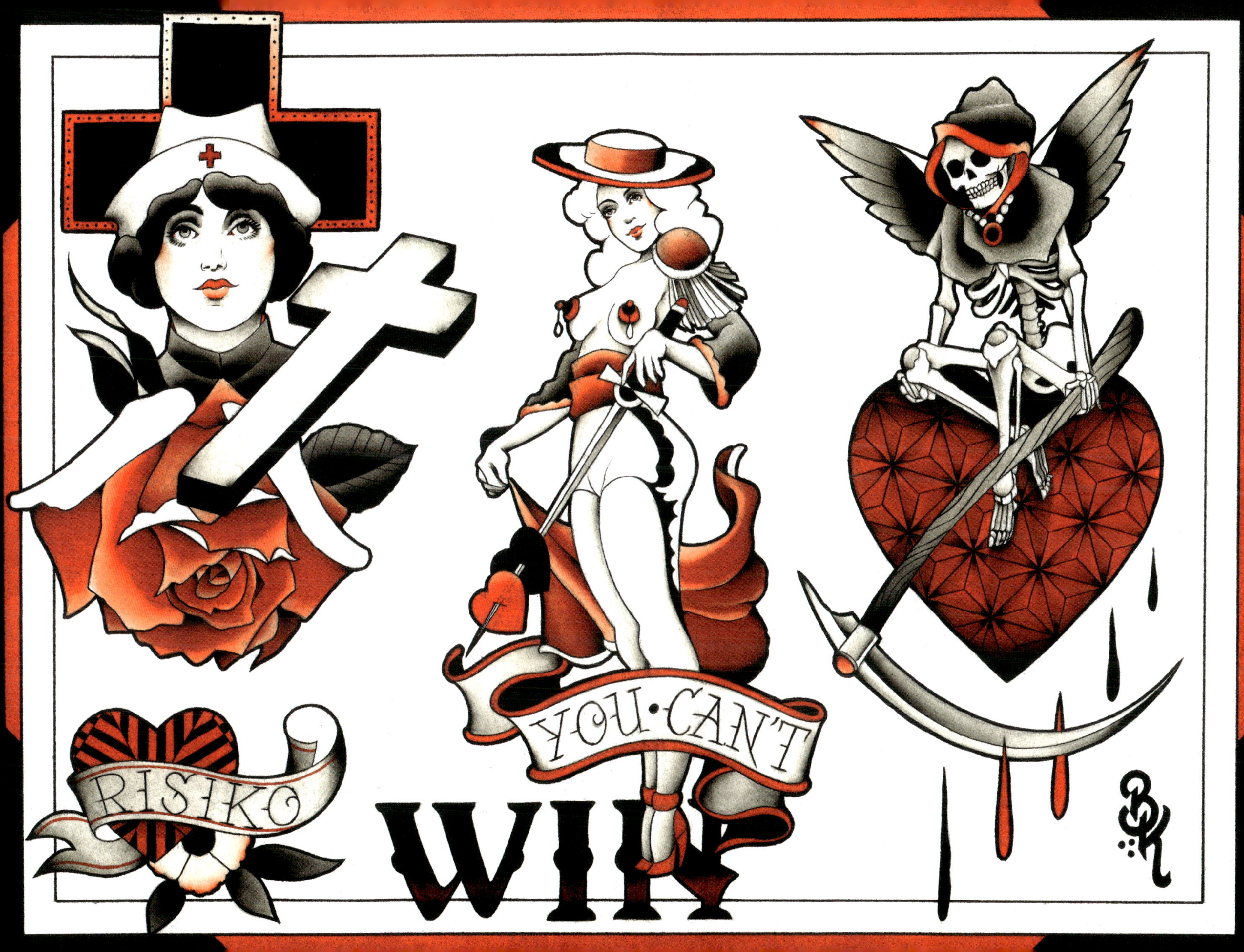
RISIKO
YOU·CAN'T
WIN

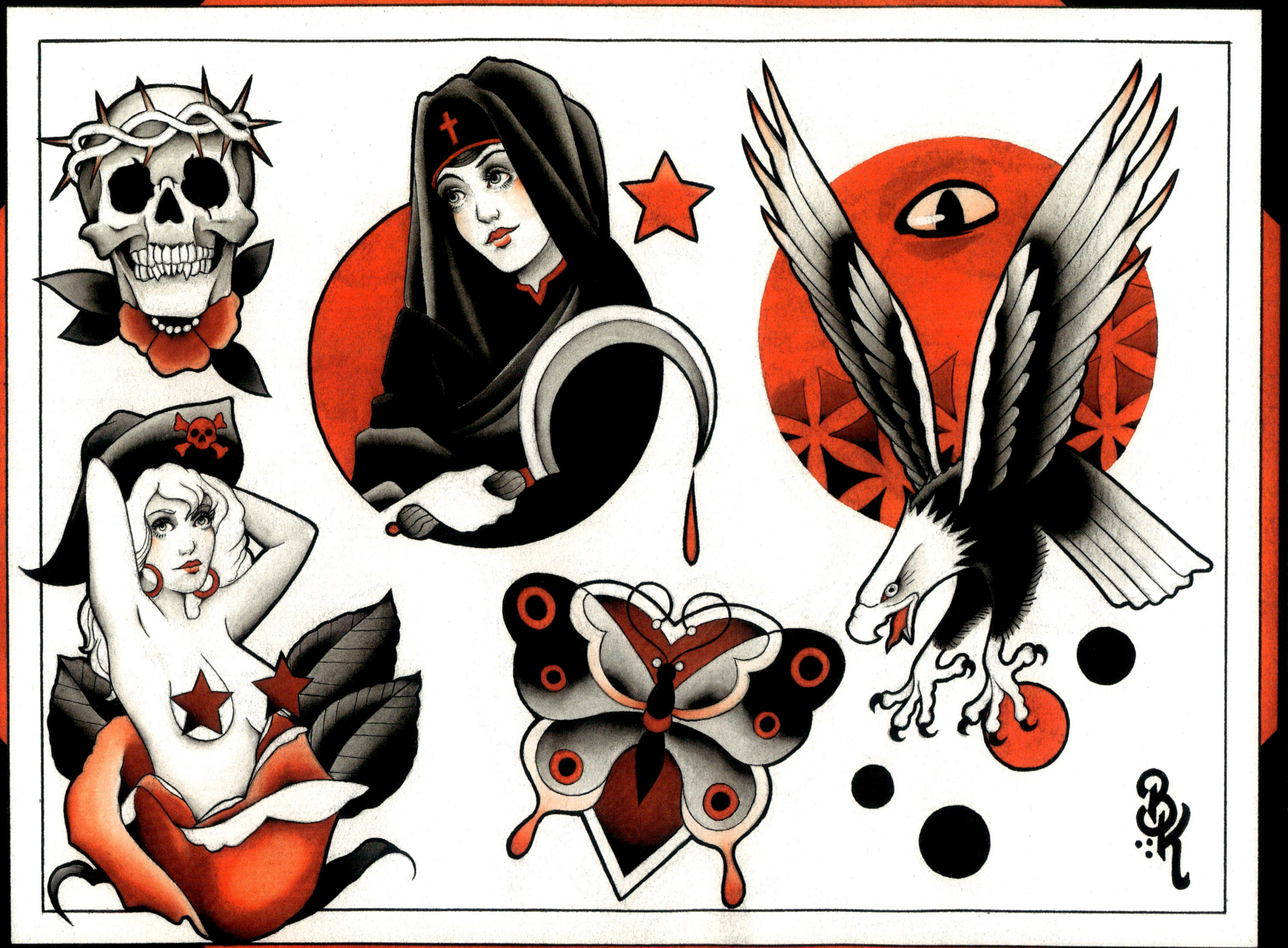

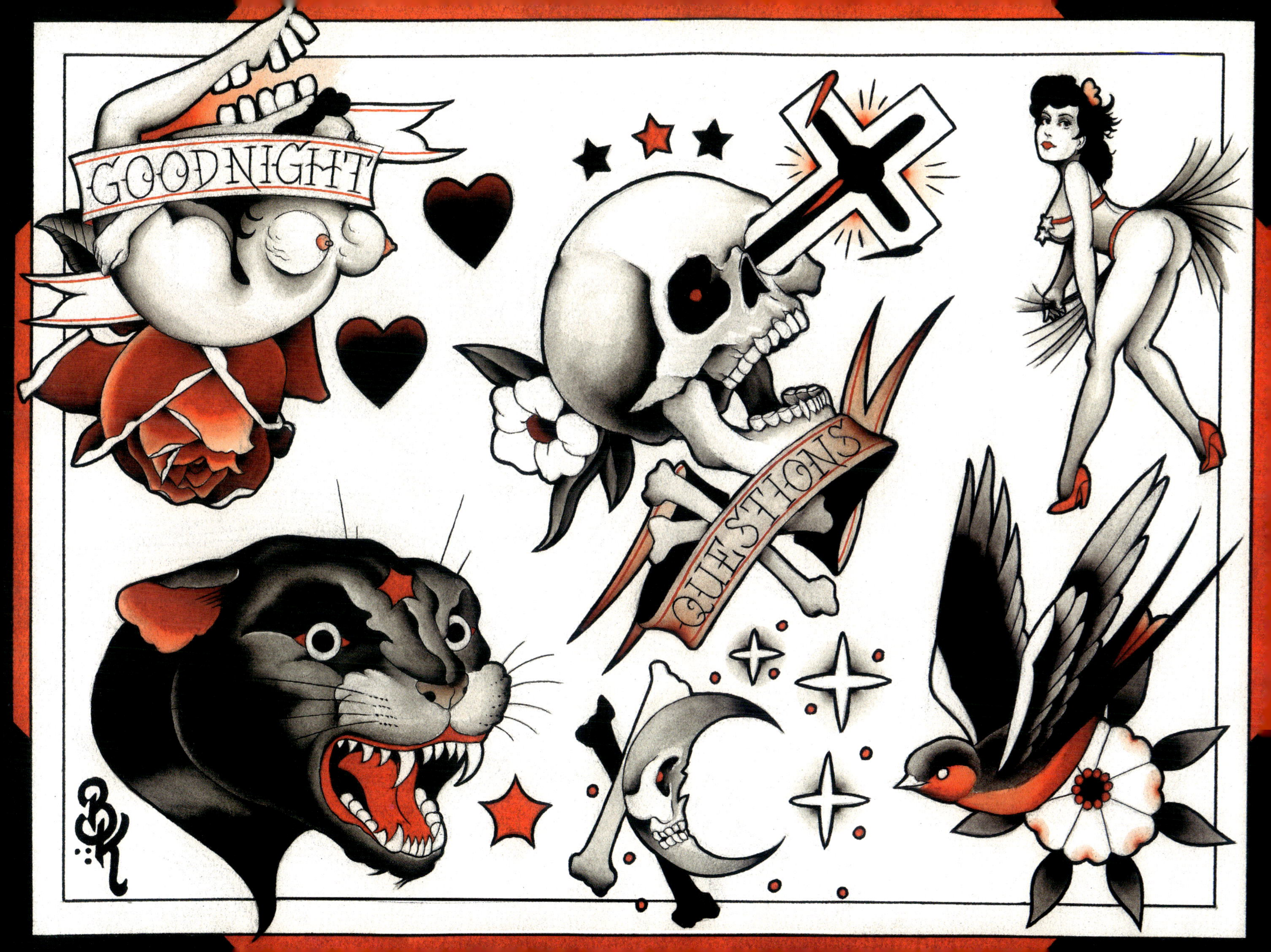
GOODNIGHT
QUESTIONS

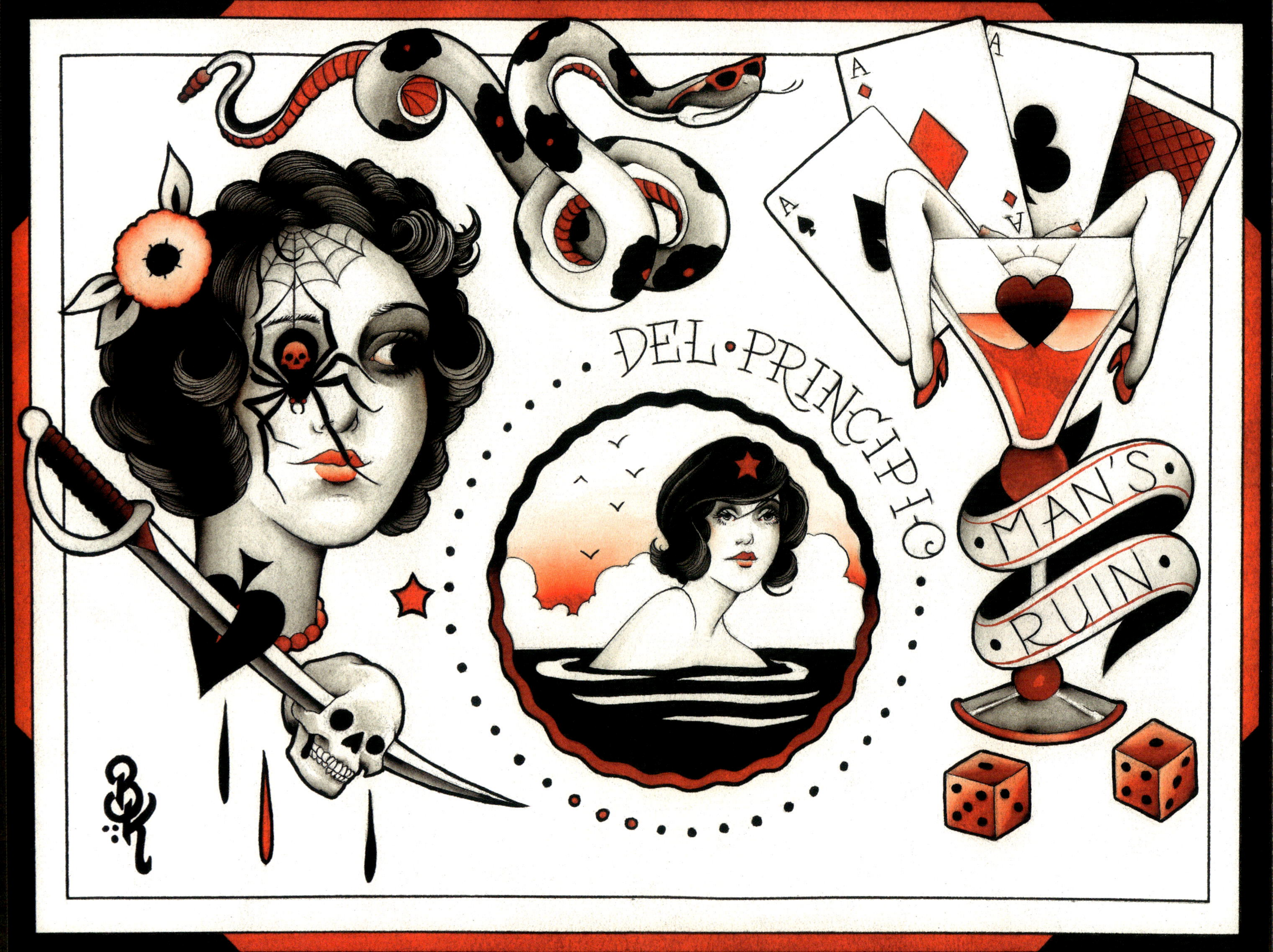
DEL·PRINCIPIO
MAN'S
RUIN

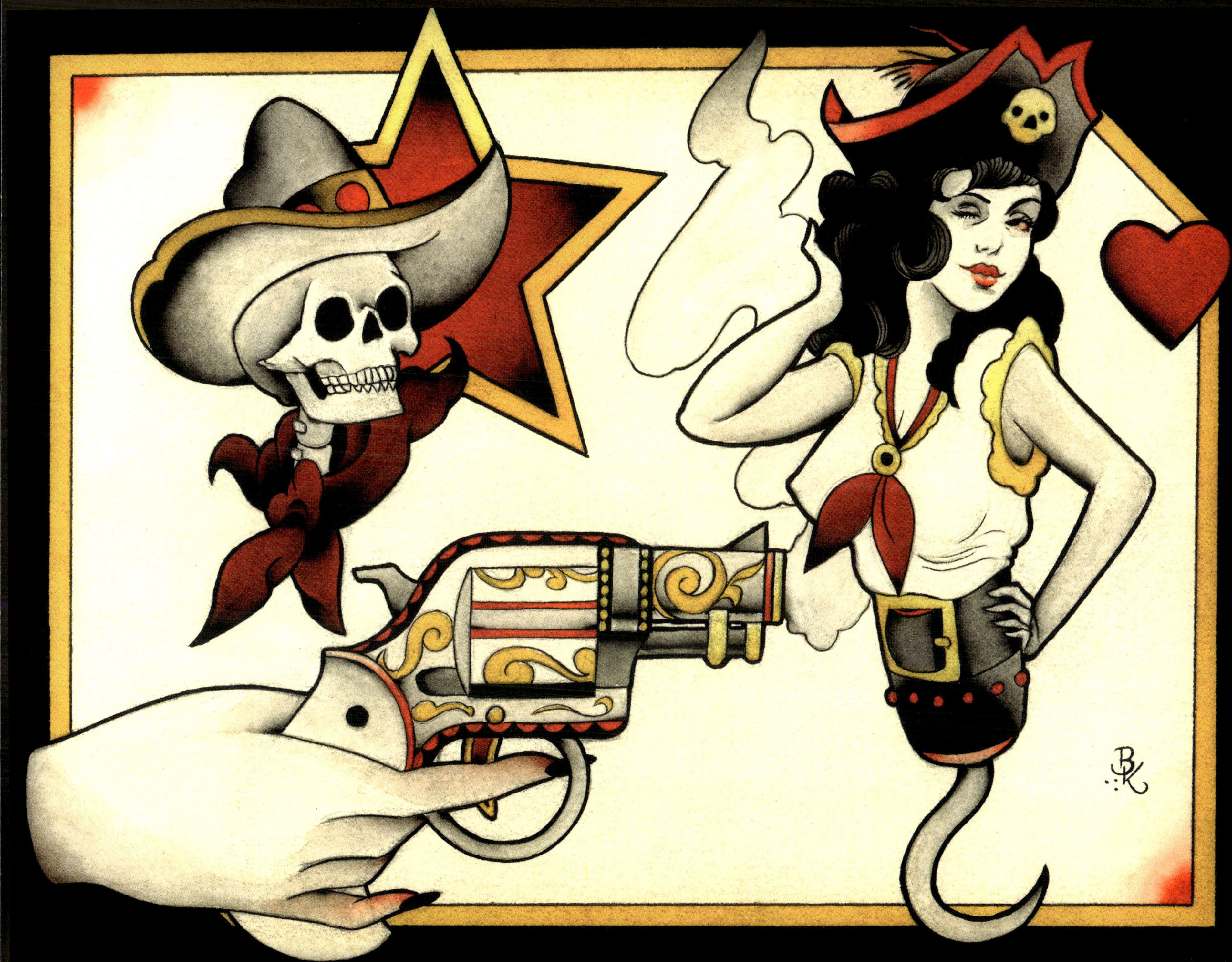

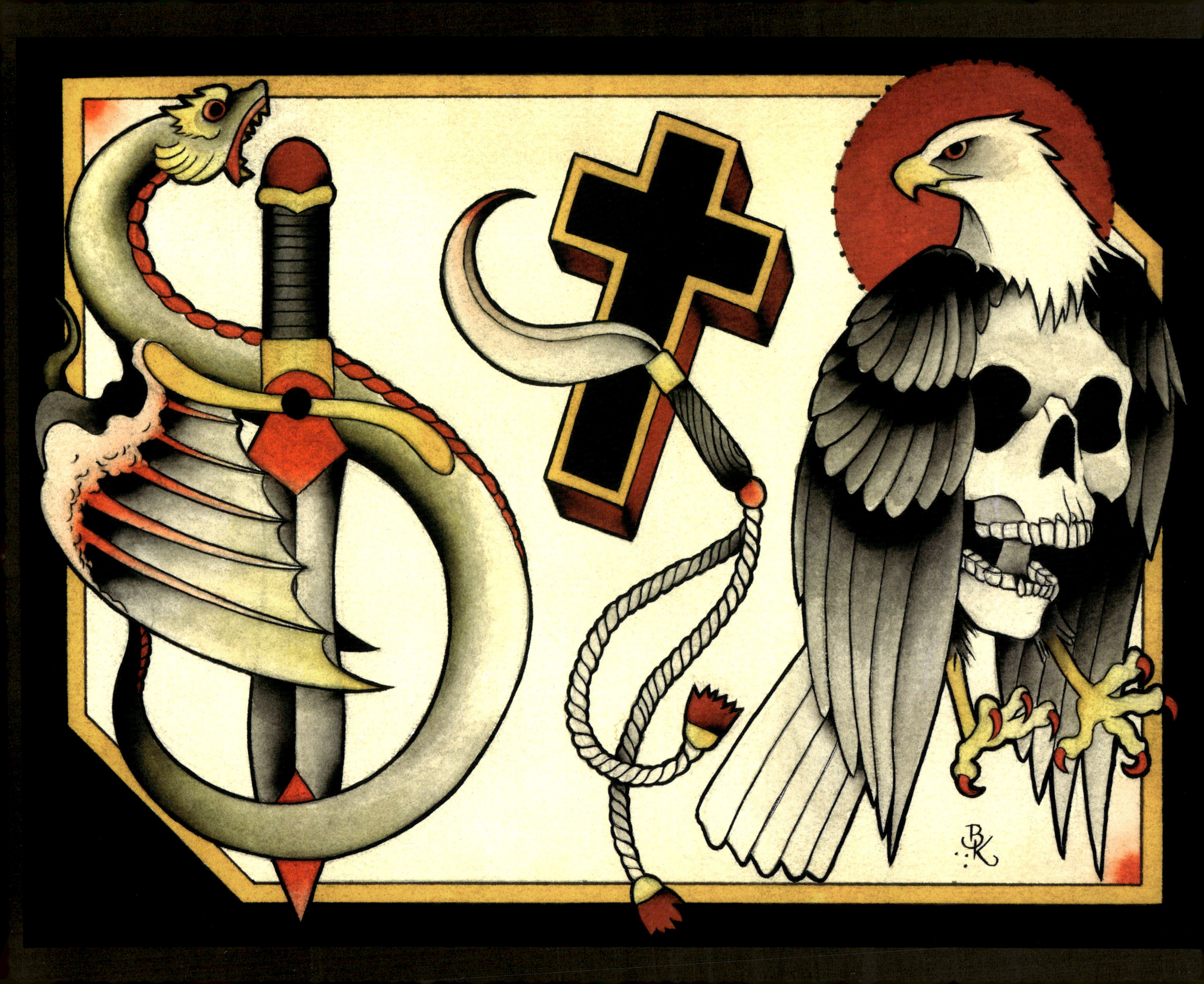

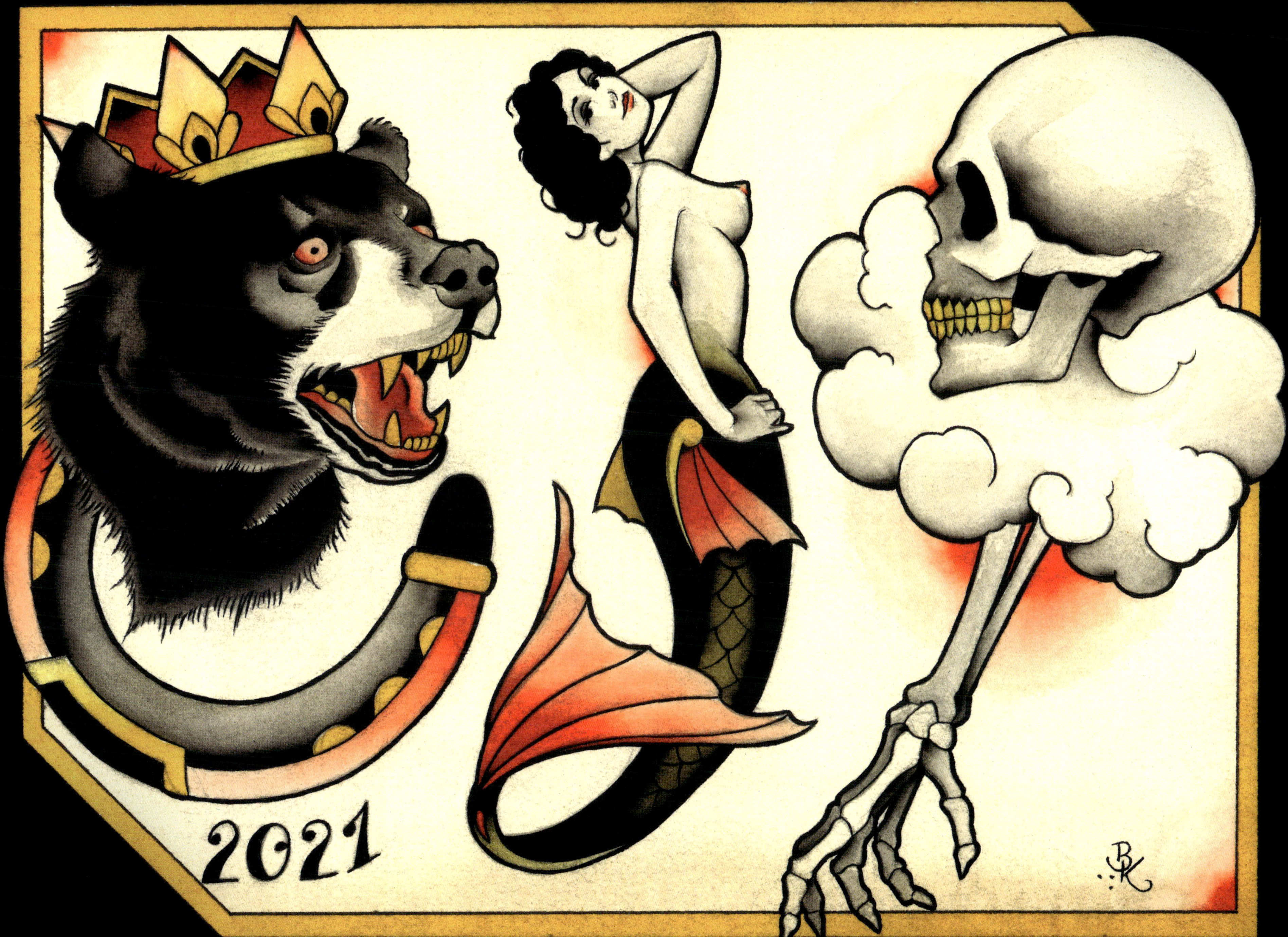
2021

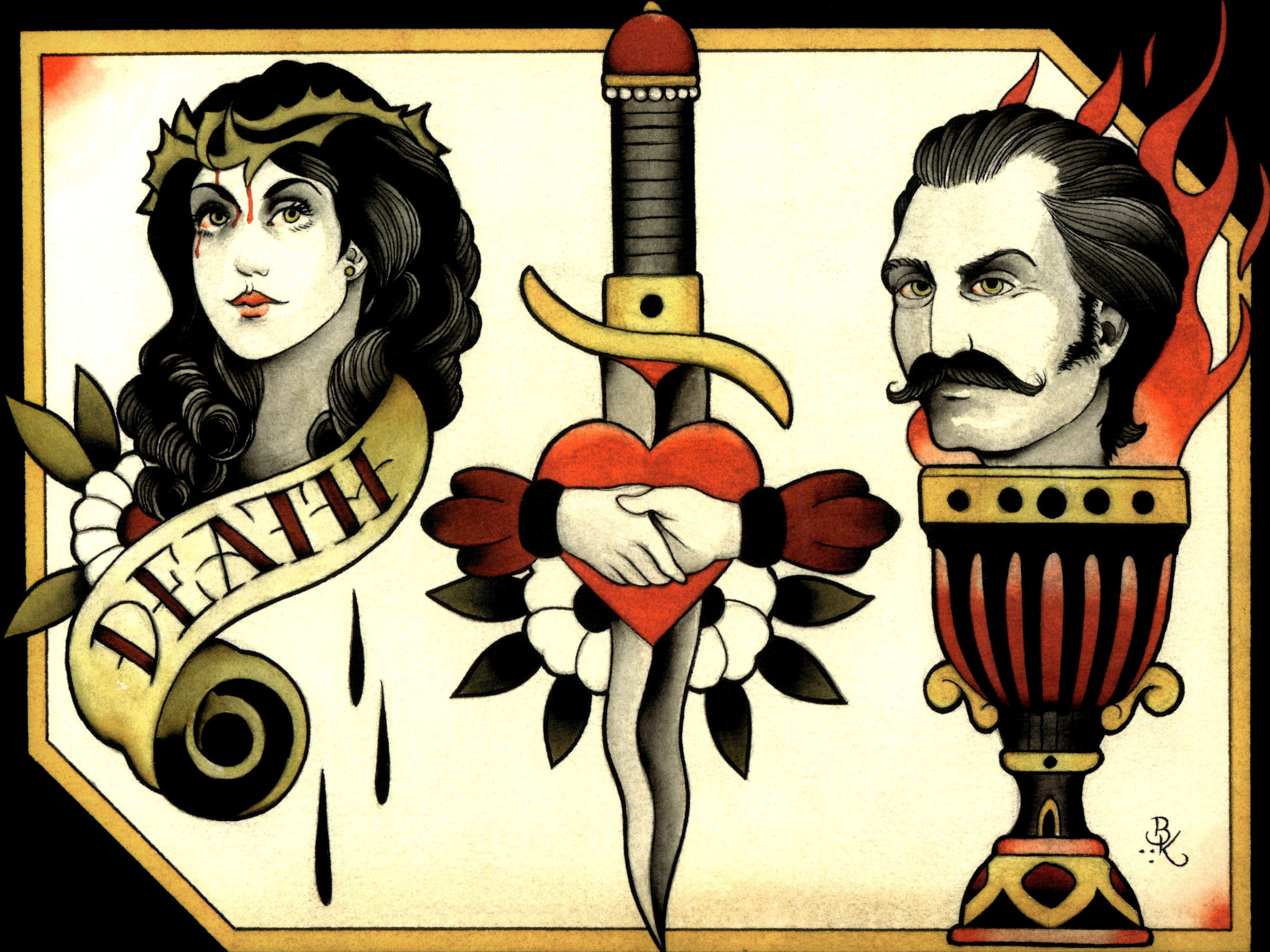
DEATH
BK

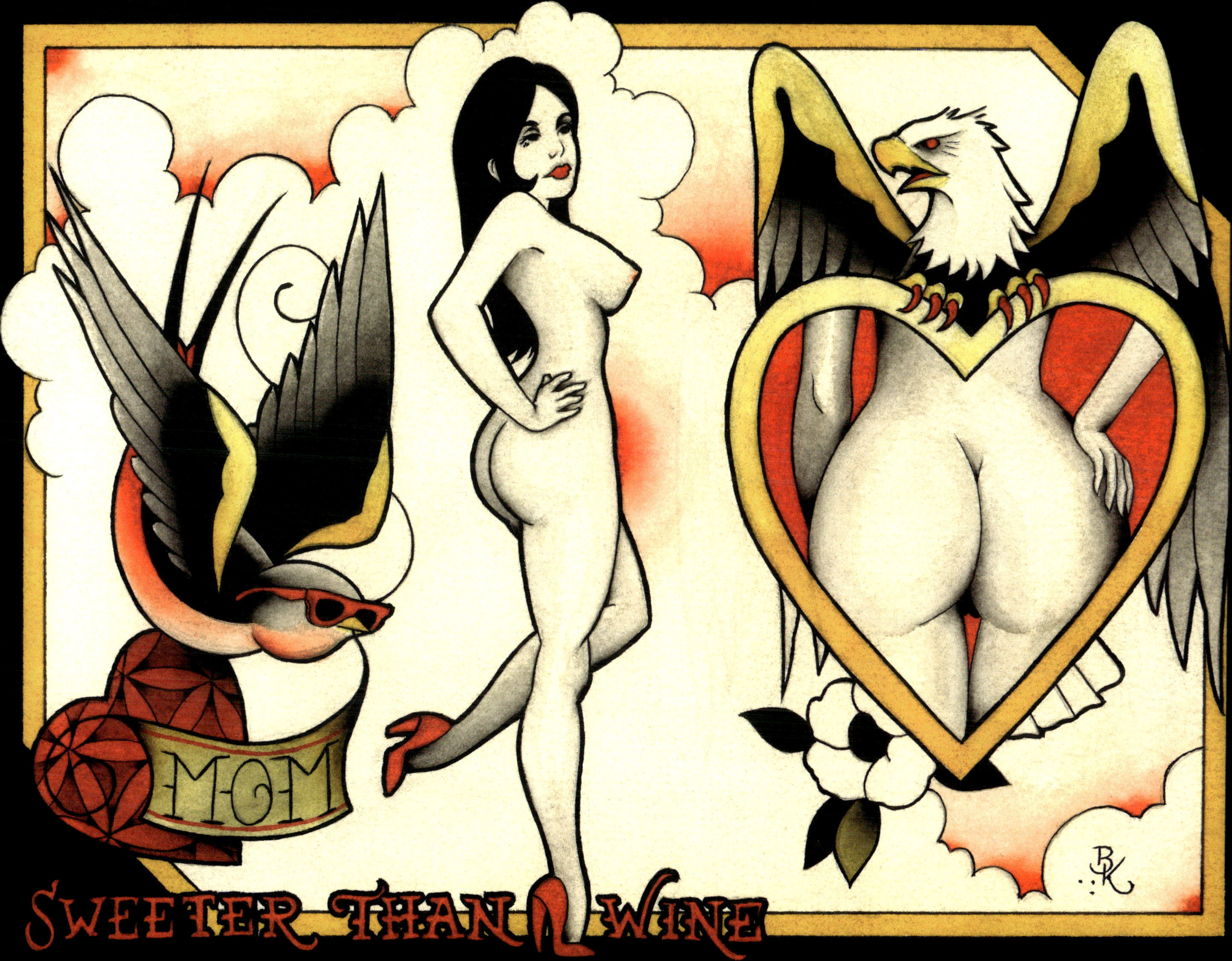
MOM
SWEETER THAN WINE
BK

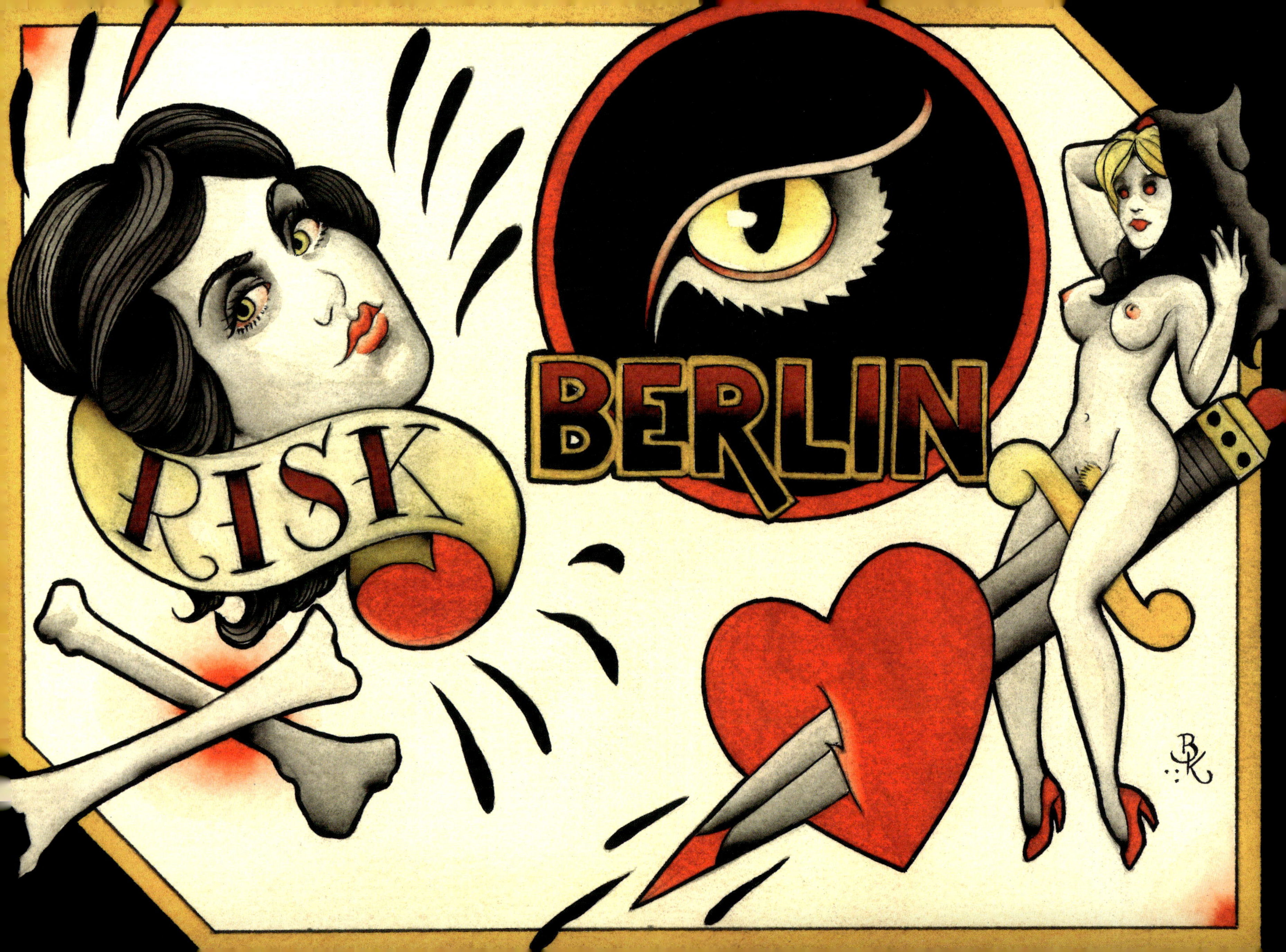
RISK
BERLIN

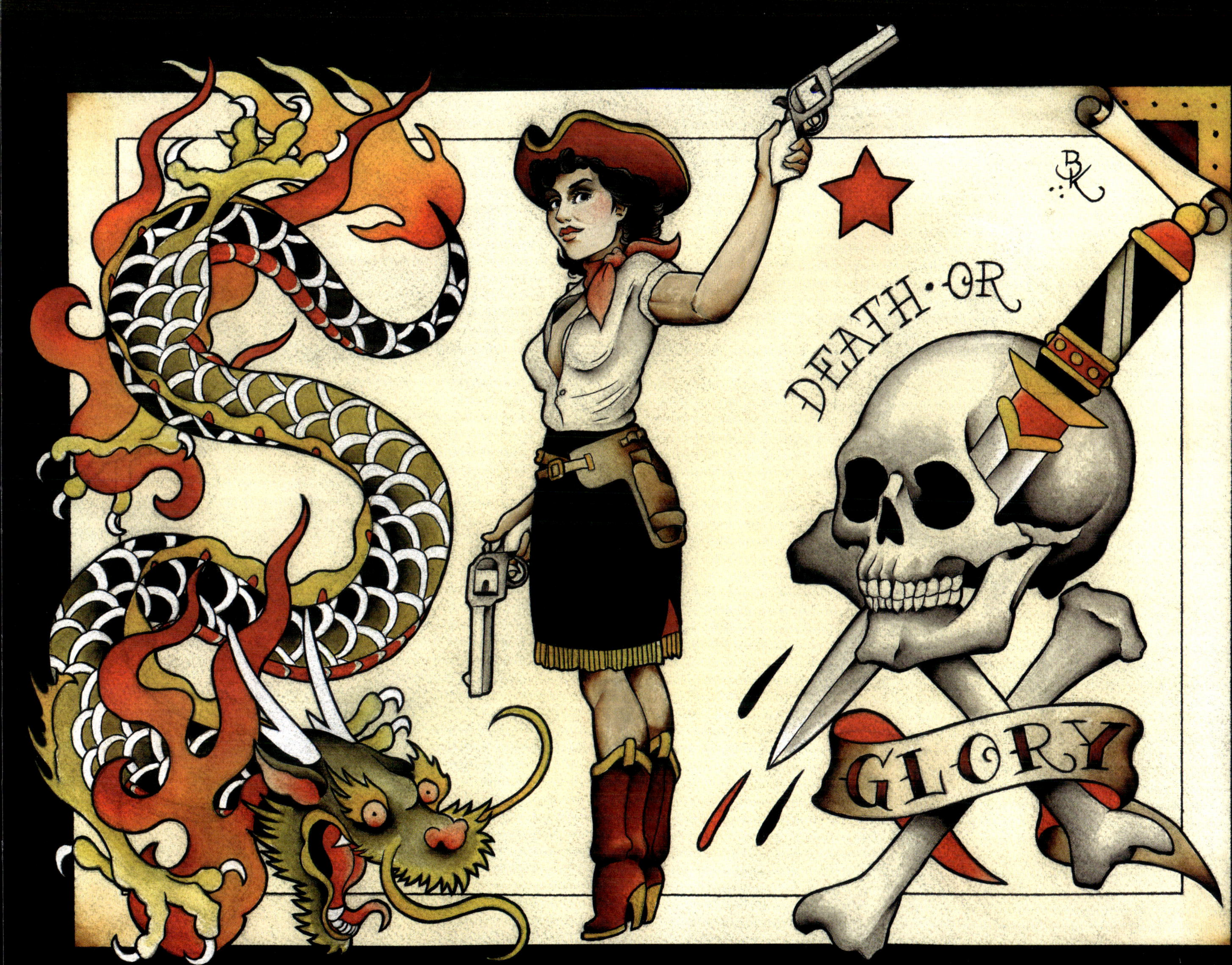
DEATH · OR
GLORY

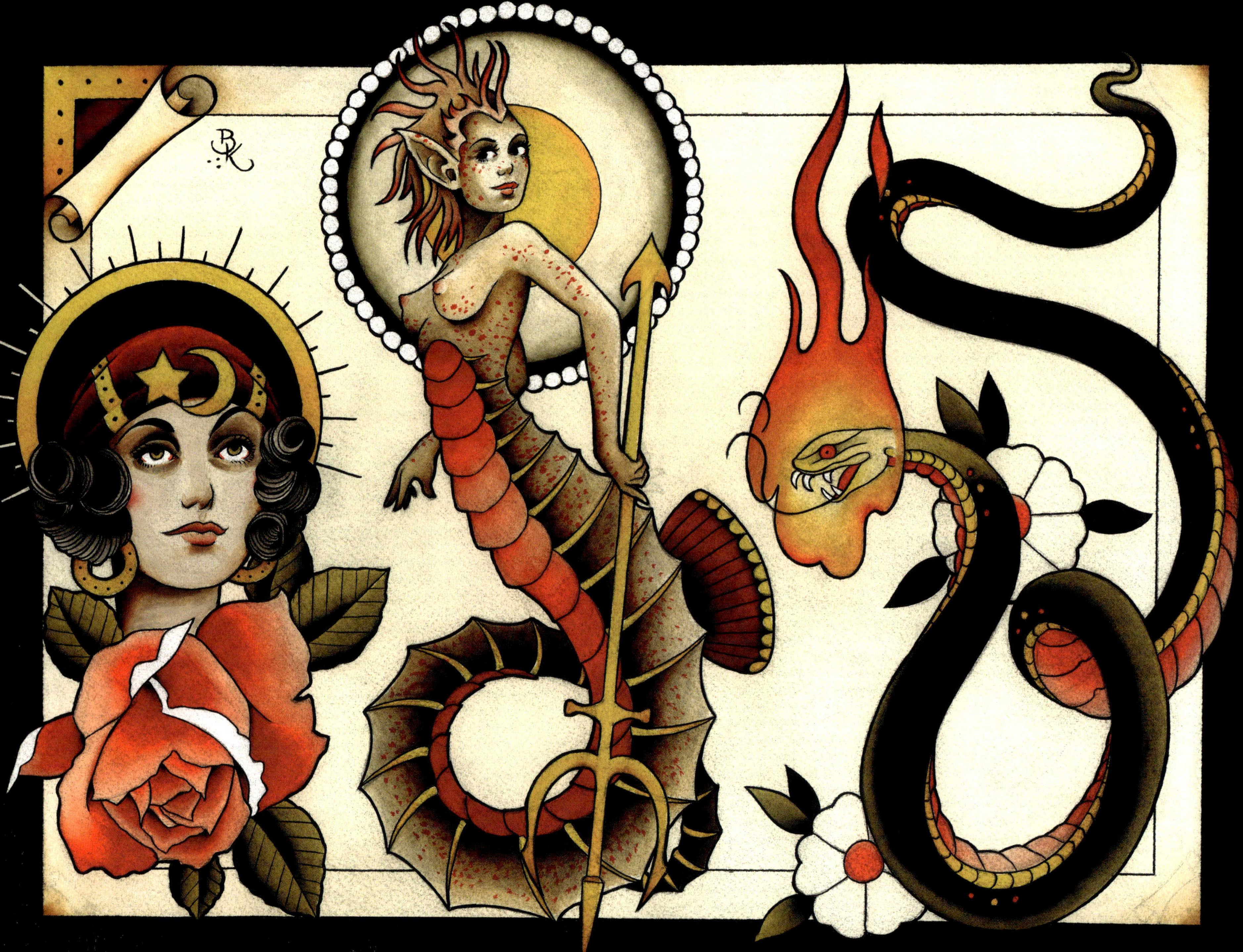

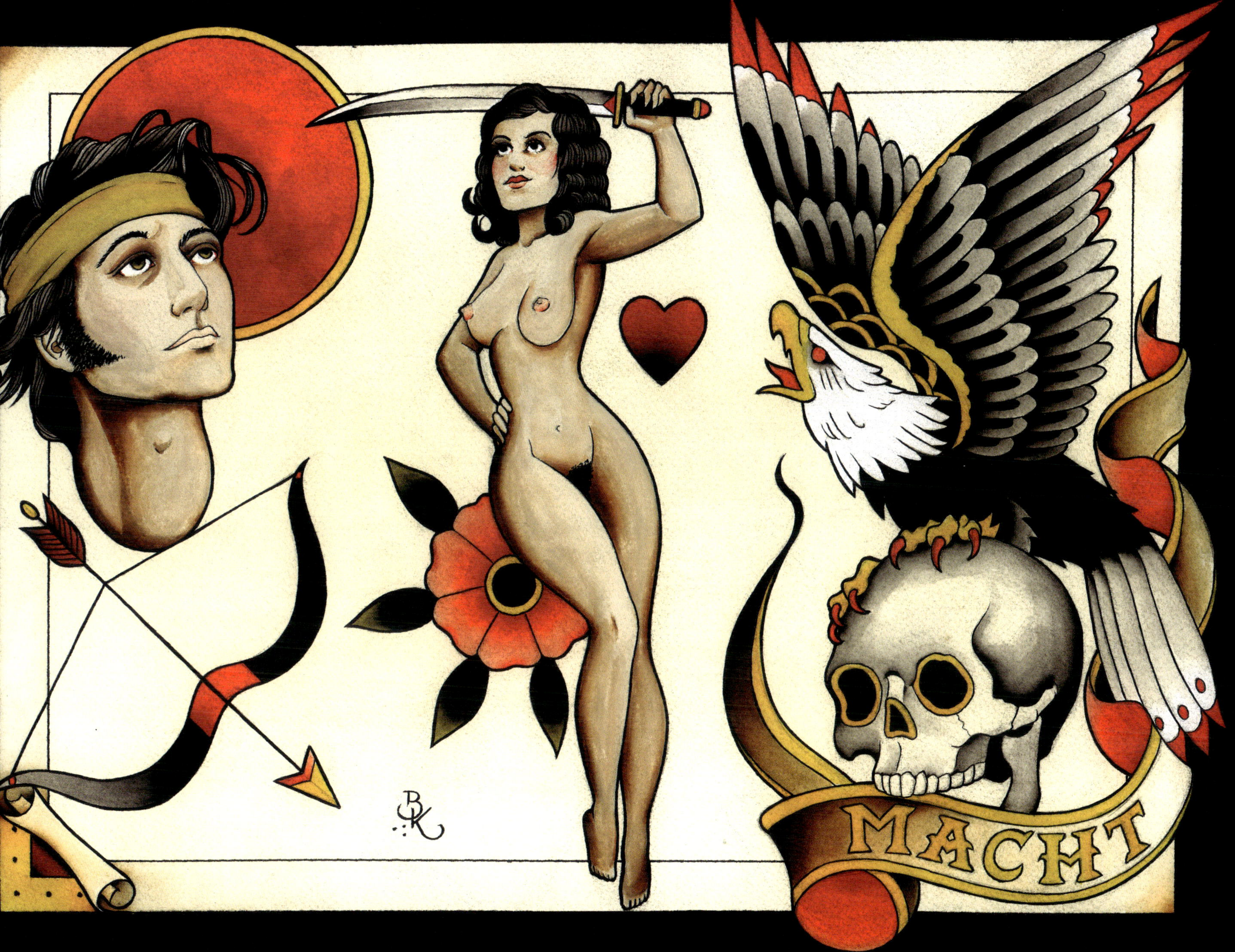
MACHT

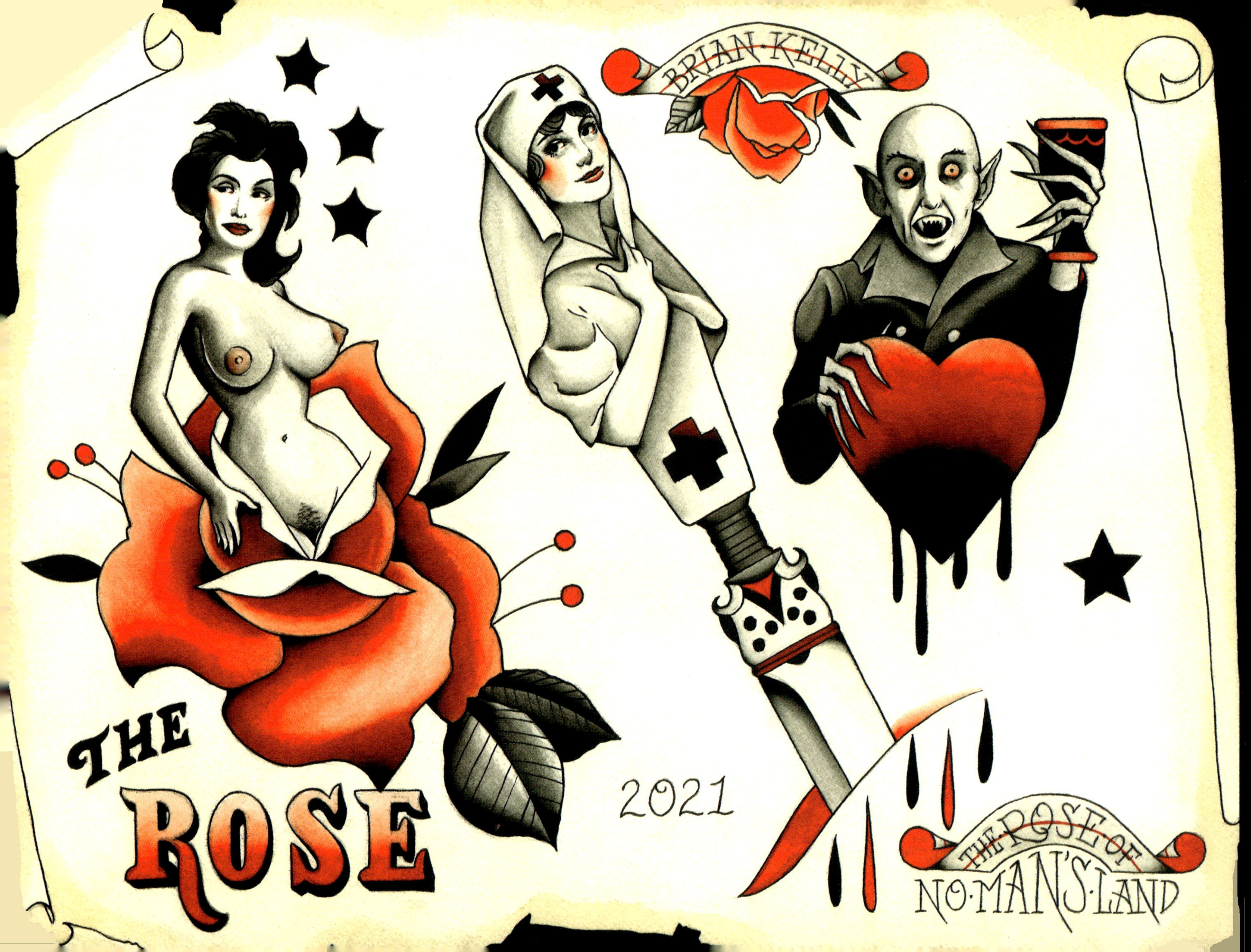
BRIAN KELLY
THE ROSE
2021
THE ROSE OF
NO·MAN'S·LAND

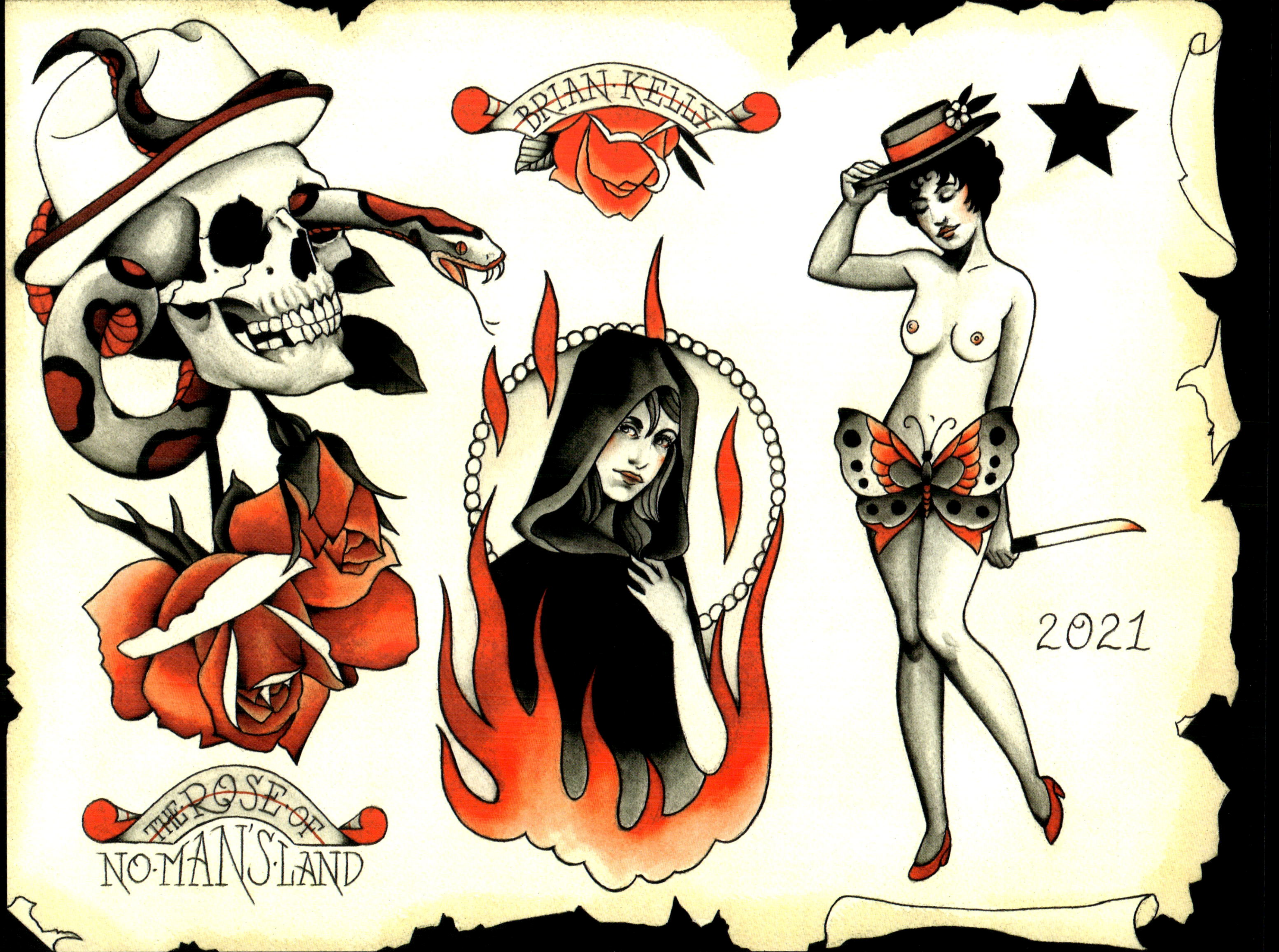
BRIAN KELLY
THE ROSE OF
NO-MAN'S-LAND
2021

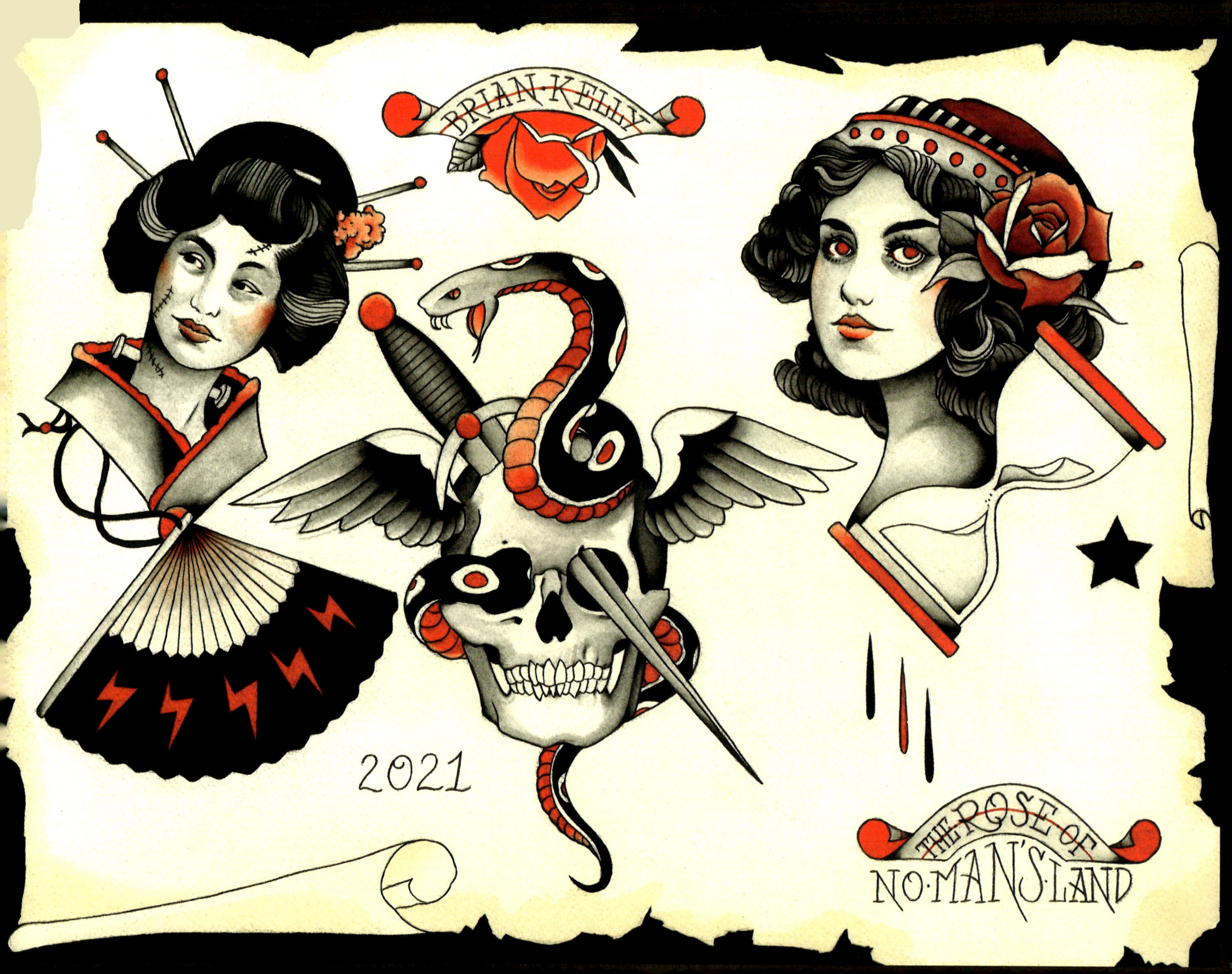

BRIAN·KELLY
2021
THE ROSE OF
NO·MAN'S·LAND

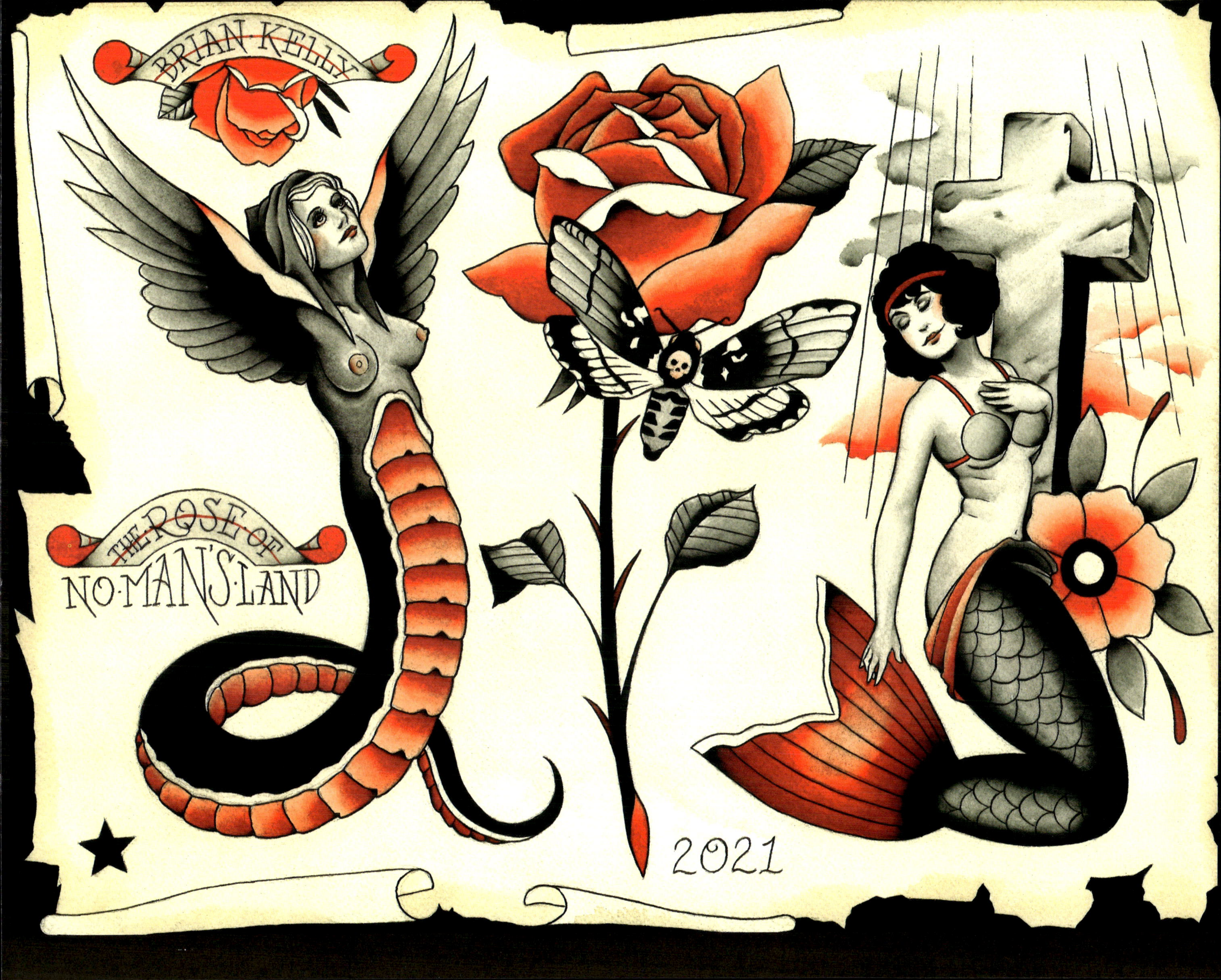

BRIAN·KELLY
THE ROSE OF
NO·MAN'S·LAND
2021

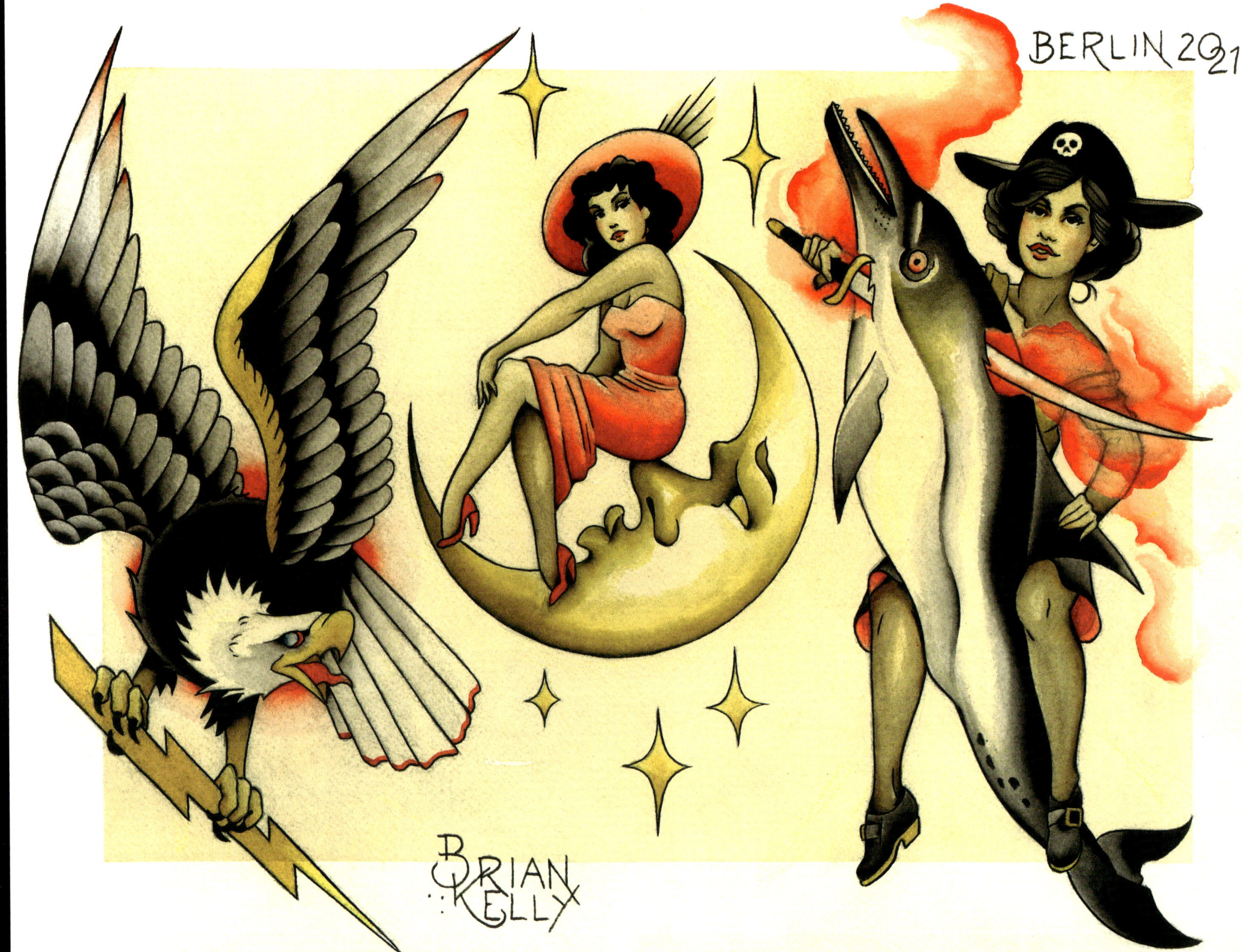
BERLIN 2021
BRIAN KELLY

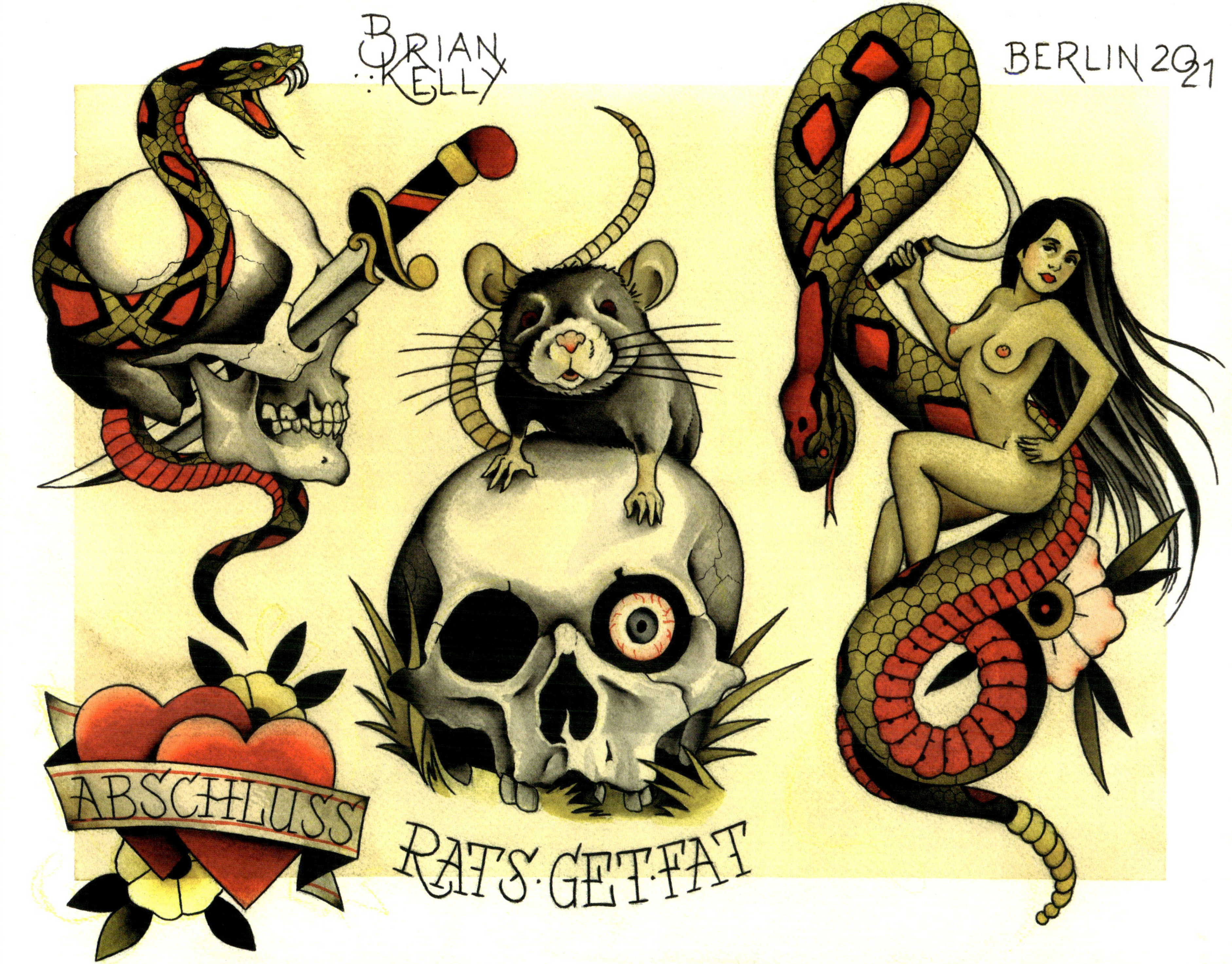
BRIAN KELLY
BERLIN 2021
ABSCHLUSS
RATS·GET·FAT

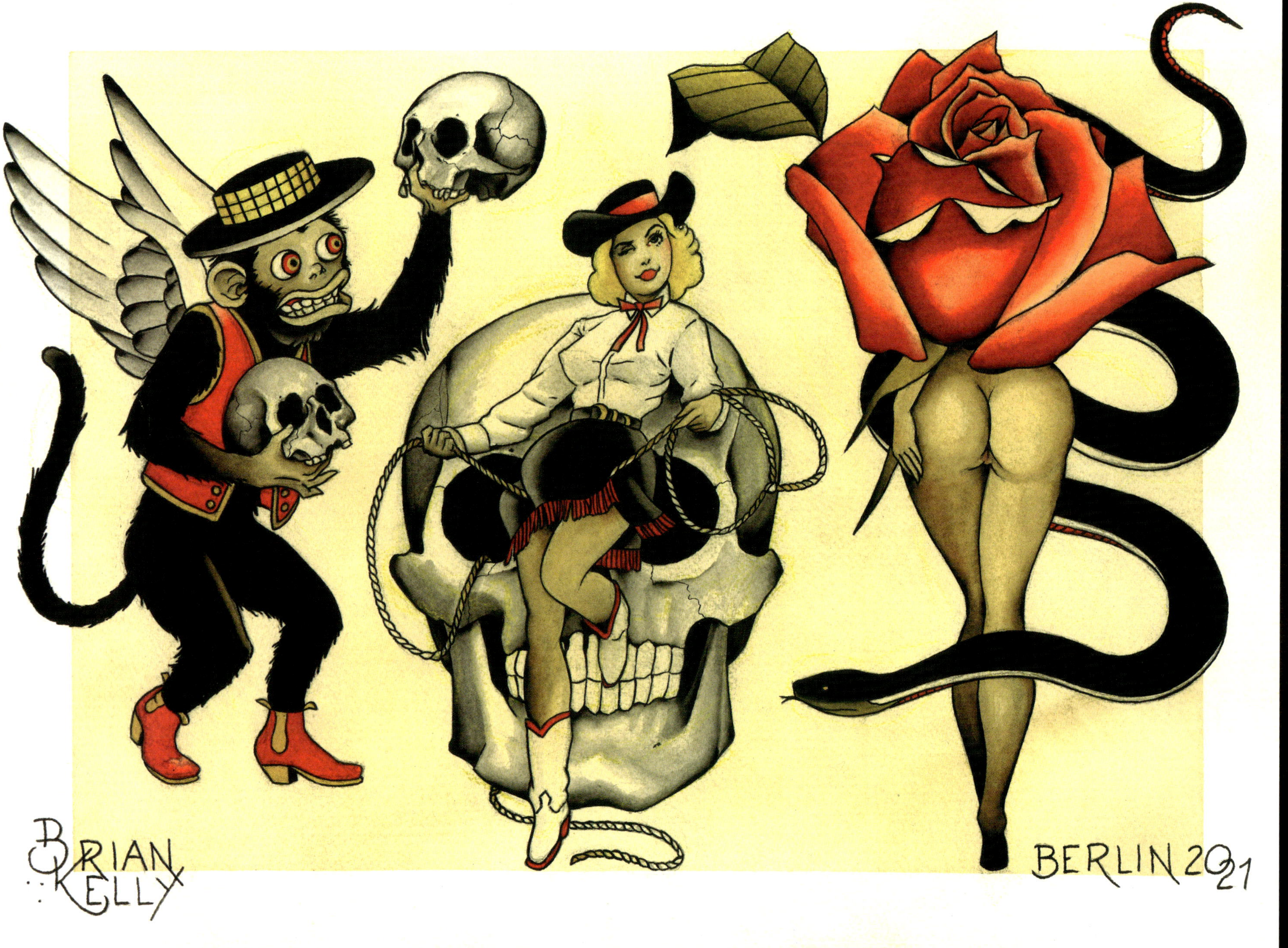
BRIAN KELLY
BERLIN 2021

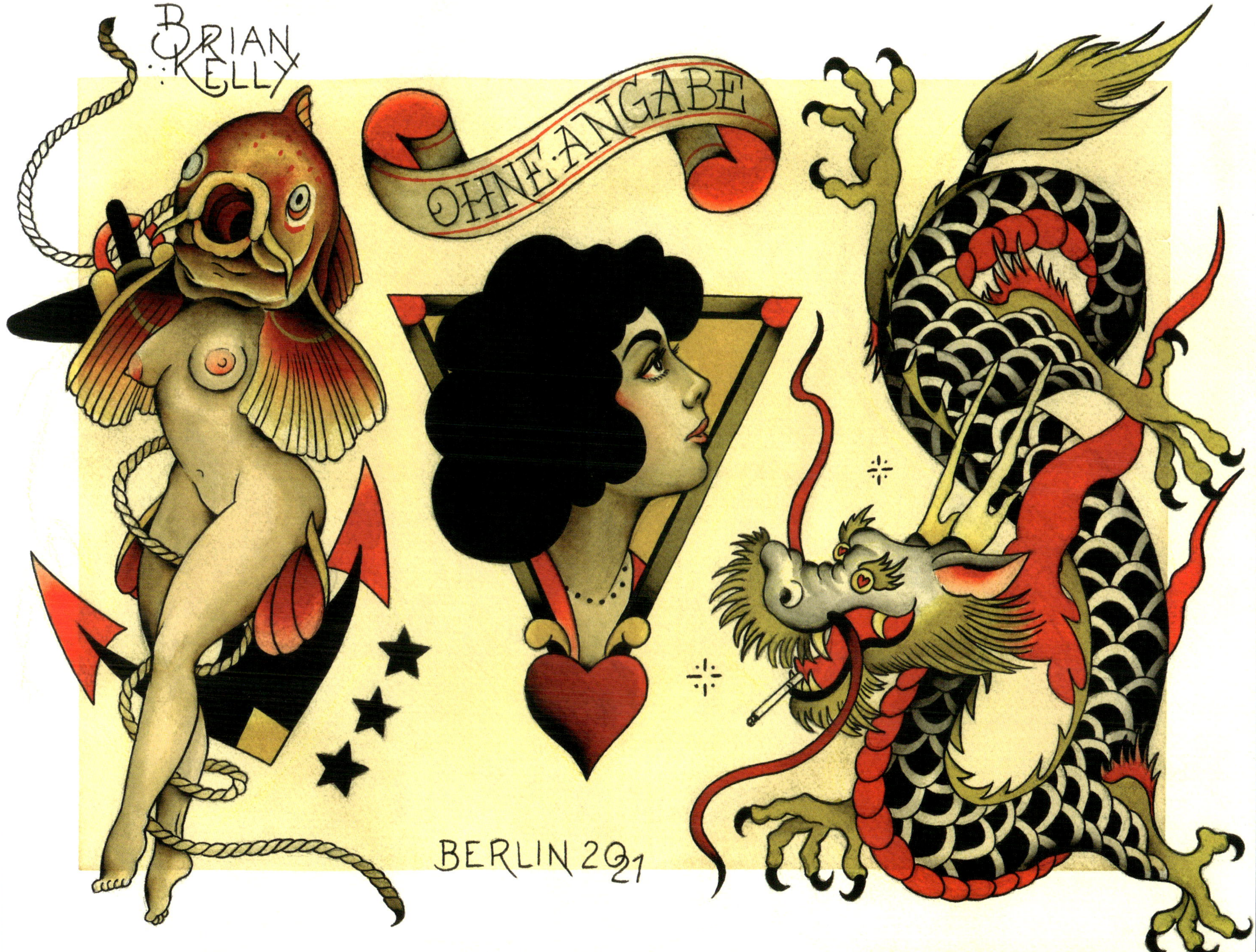
BRIAN KELLY
OHNE ANGABE
BERLIN 2021

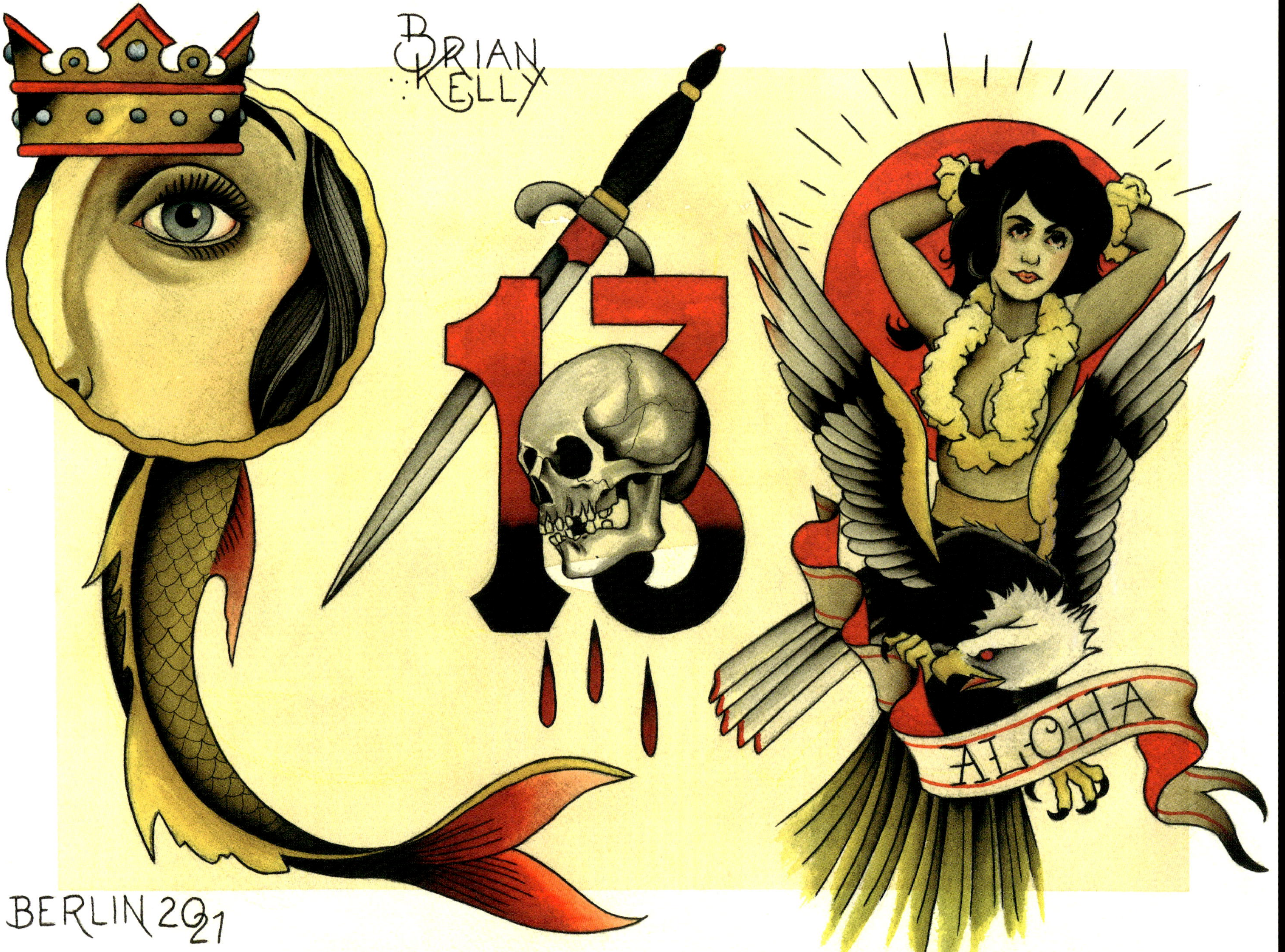
BRIAN KELLY
13
ALOHA
BERLIN 2021

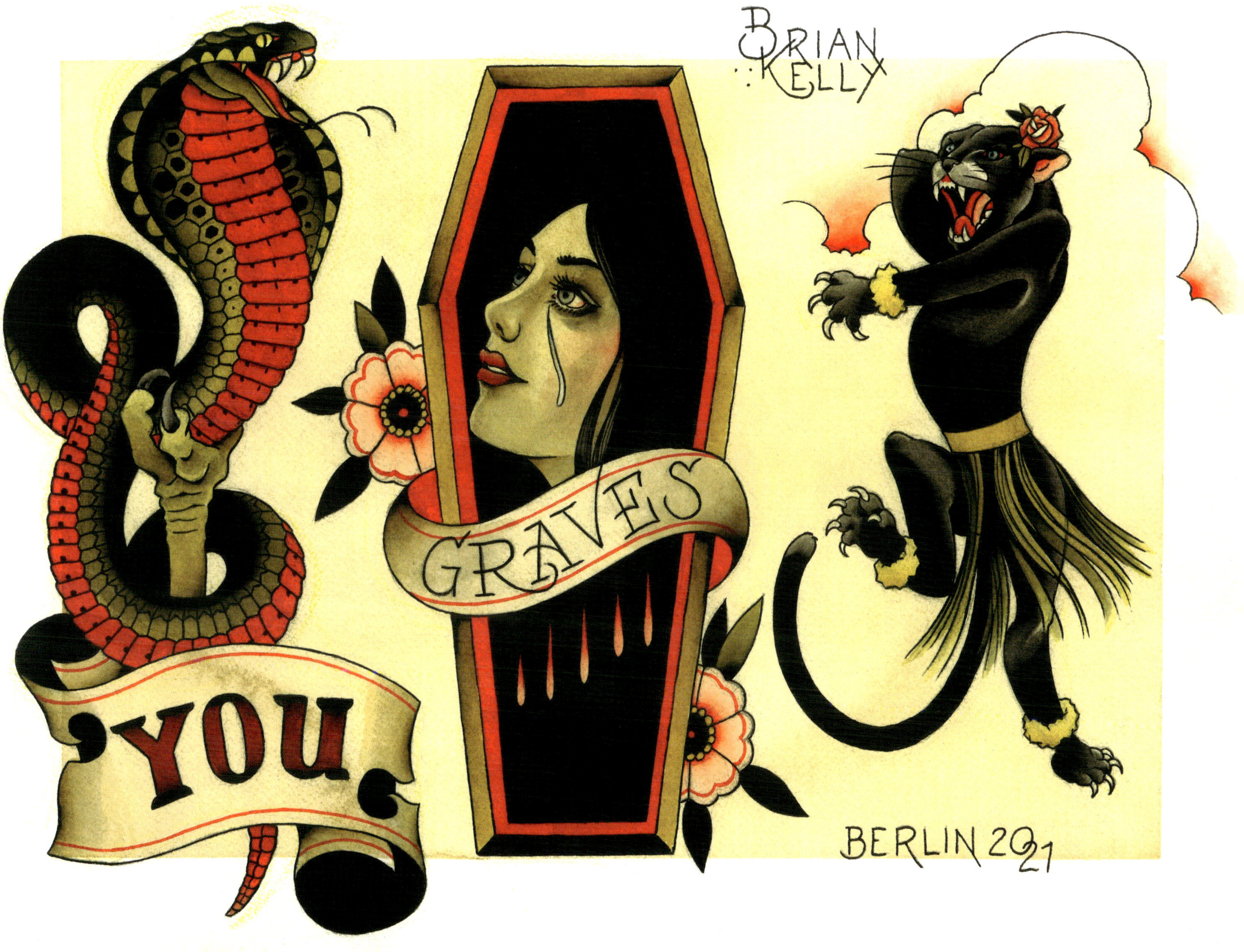

BRIAN KELLY
GRAVES
YOU
BERLIN 2021

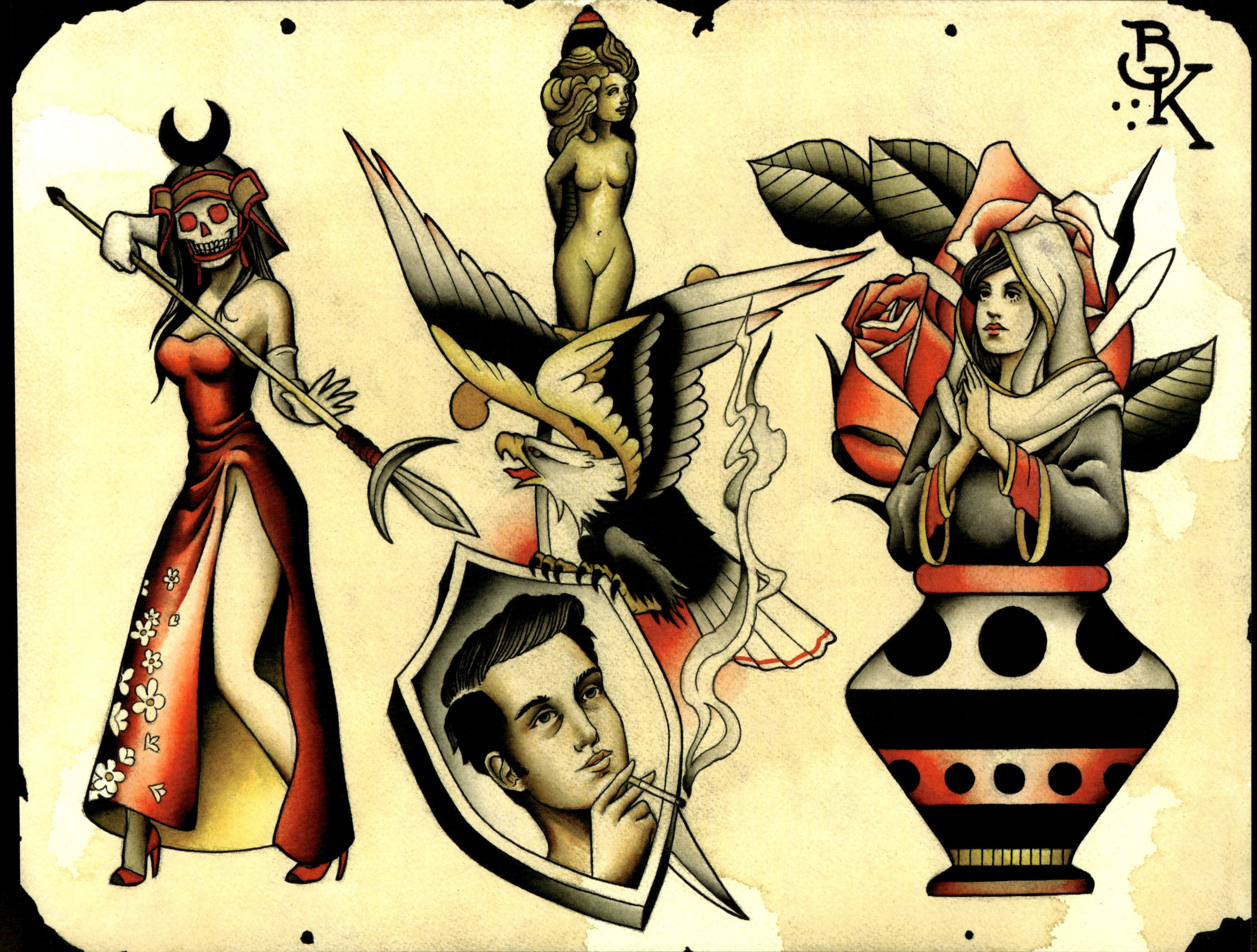

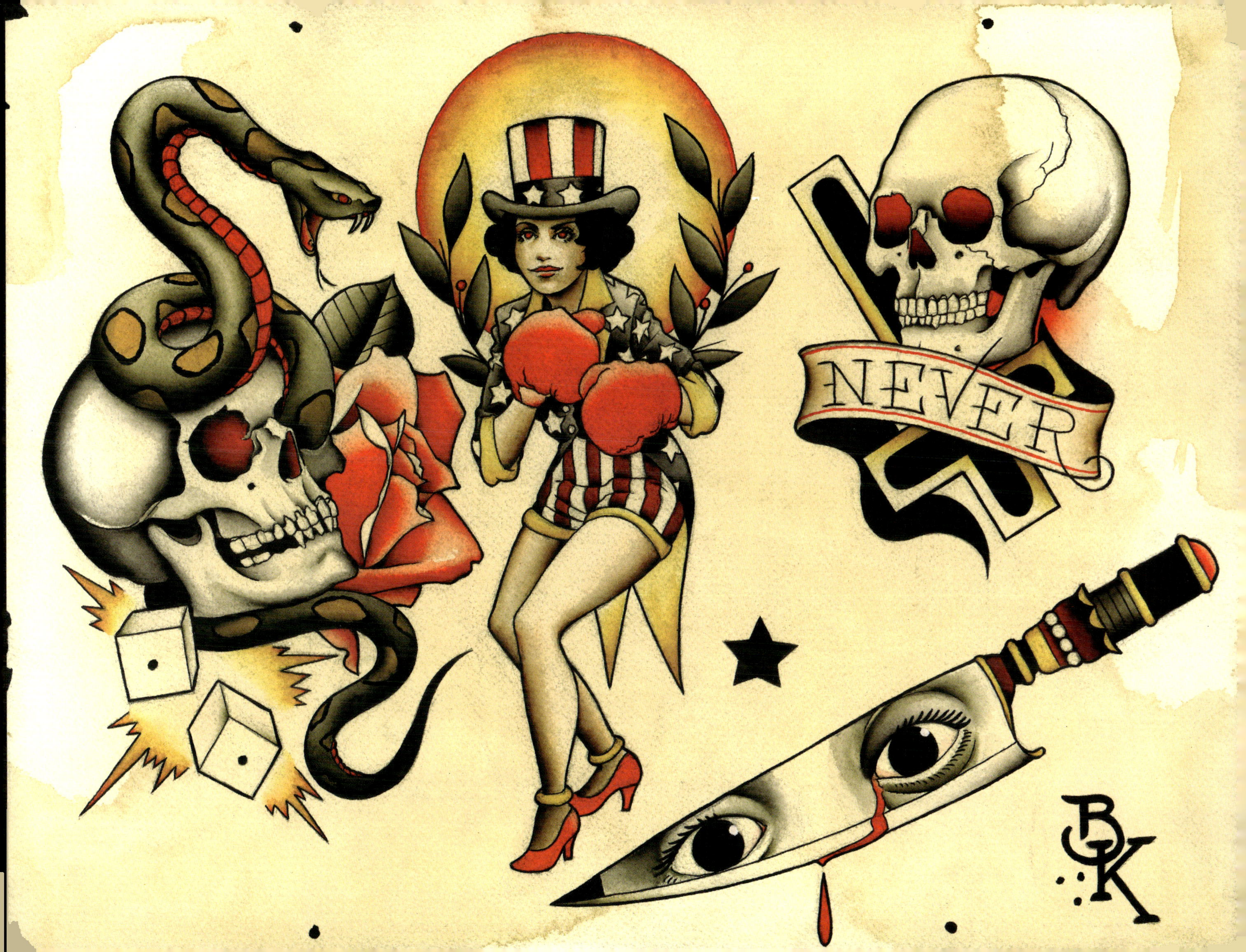
NEVER
BK

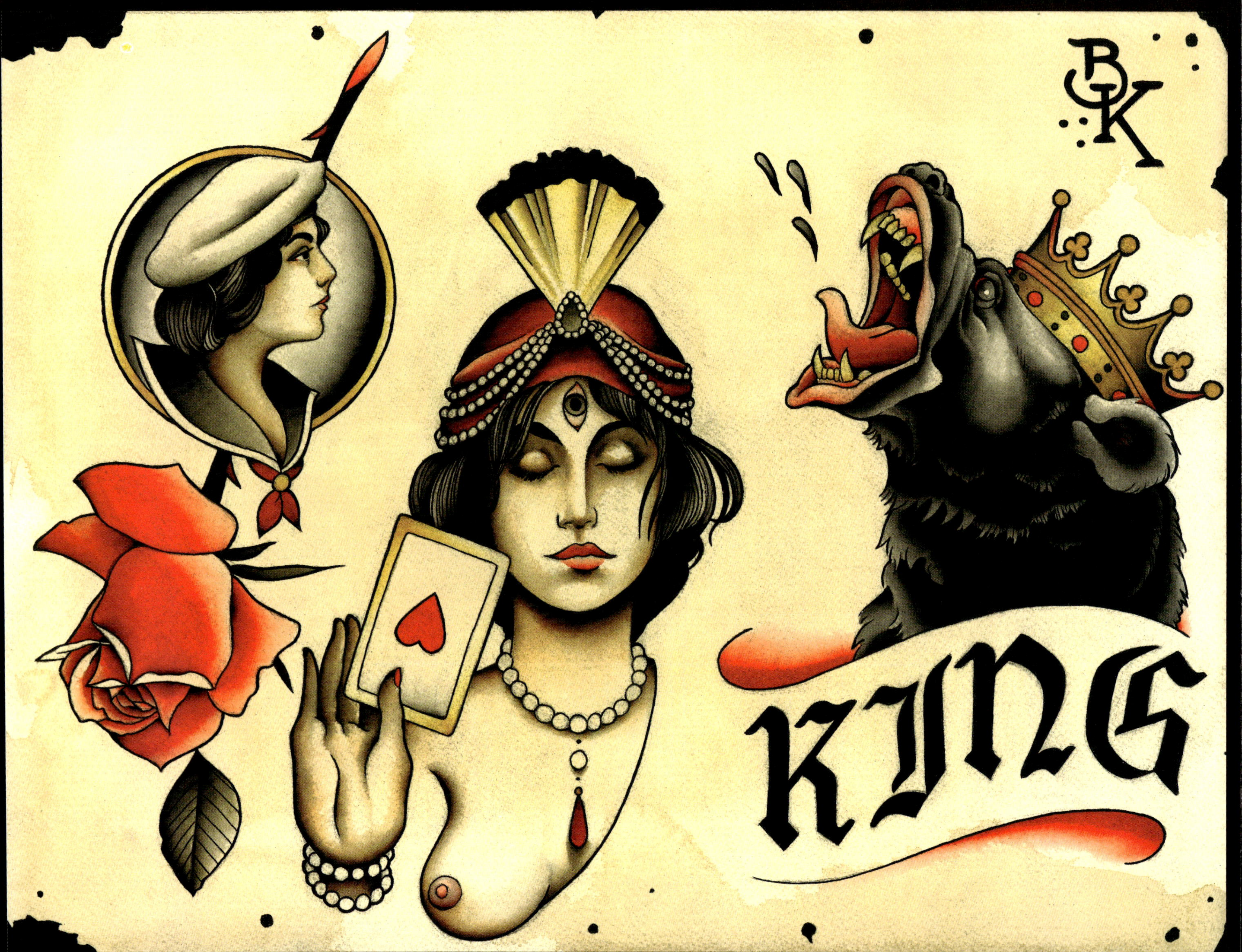
BK
KING

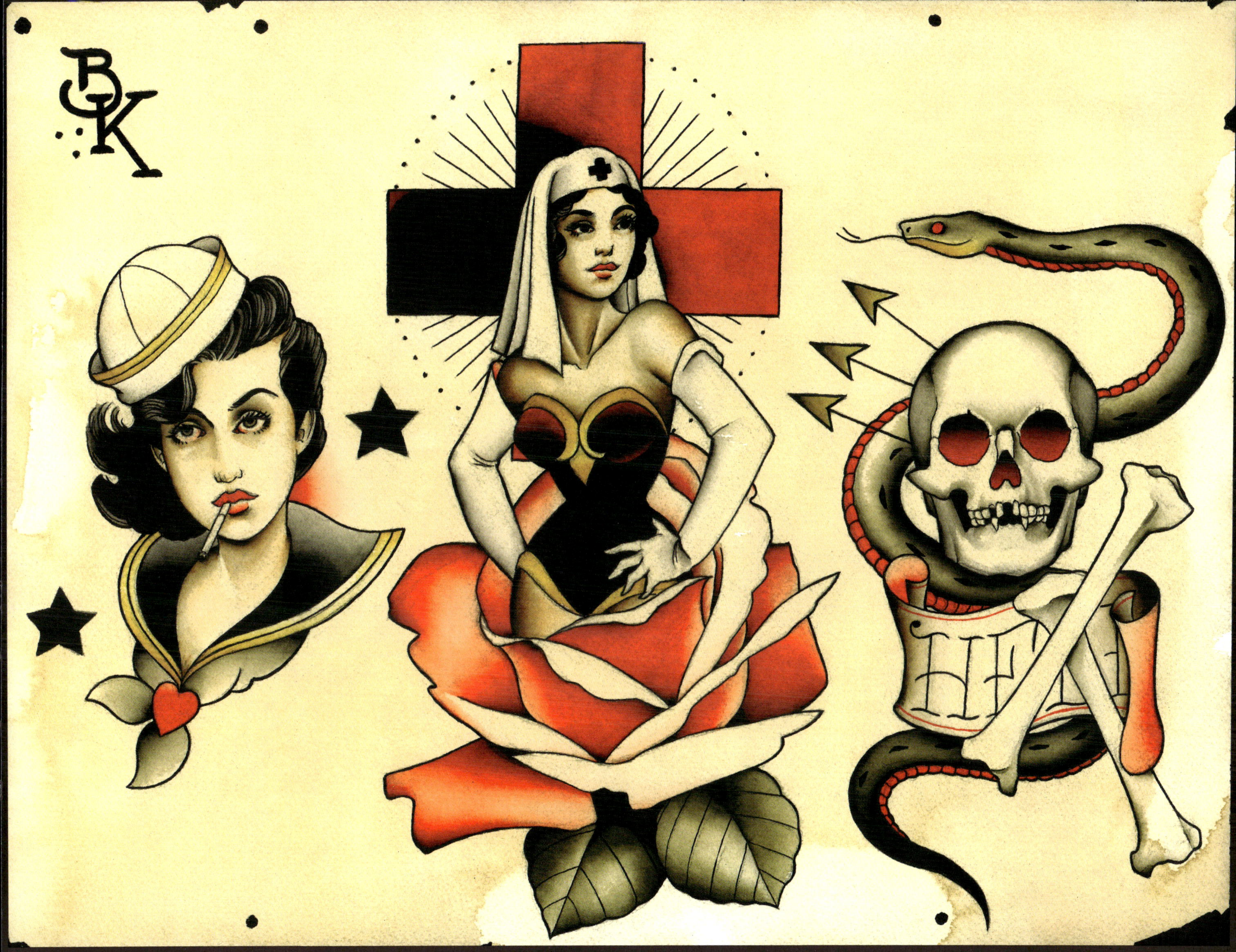

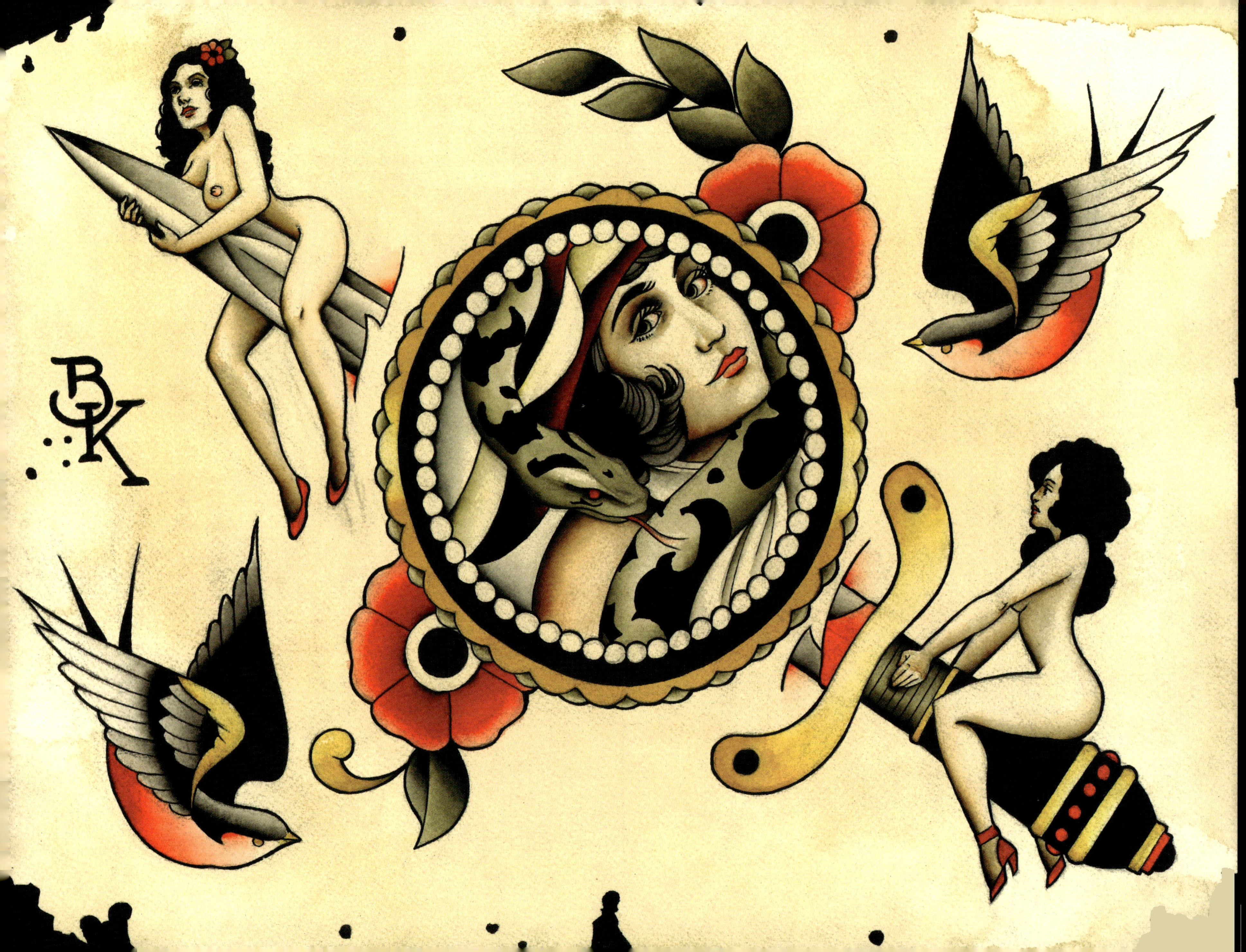

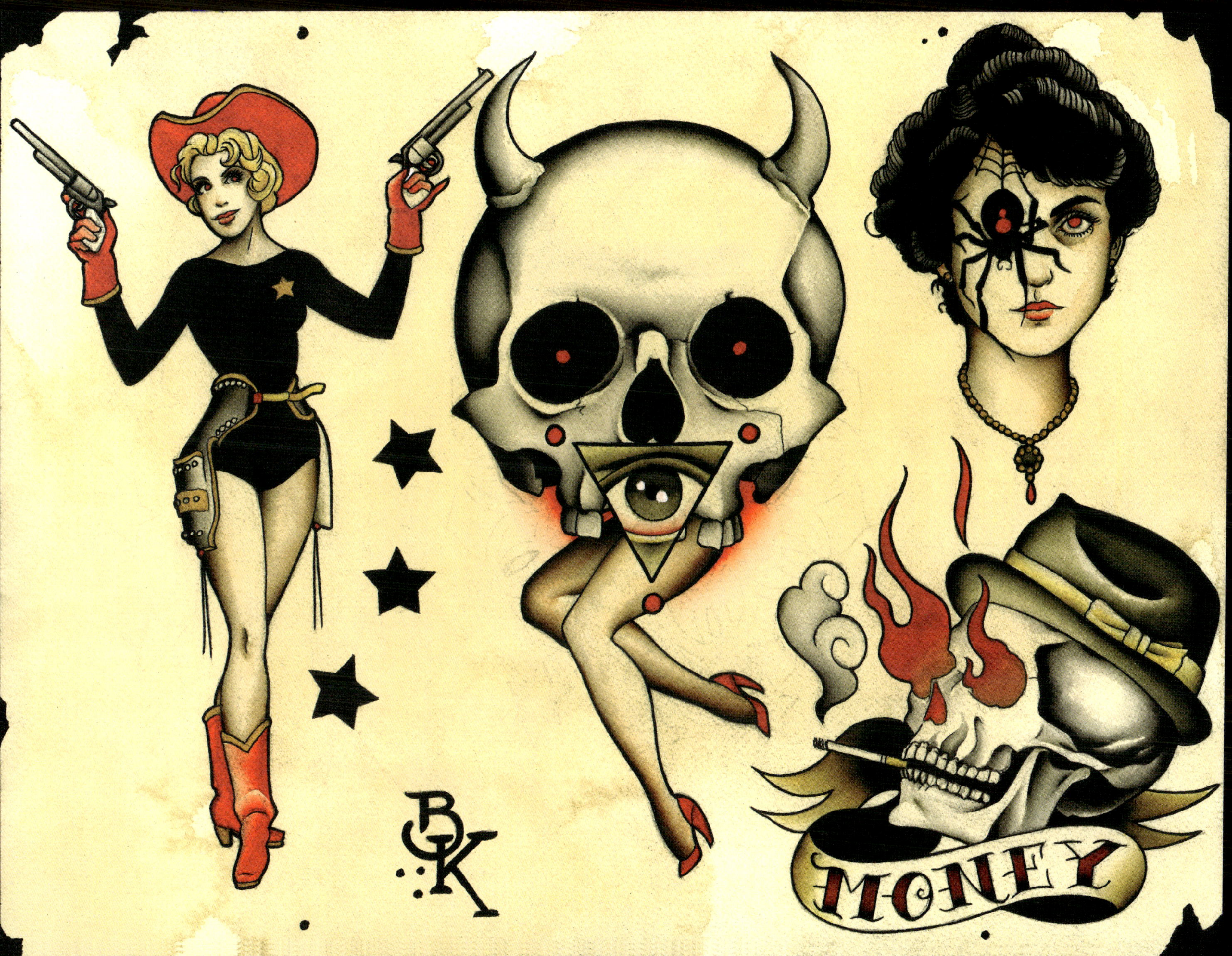
BK
MONEY

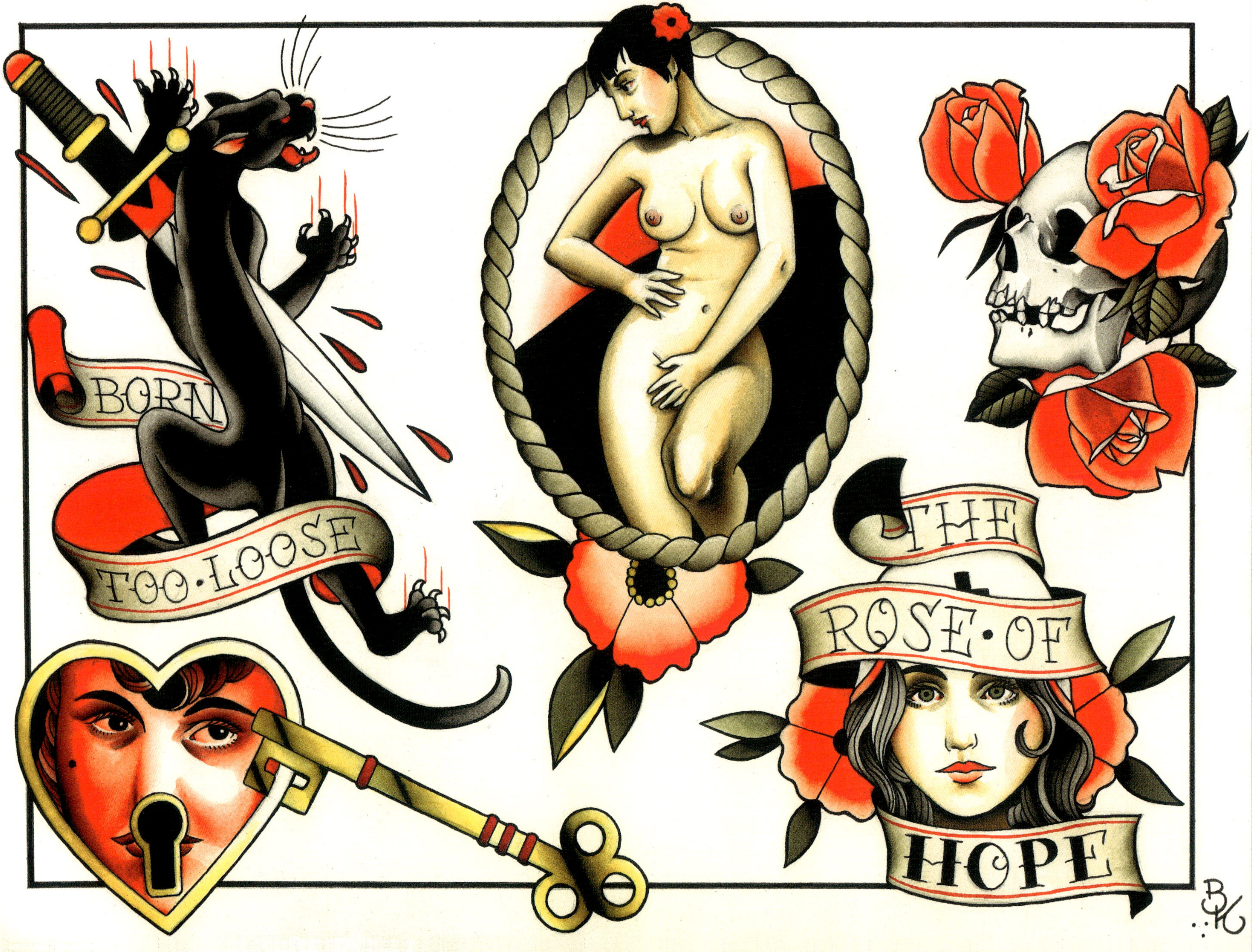

BORN
TOO·LOOSE
THE
ROSE·OF
HOPE

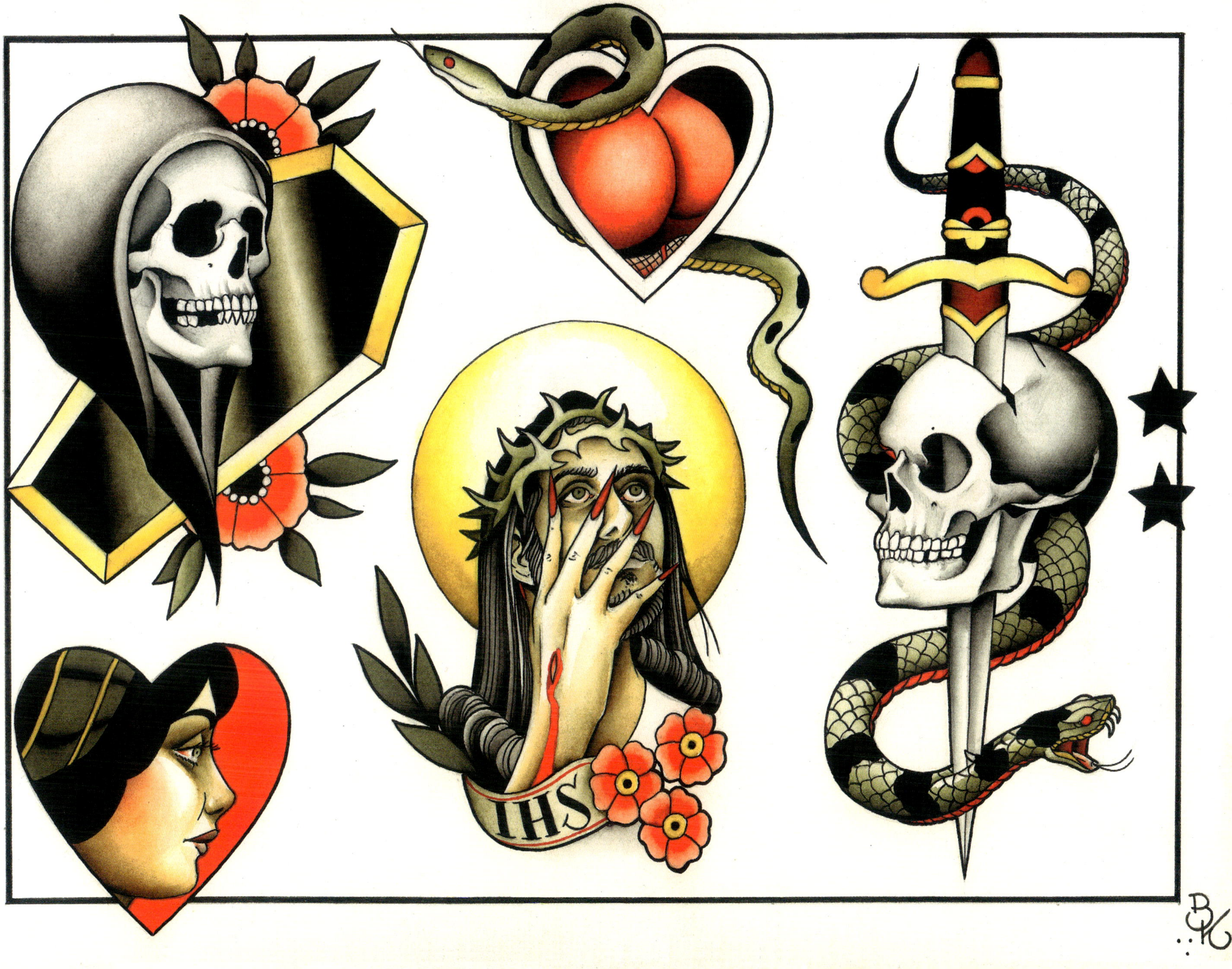
IHS

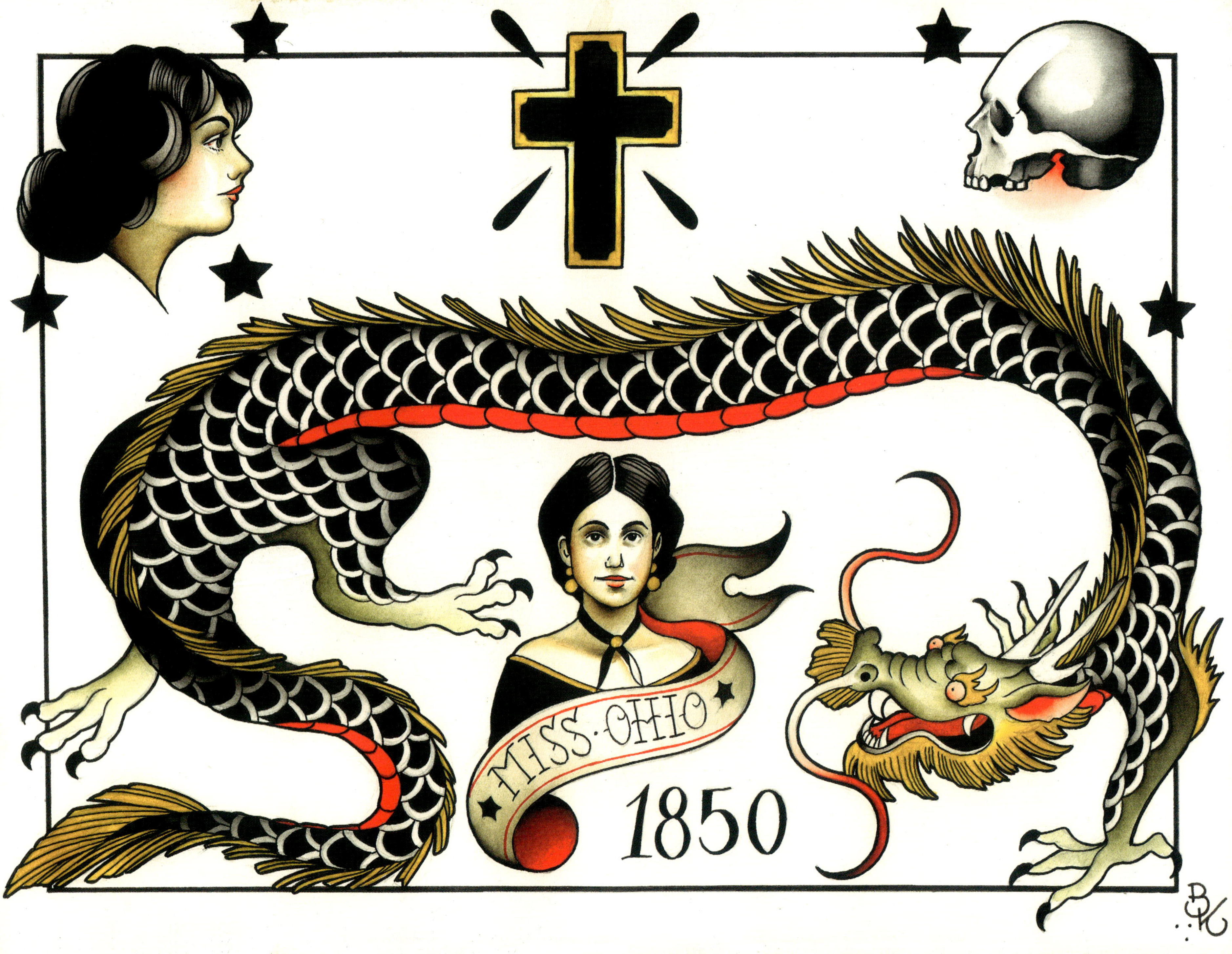
MISS·OHIO
1850

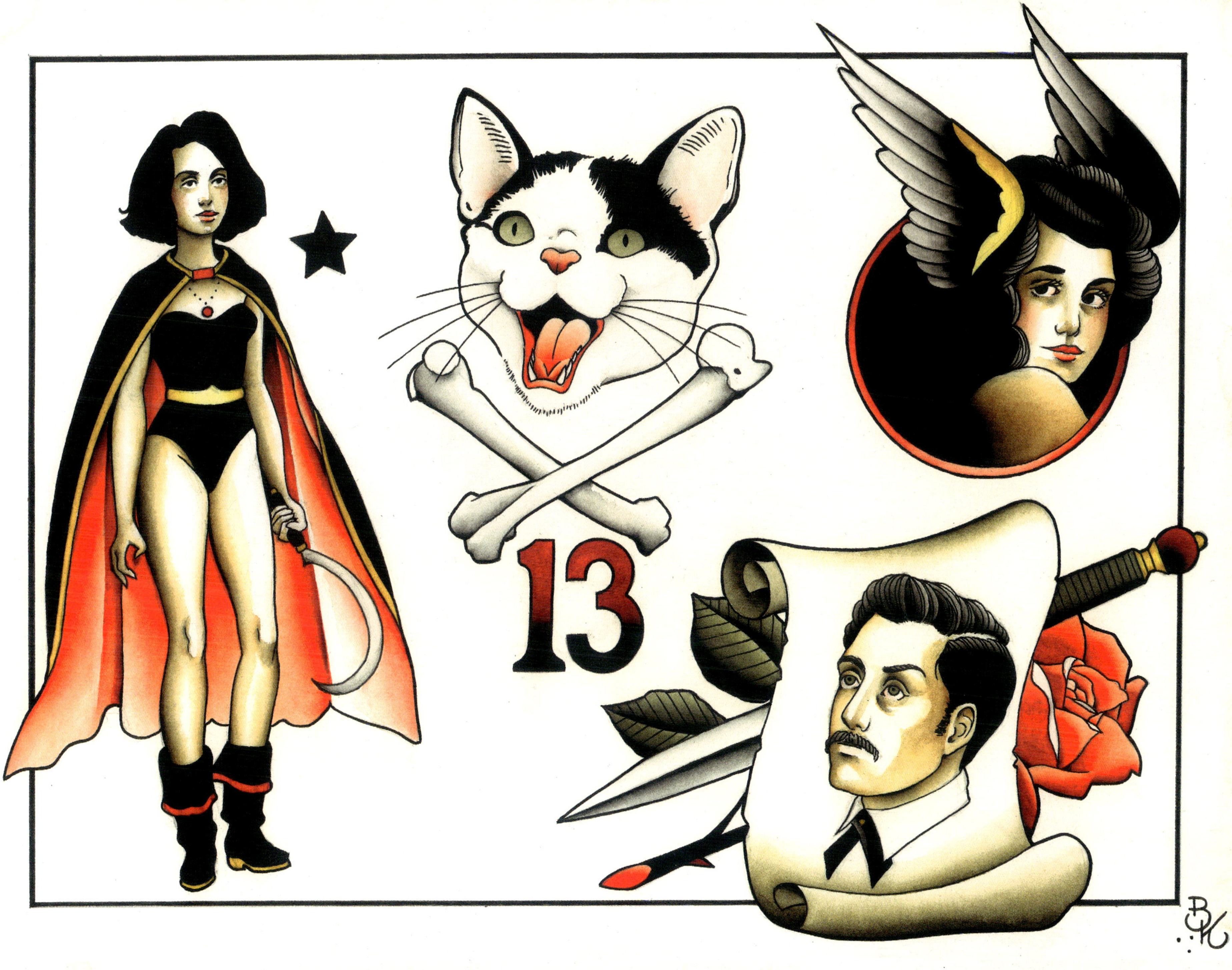
13
BK

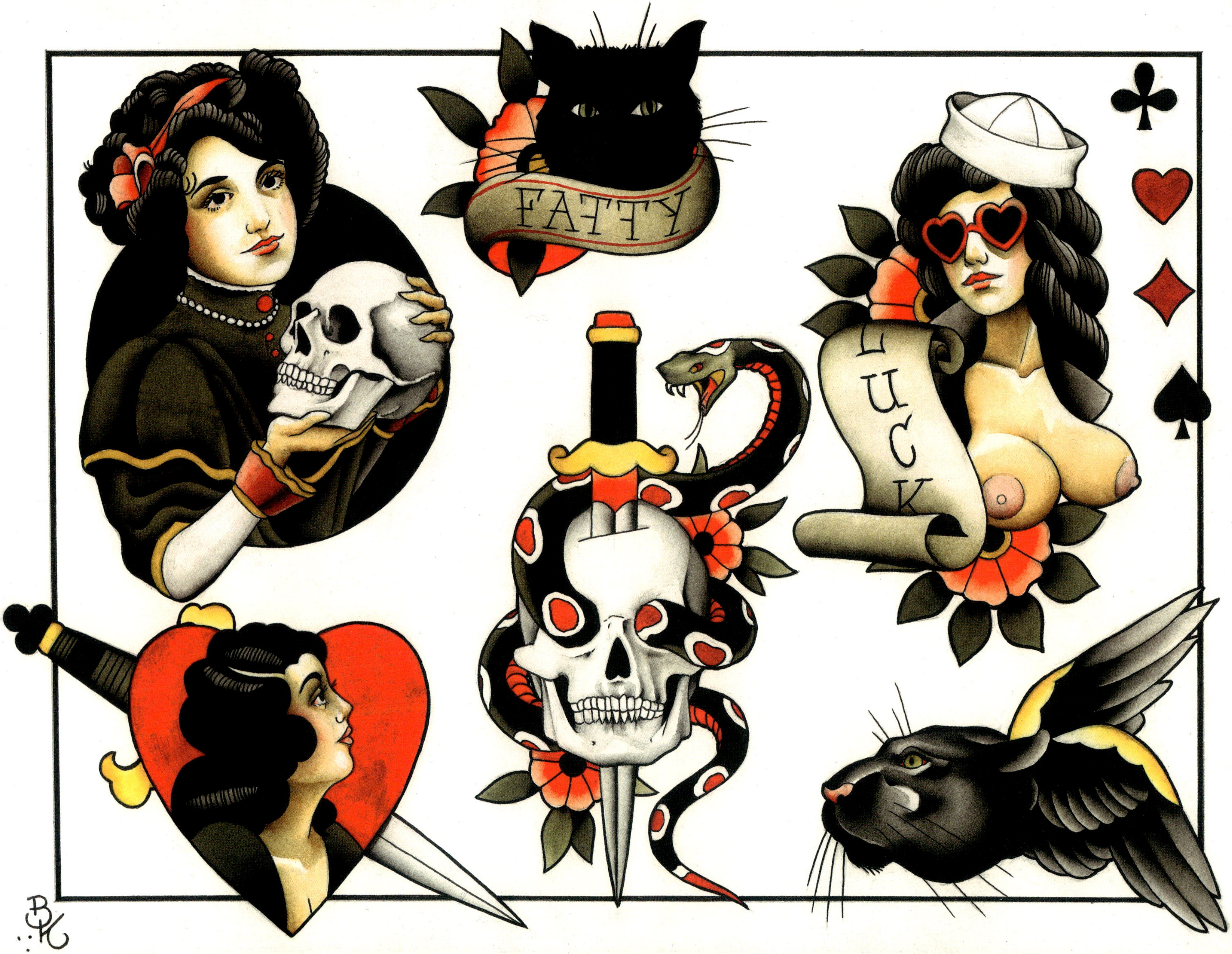
FATTY
LUCK

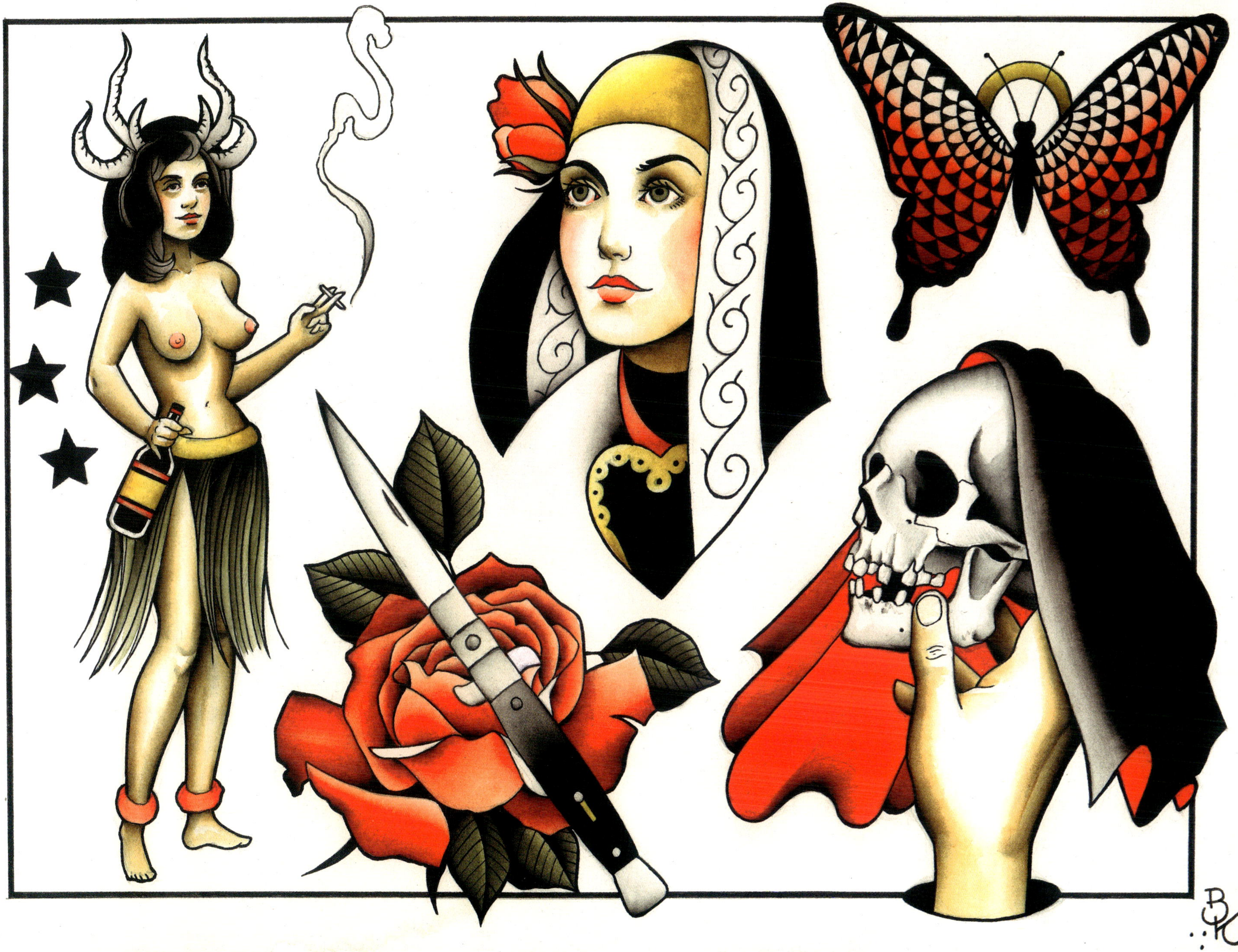

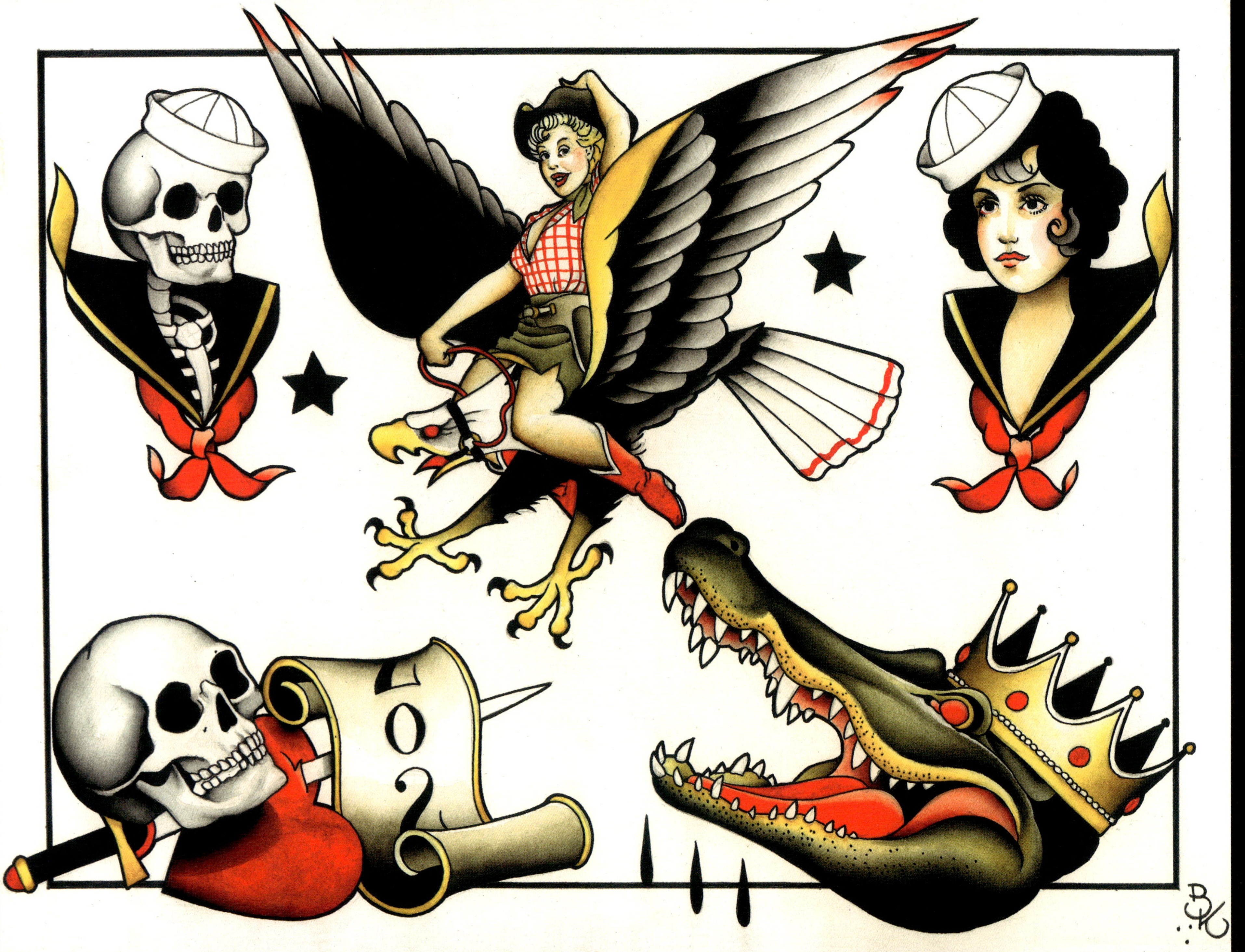

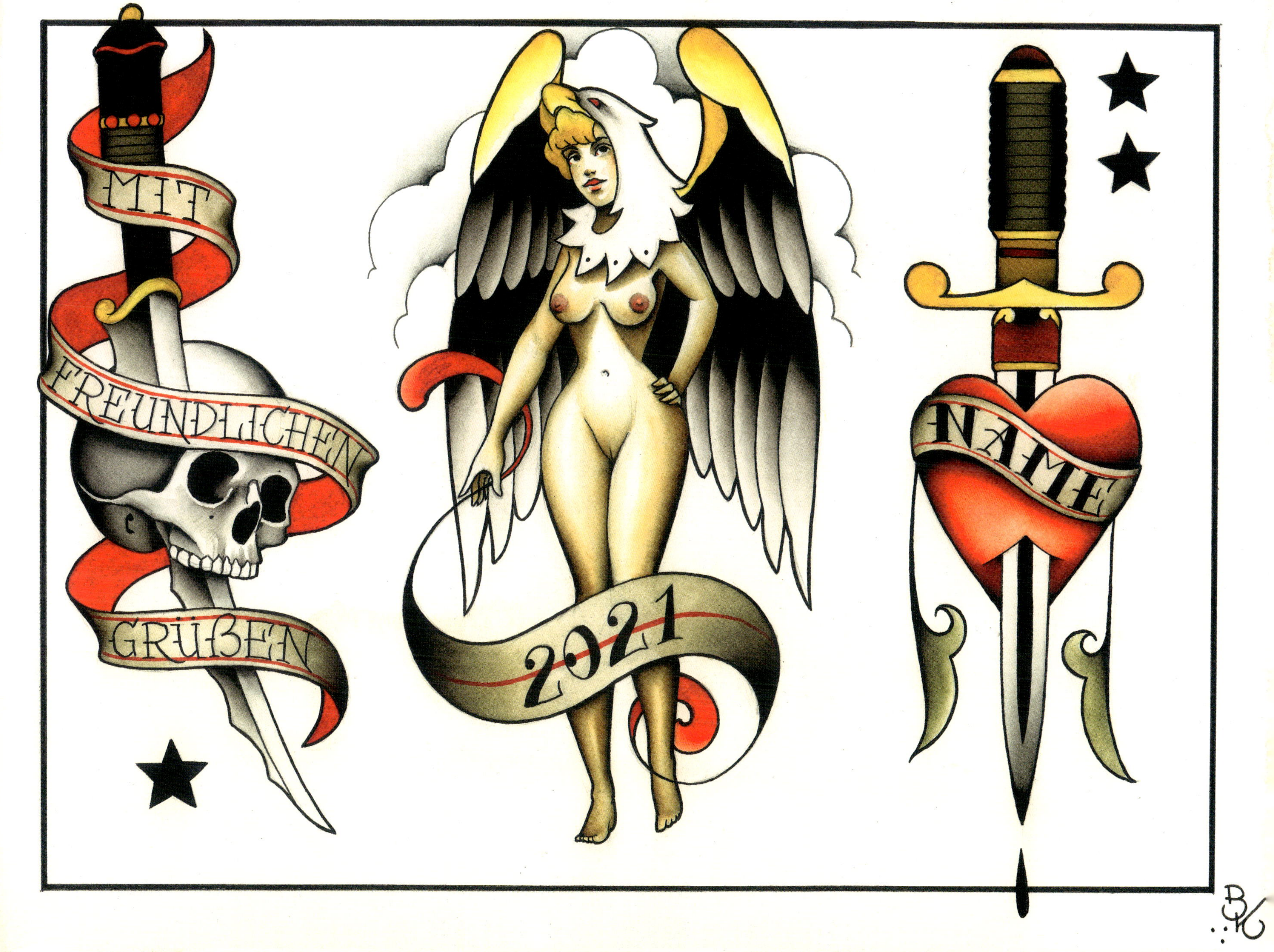
MIT
FREUNDLICHEN
GRÜßEN
2021
NAME
BK

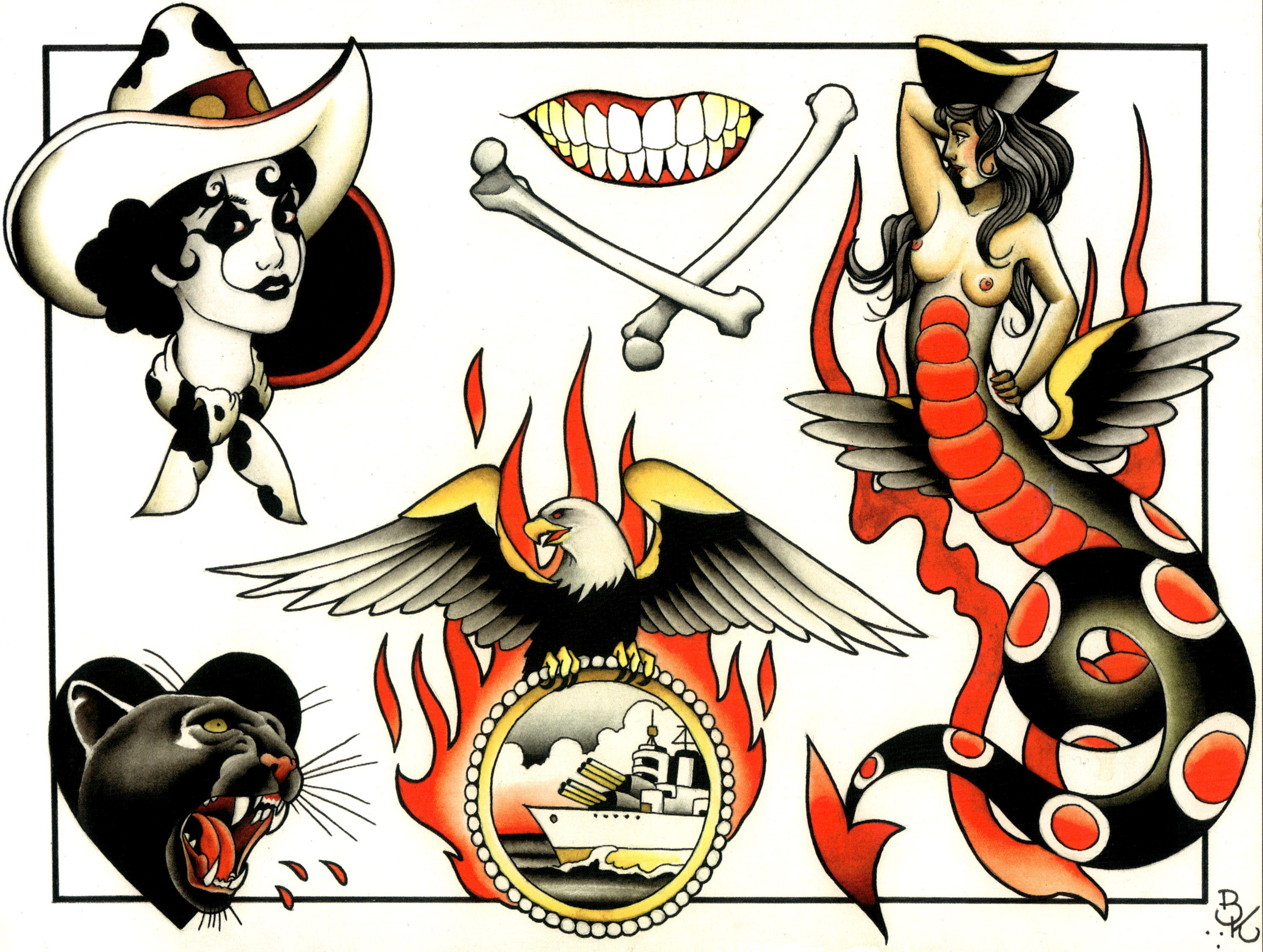

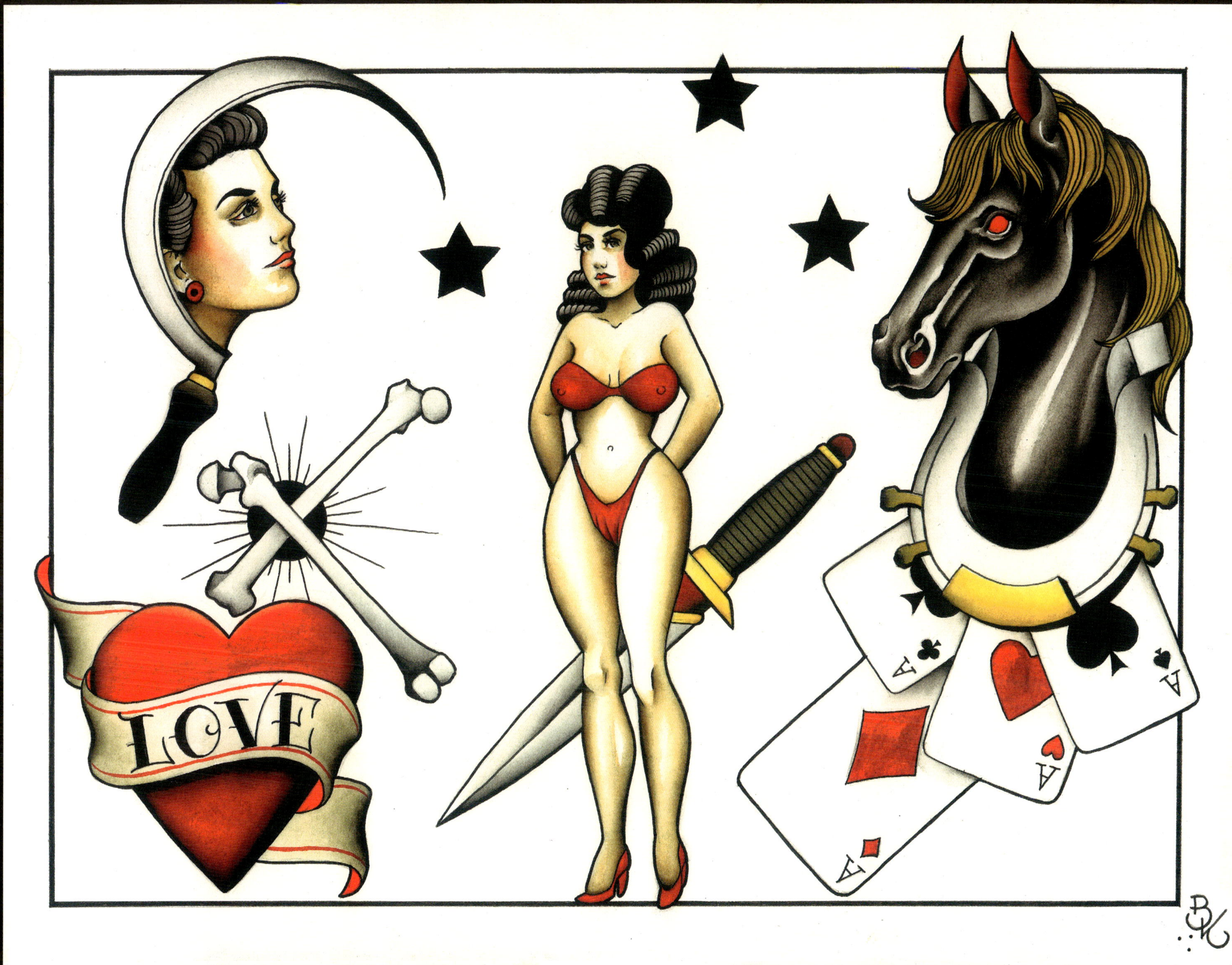
LOVE

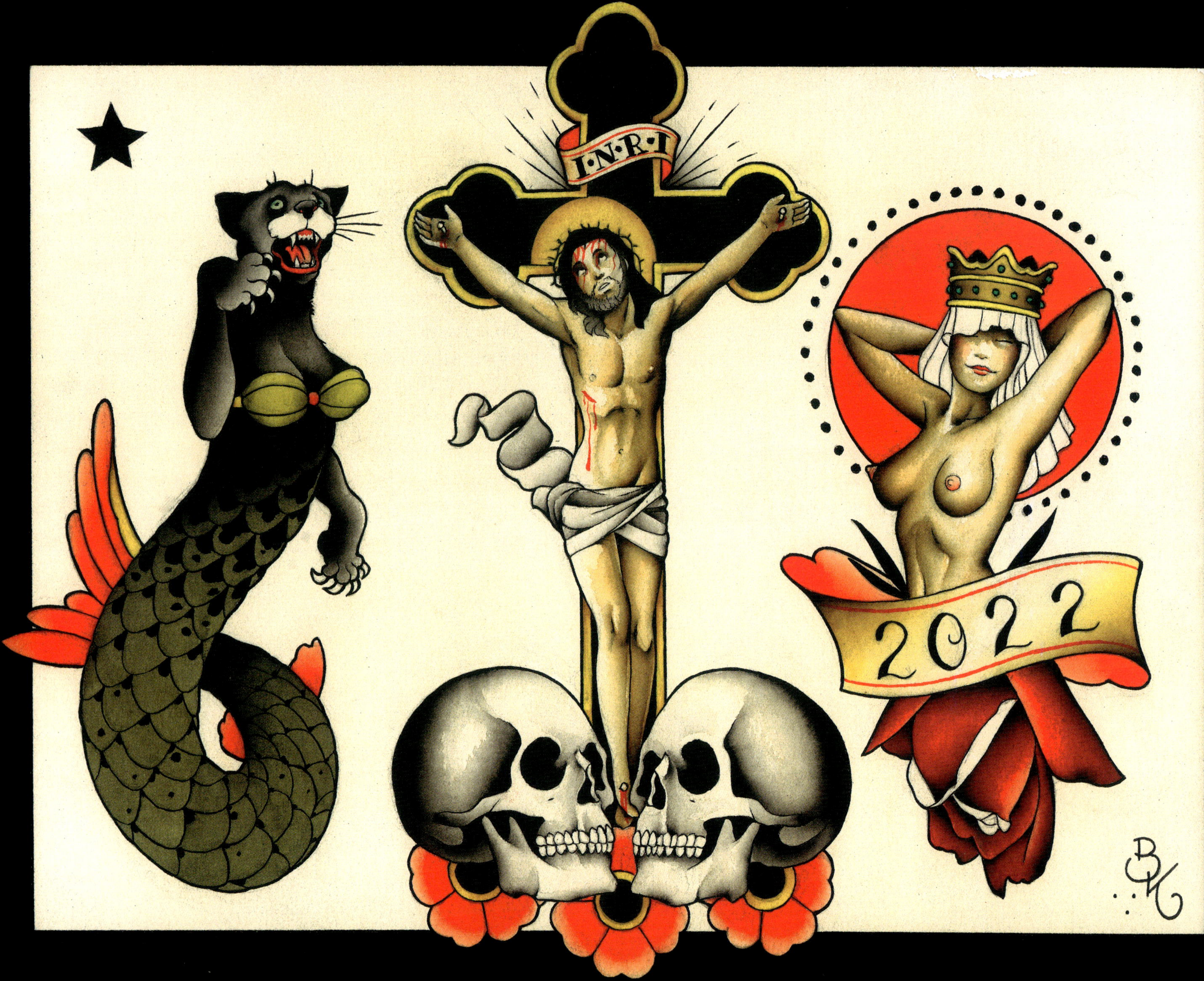

I·N·R·I
2022

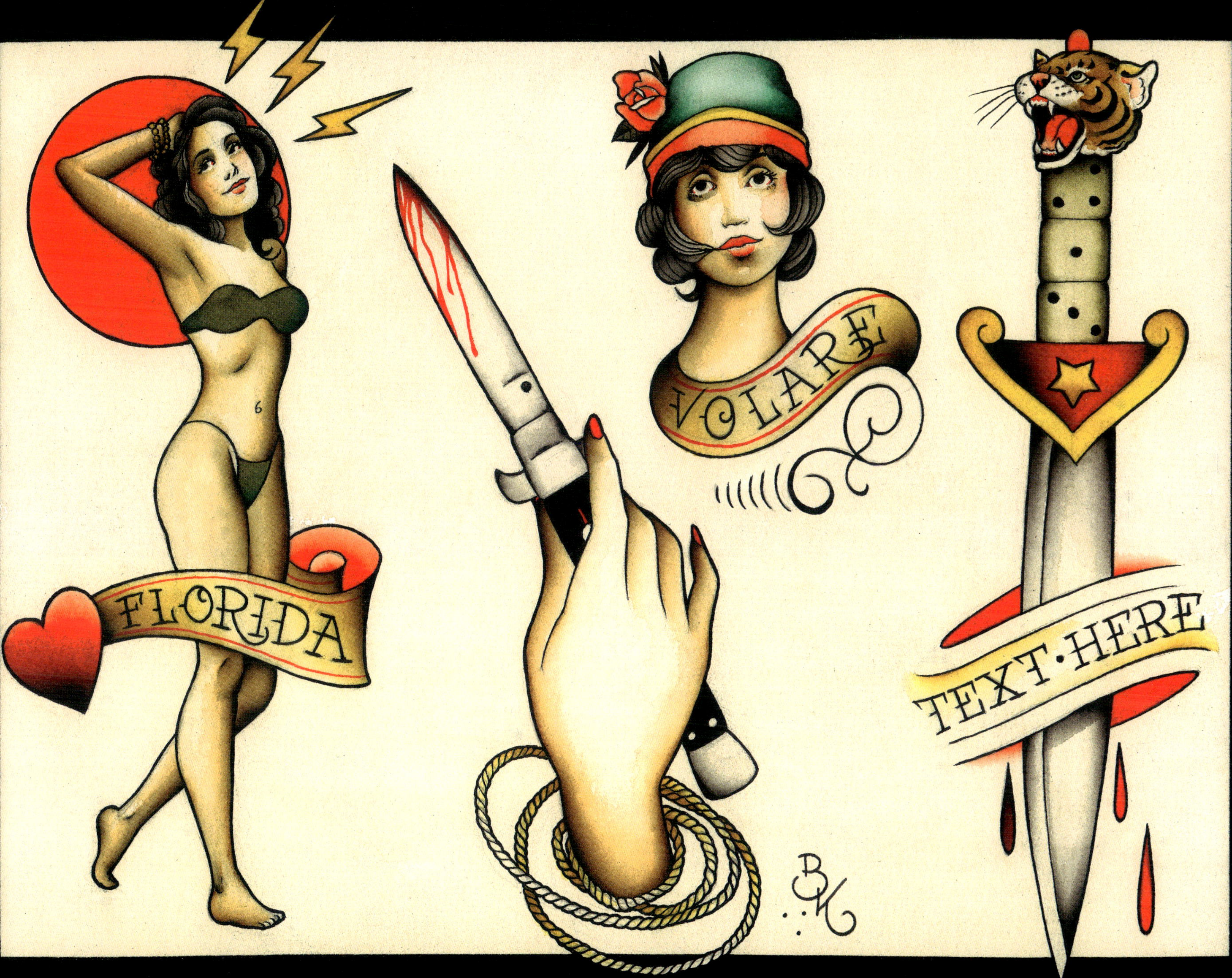
FLORIDA
VOLARE
TEXT·HERE

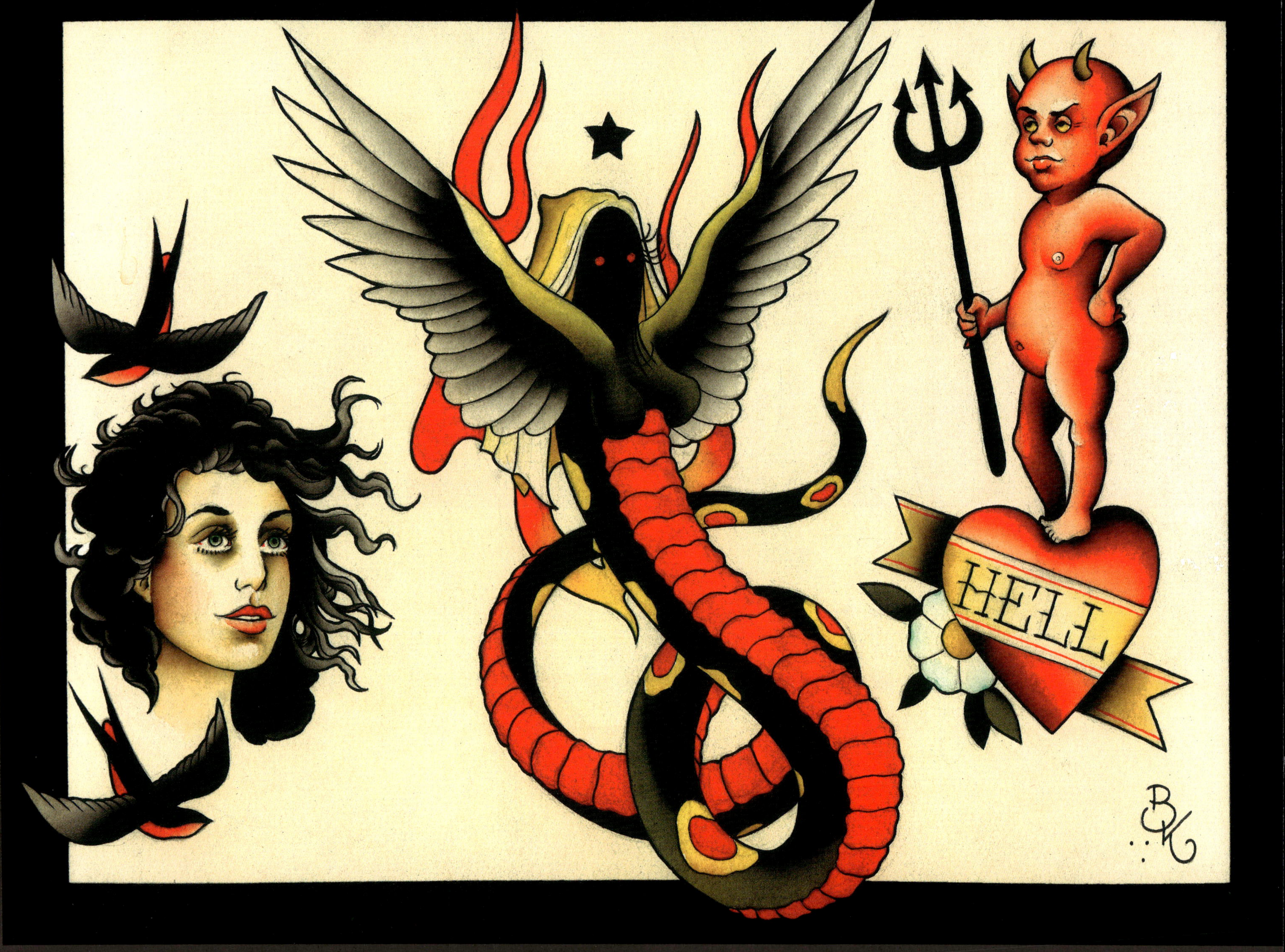
HELL

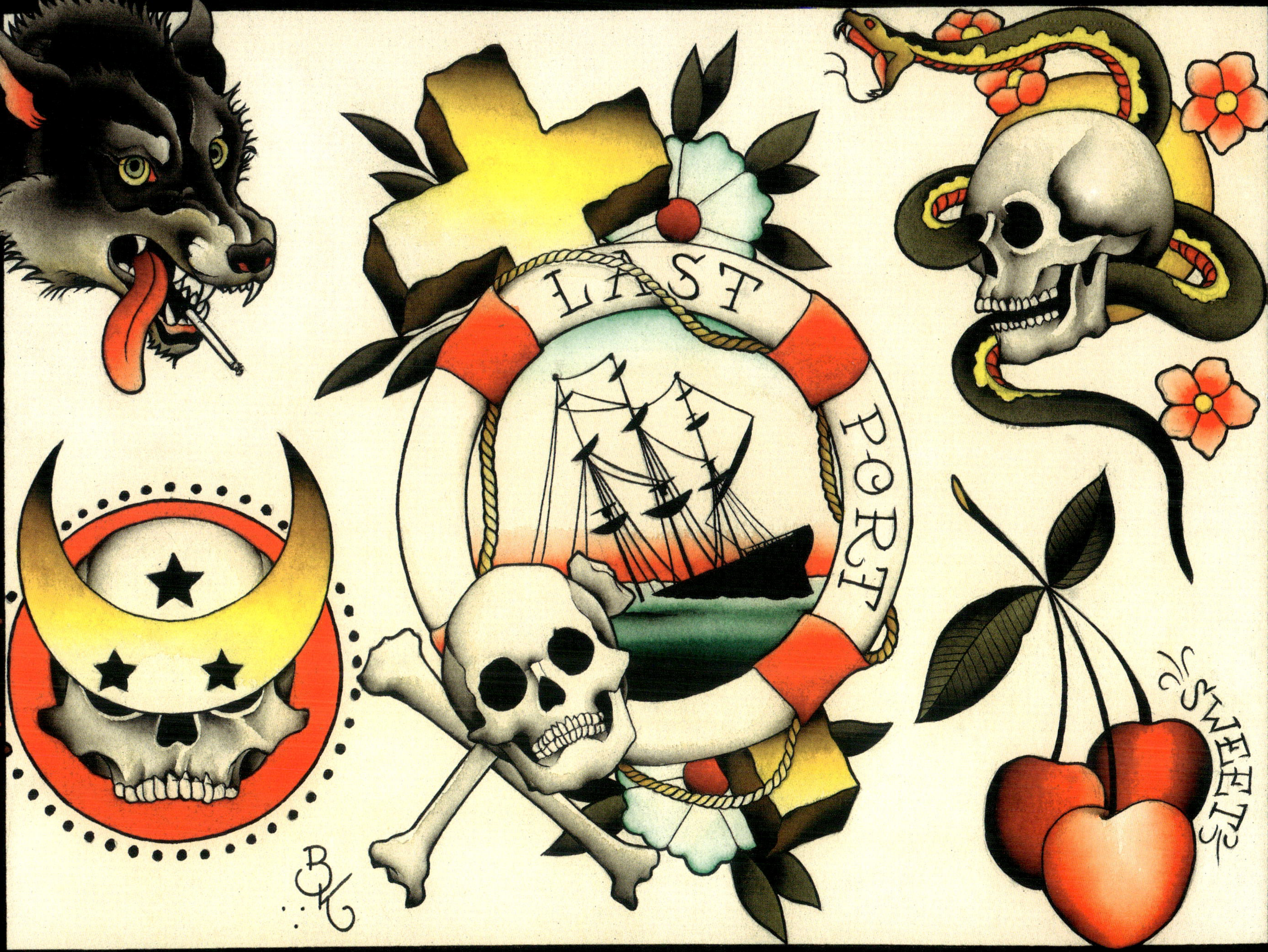
LAST PORT
SWEET

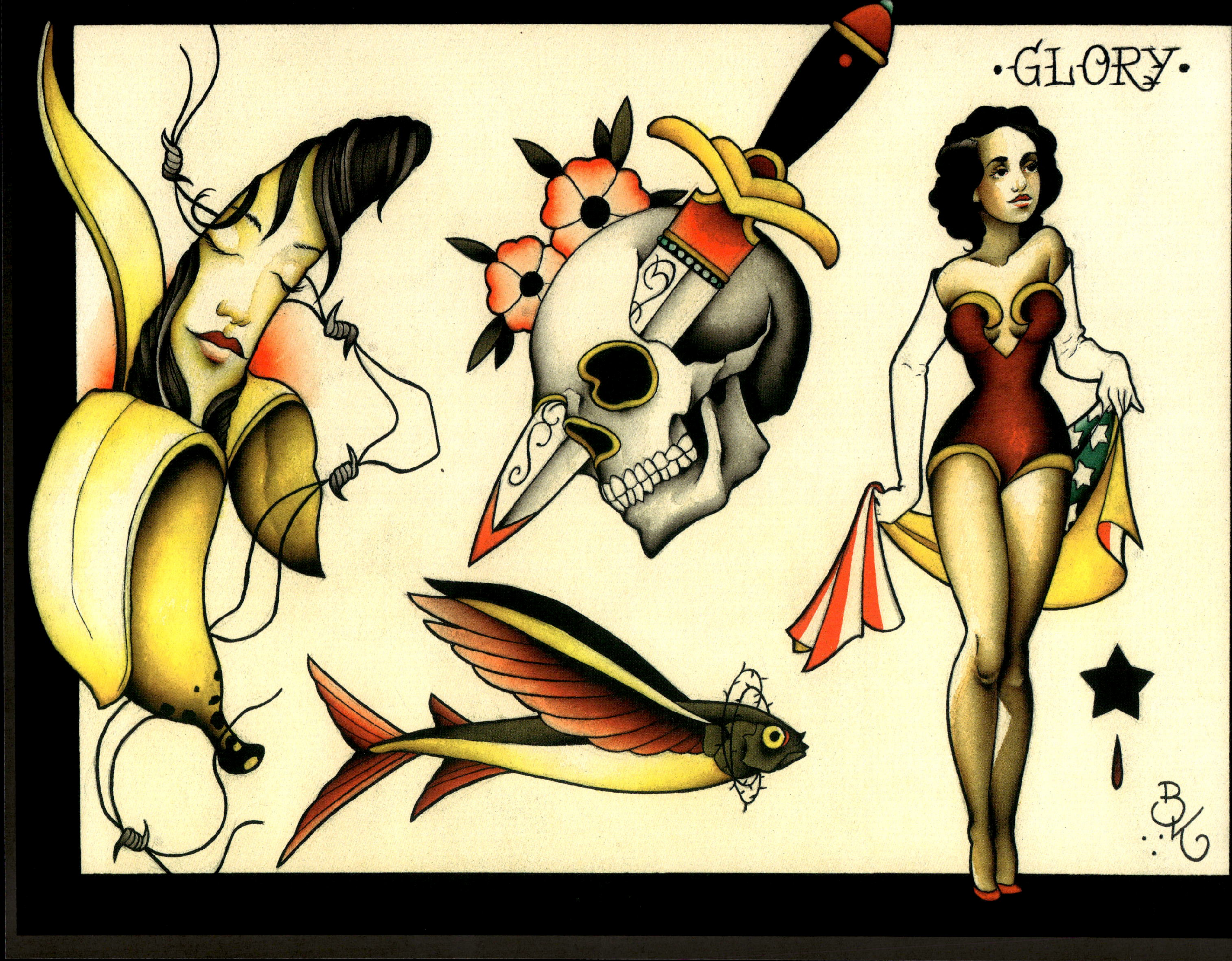

•GLORY•

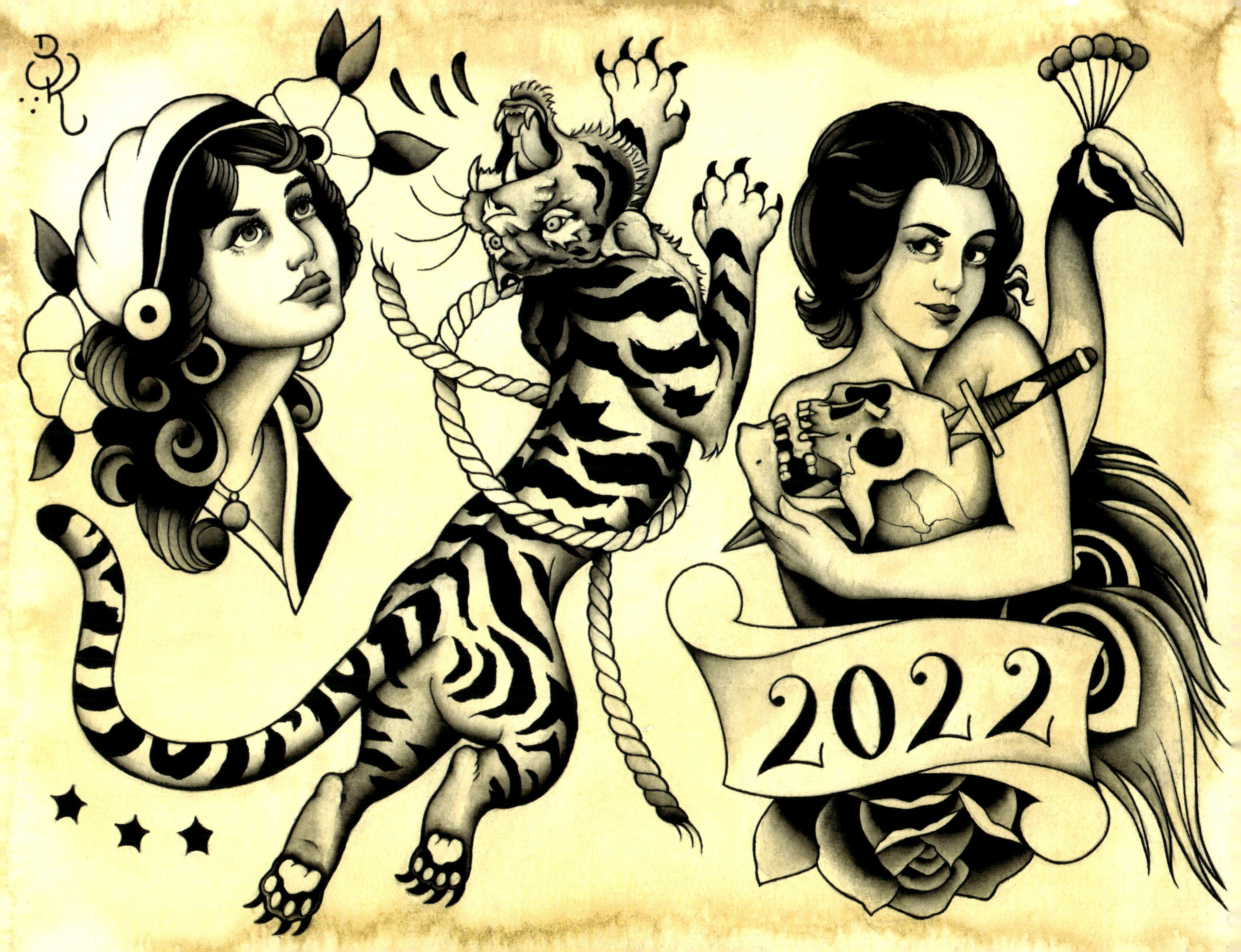
2022

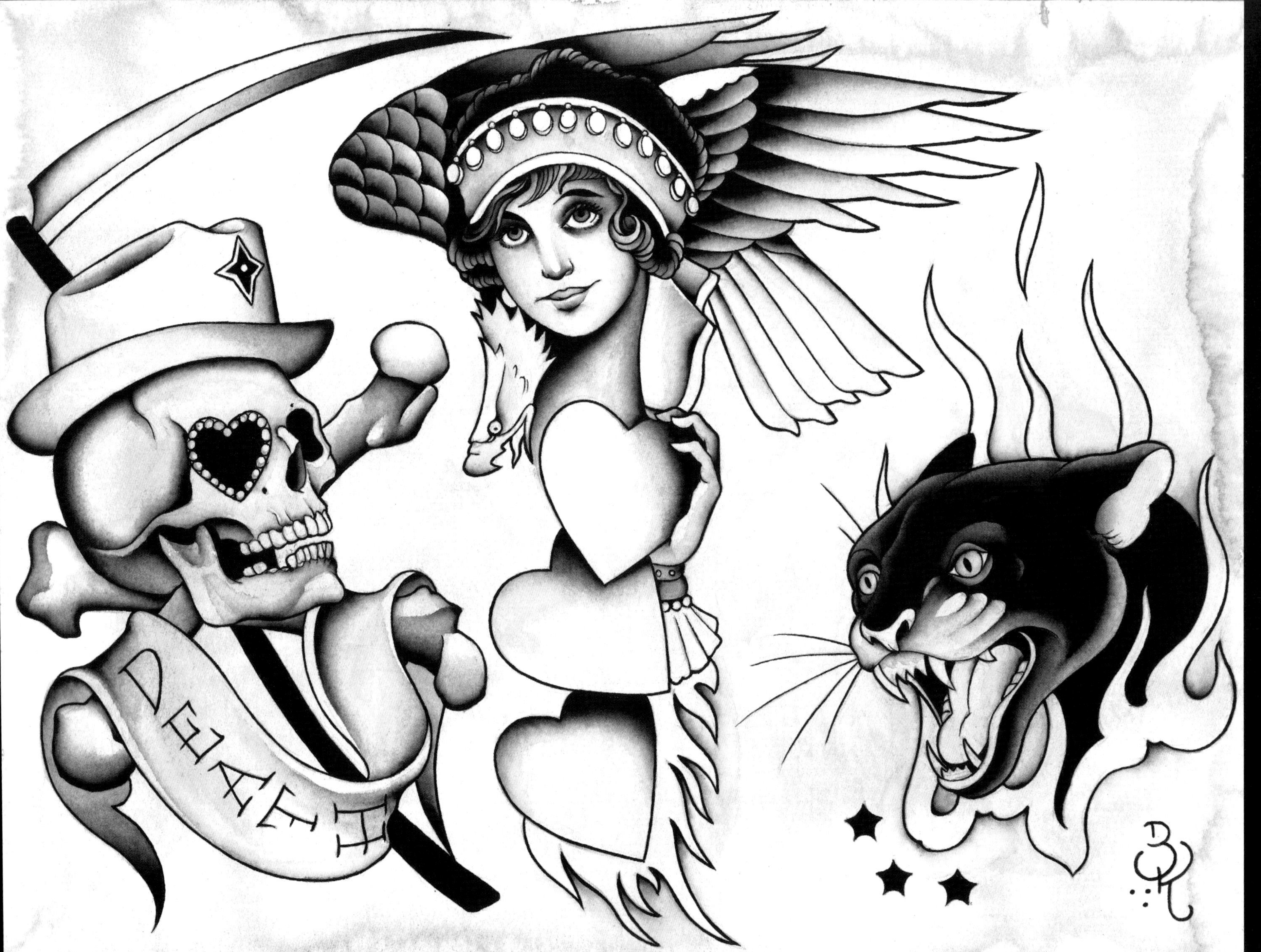
DEATH

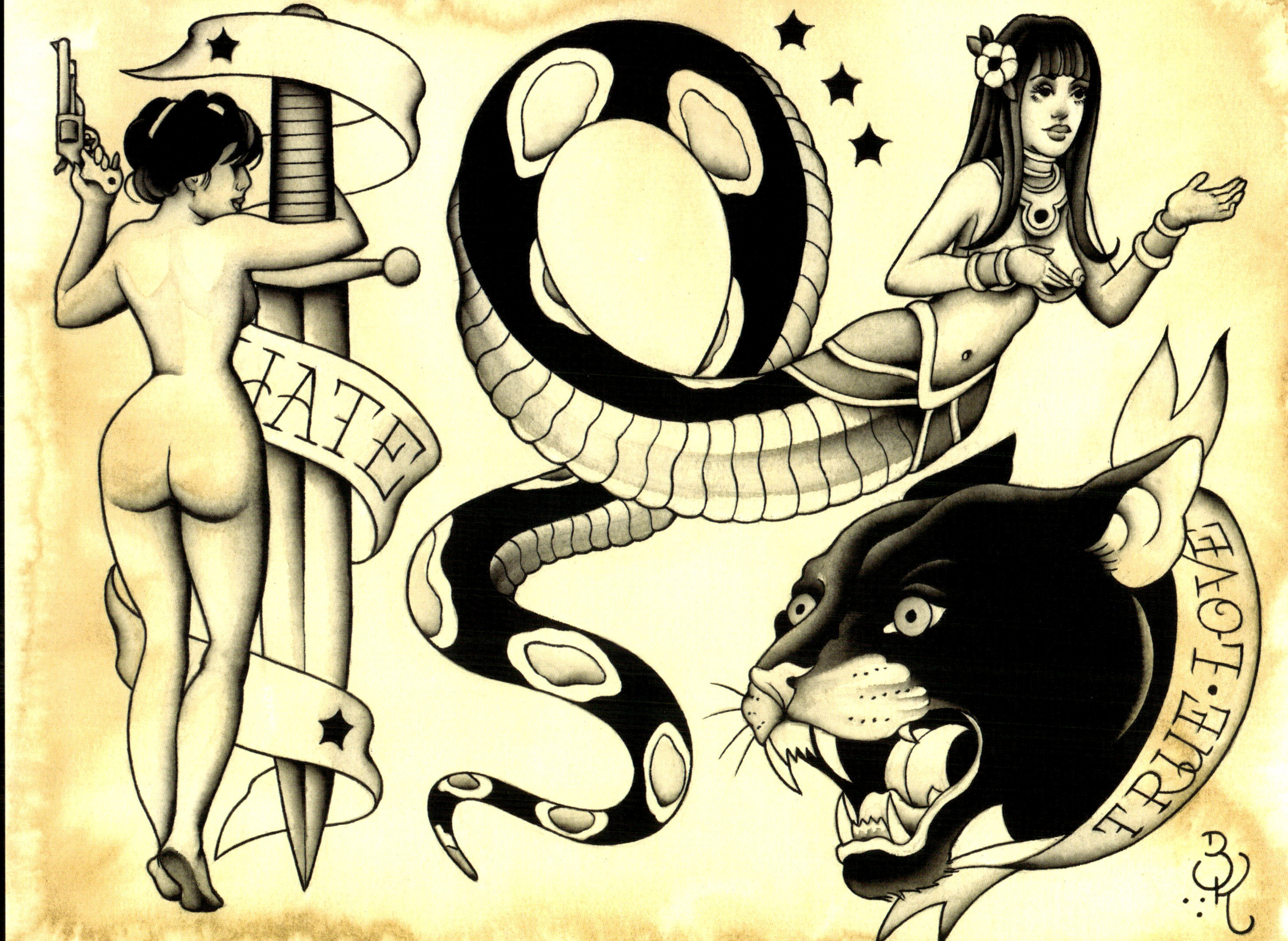

HATE
TRUE·LOVE

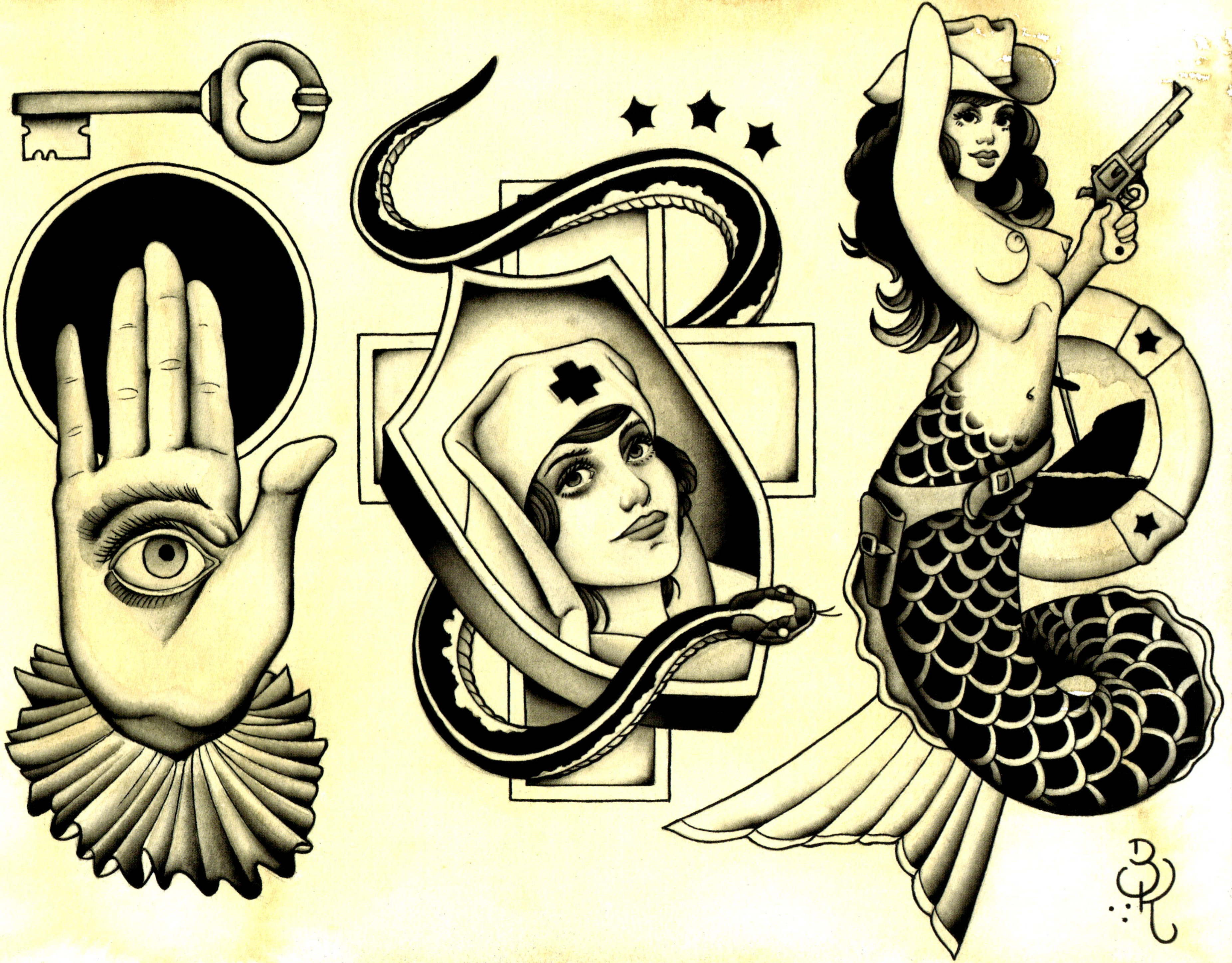

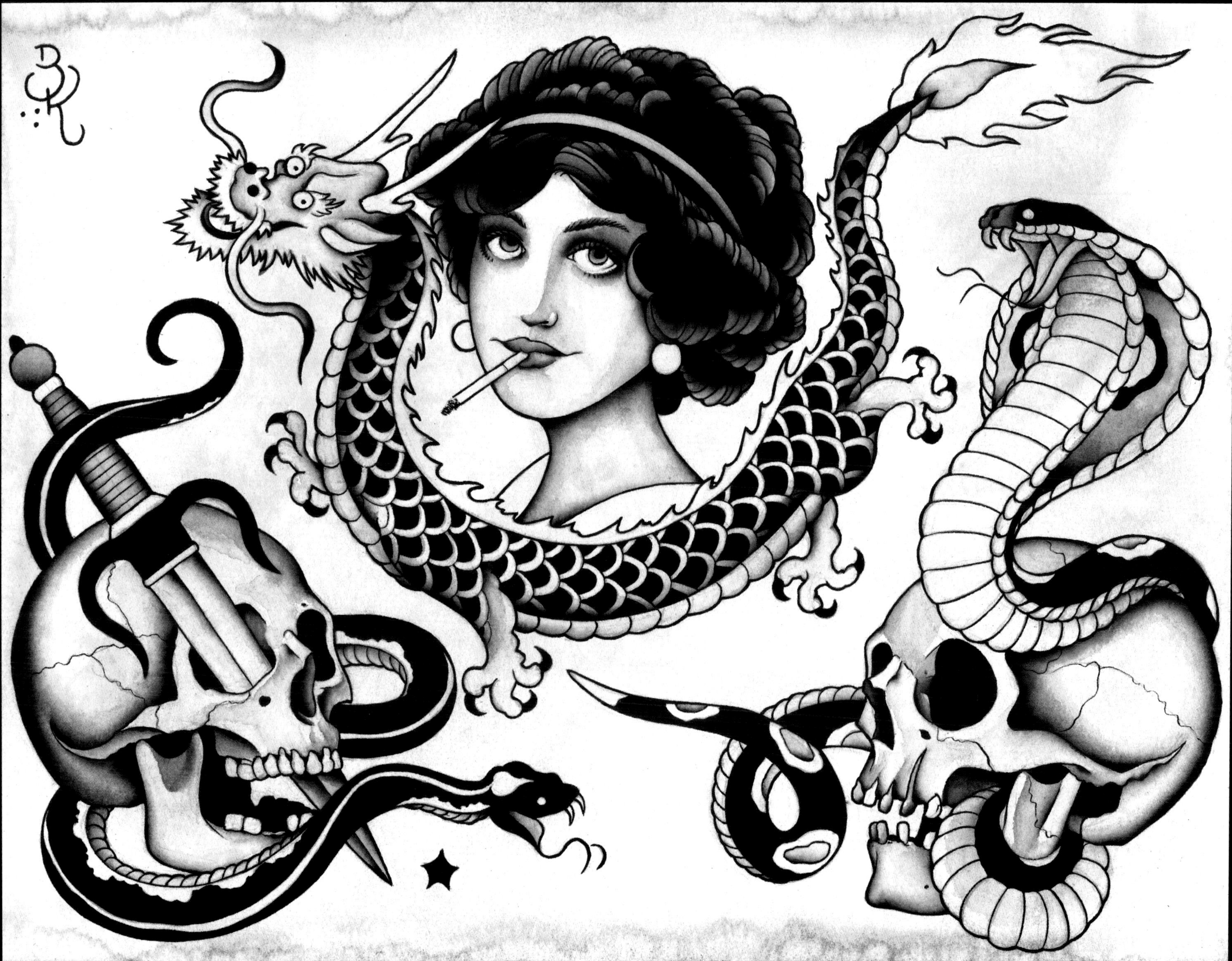

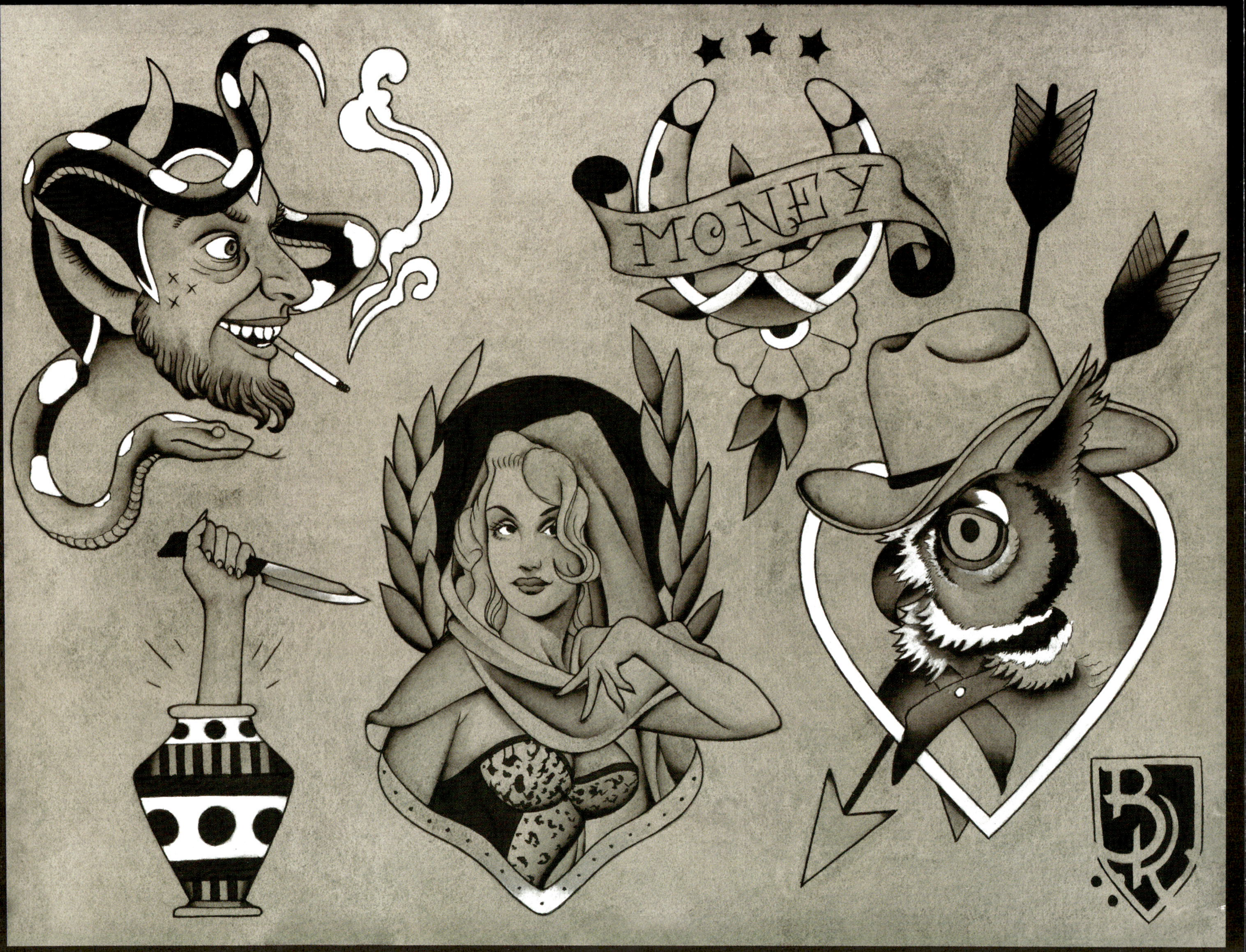
MONEY

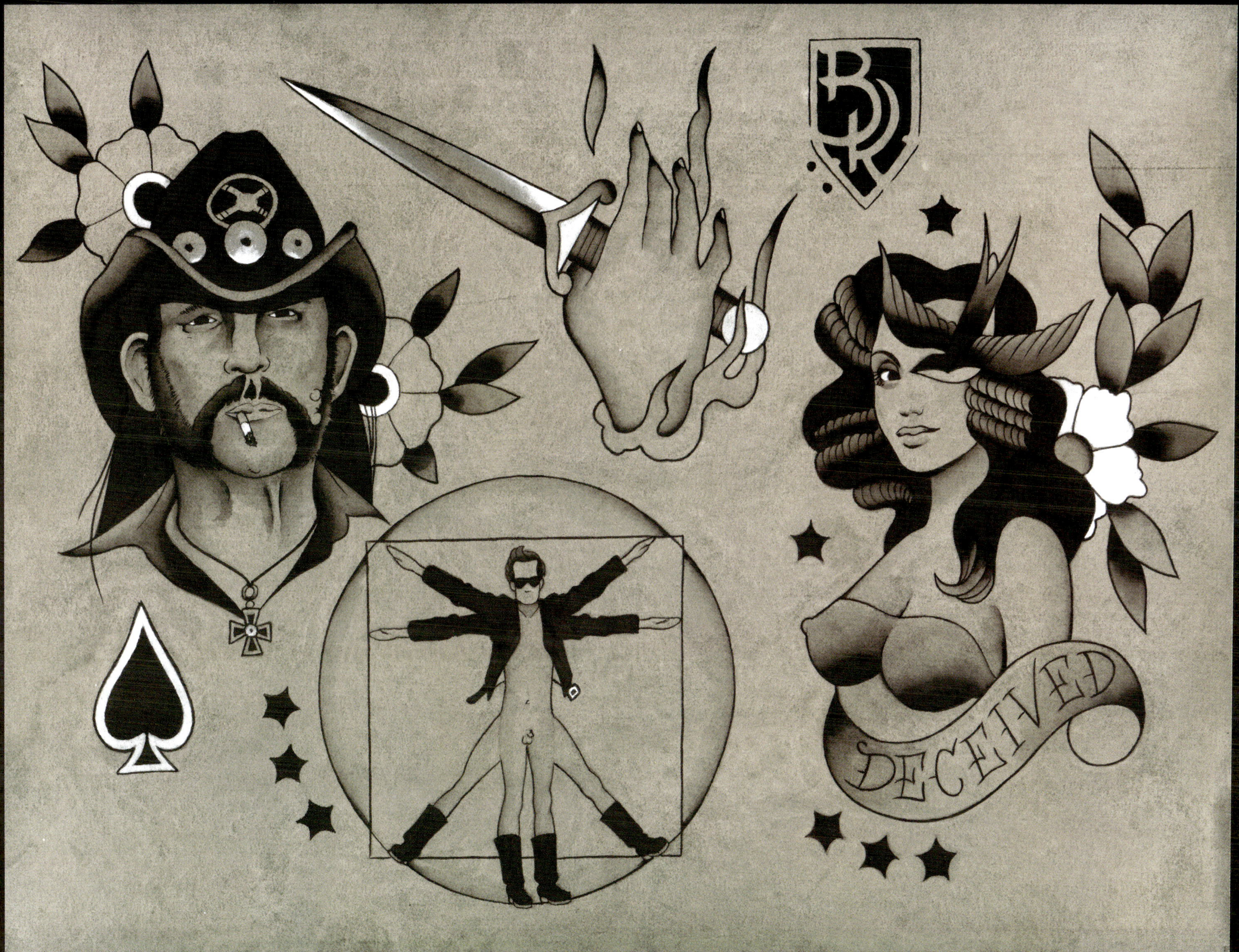
DECEIVED

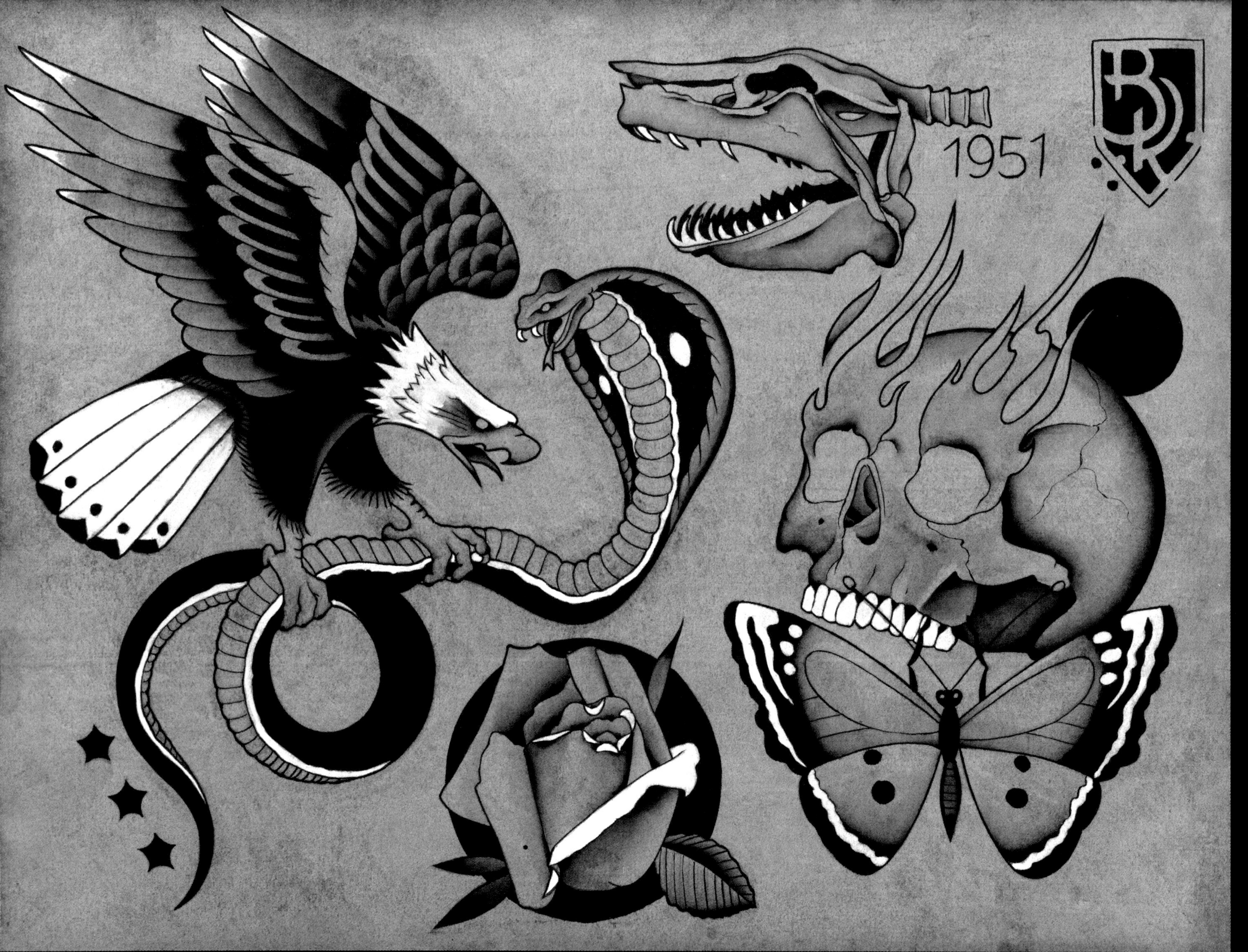
1951

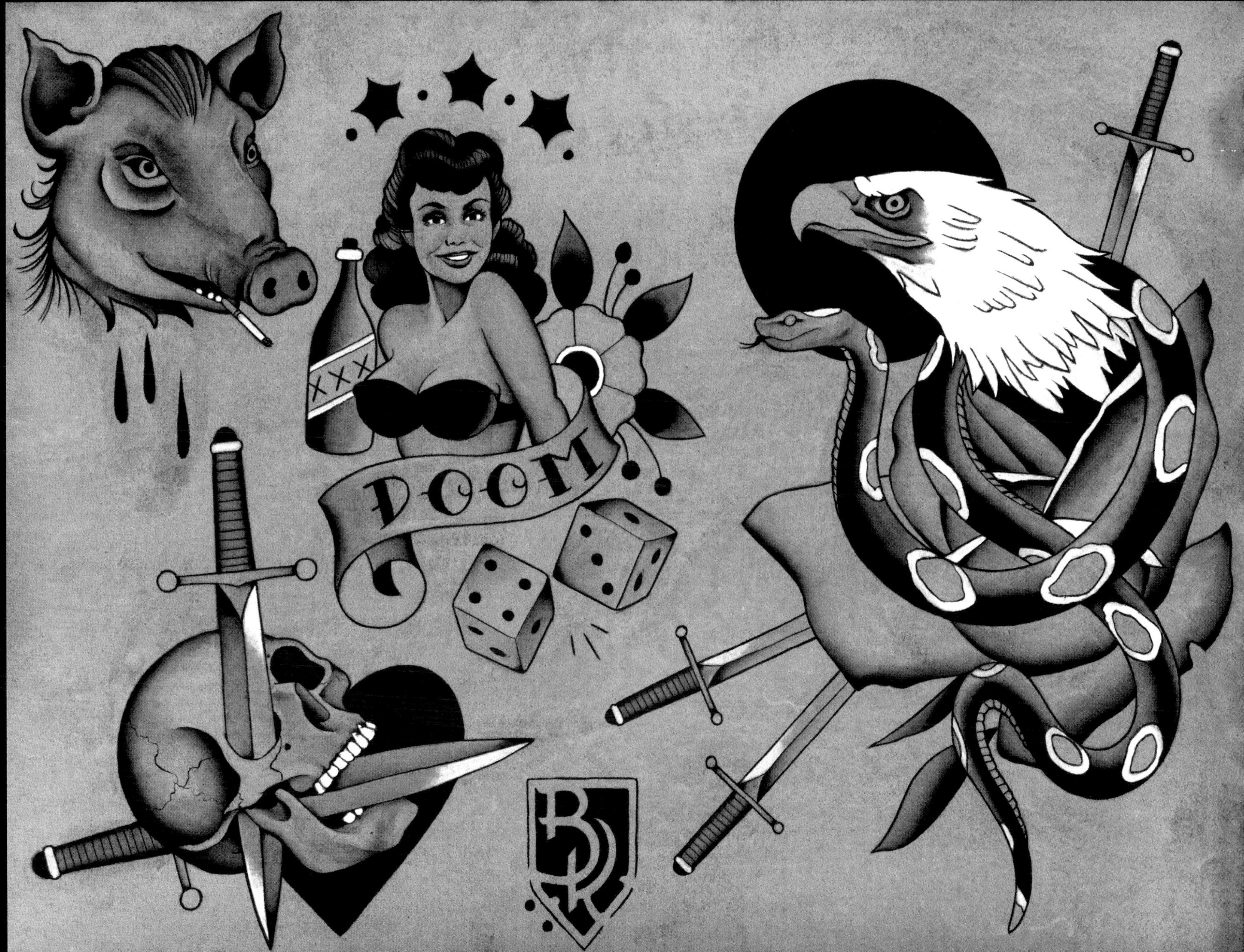
DOOM
XXX

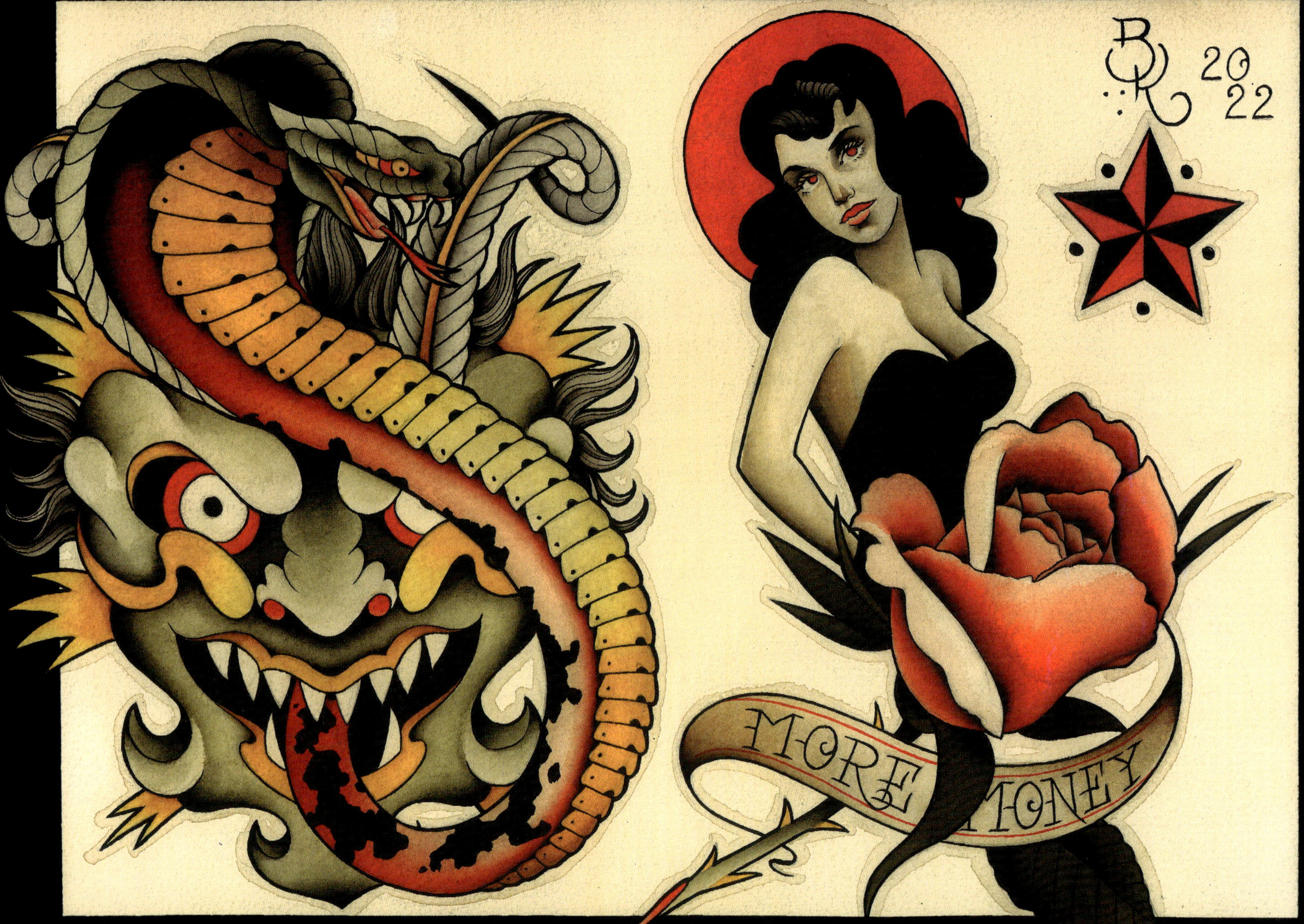
20
22
MORE MONEY

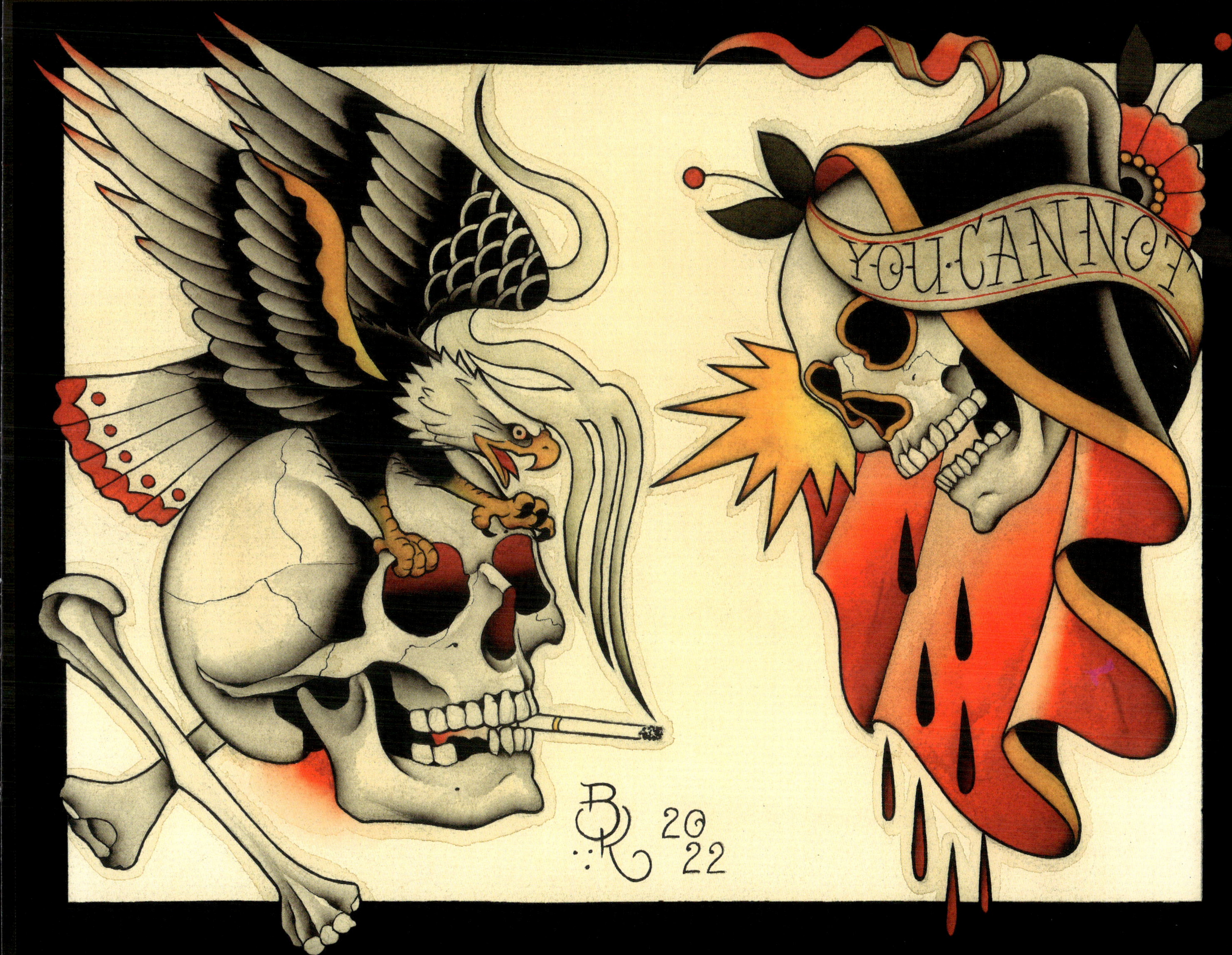
YOU·CAN·NOT
BK
2022

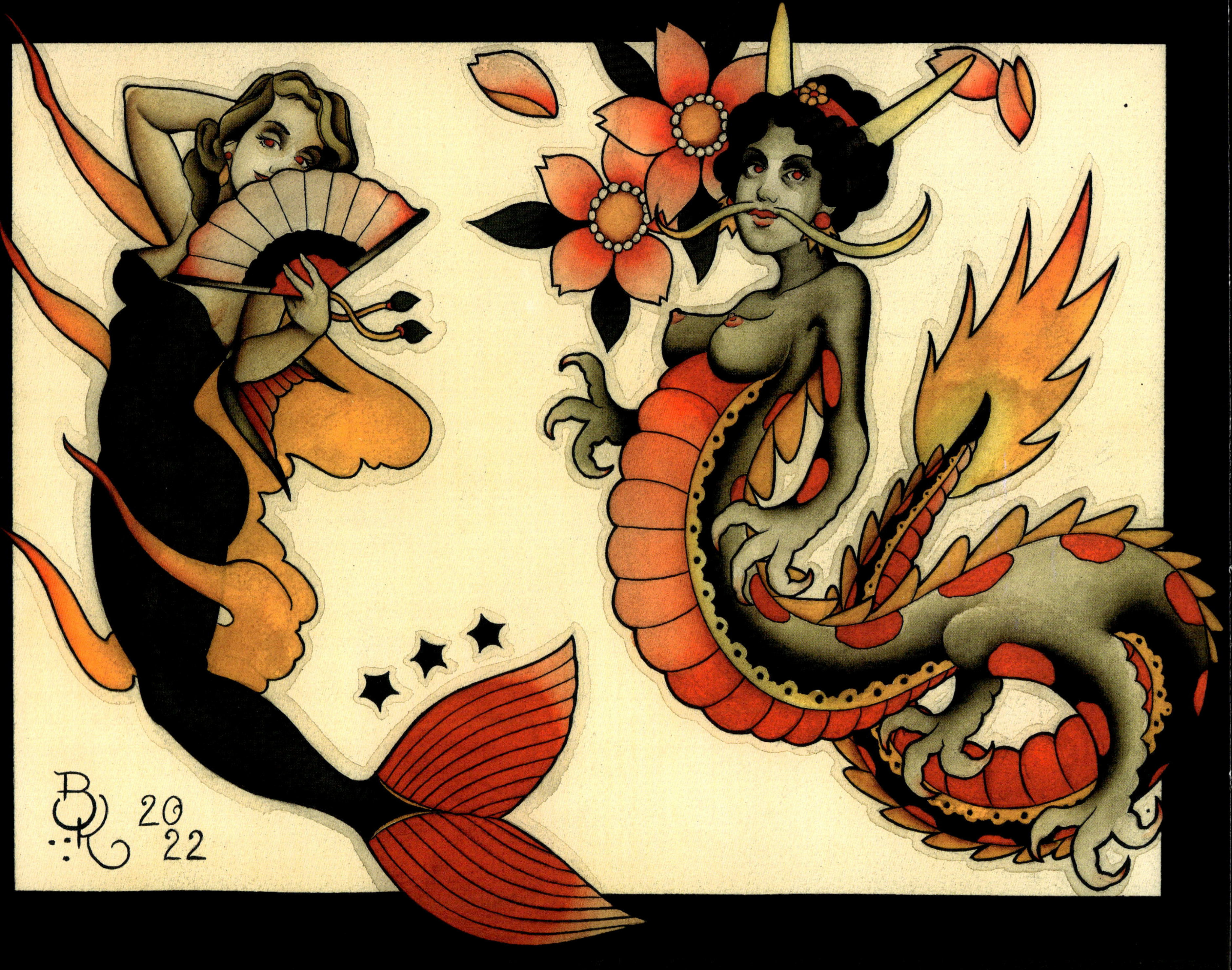

BOK
20
22

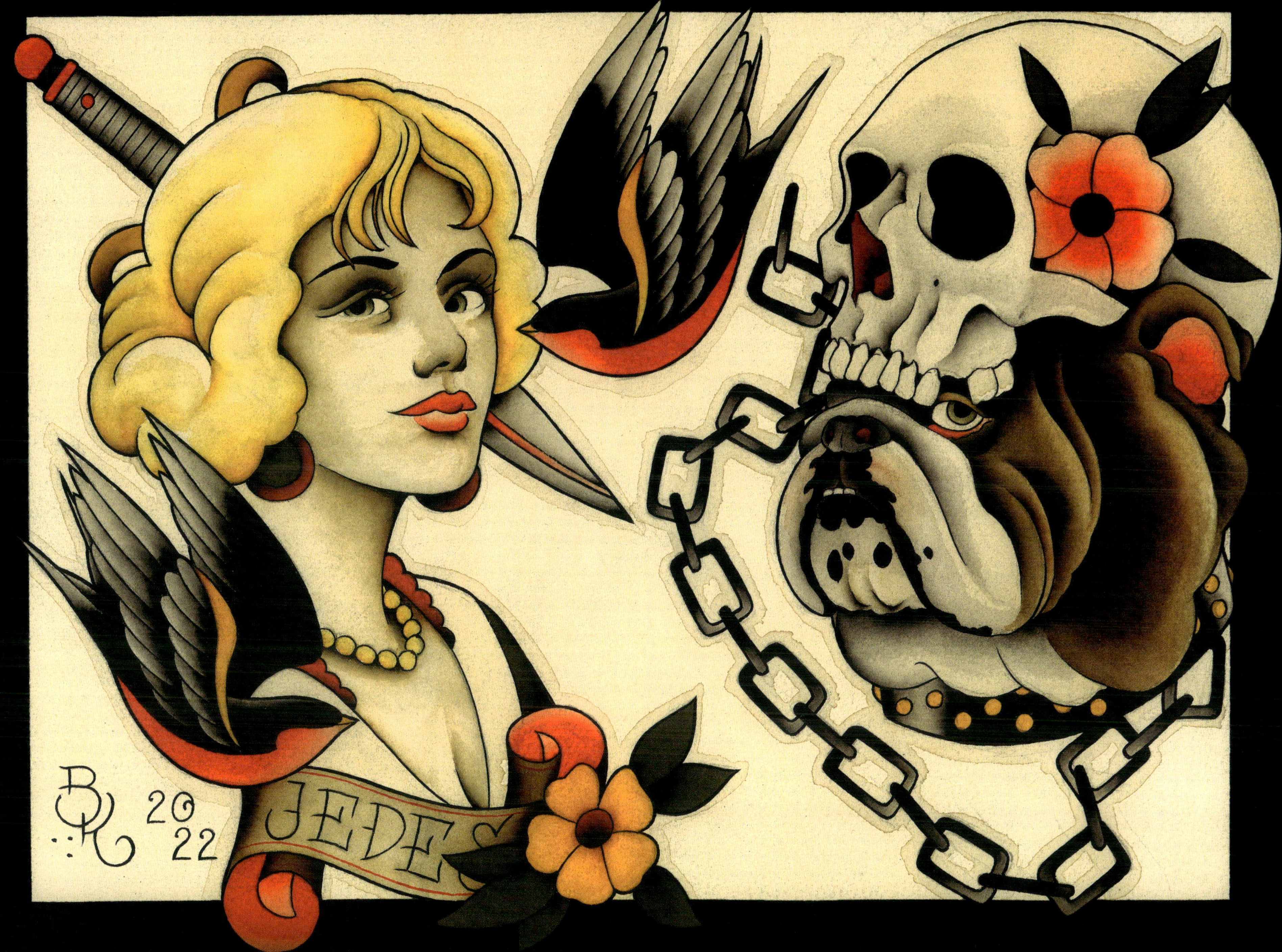
JEDE
BK 2022

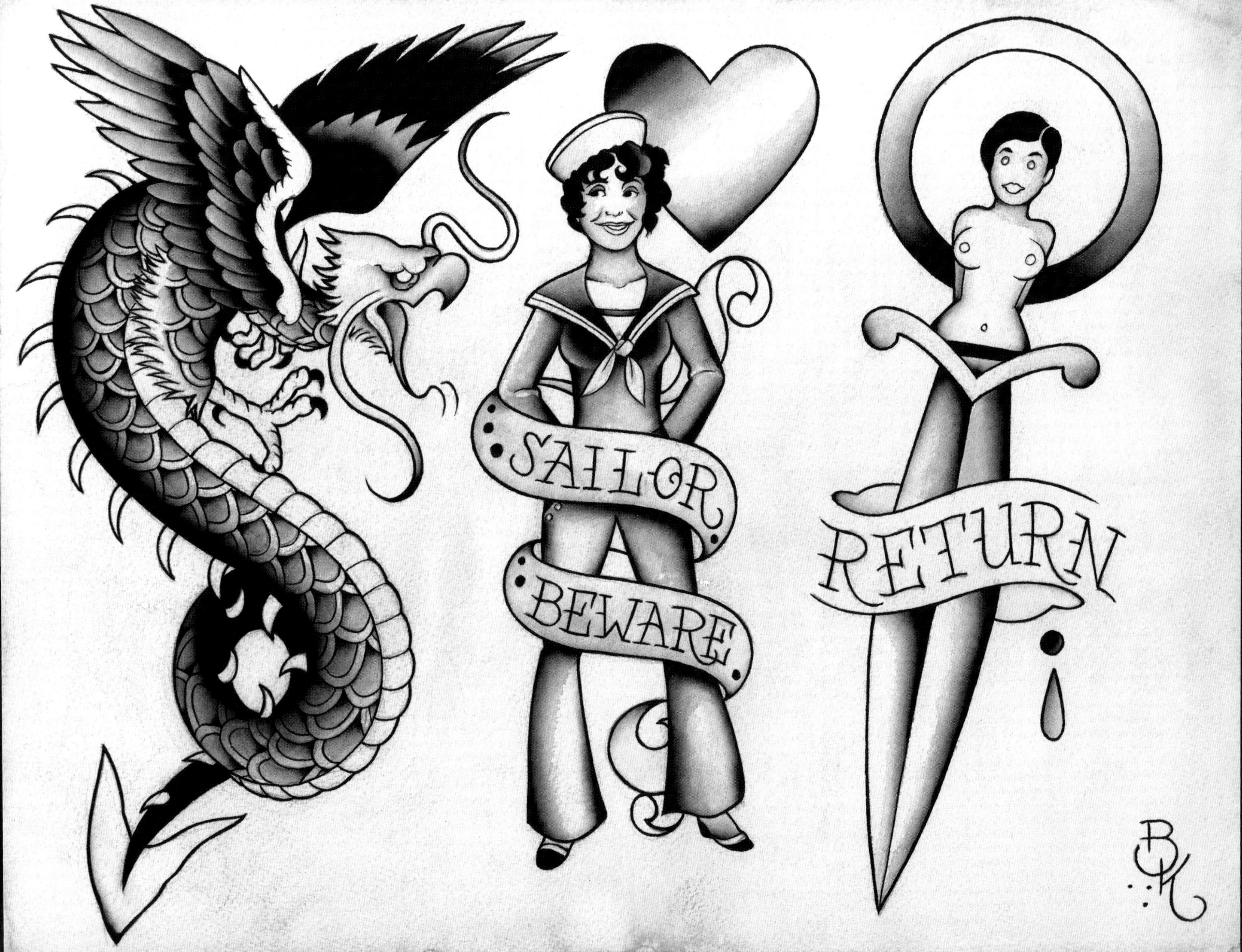
SAILOR
BEWARE
RETURN
BK

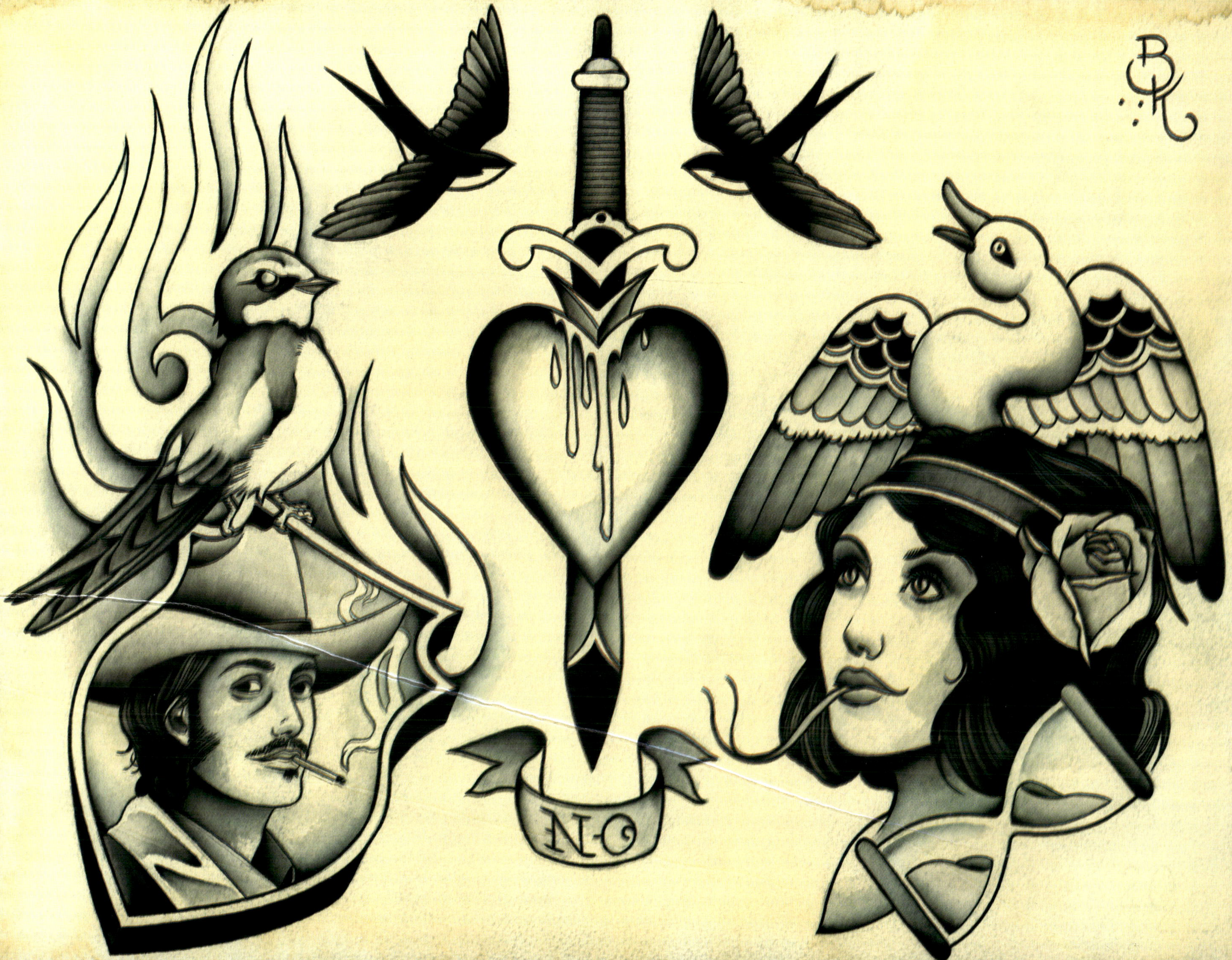
N-O

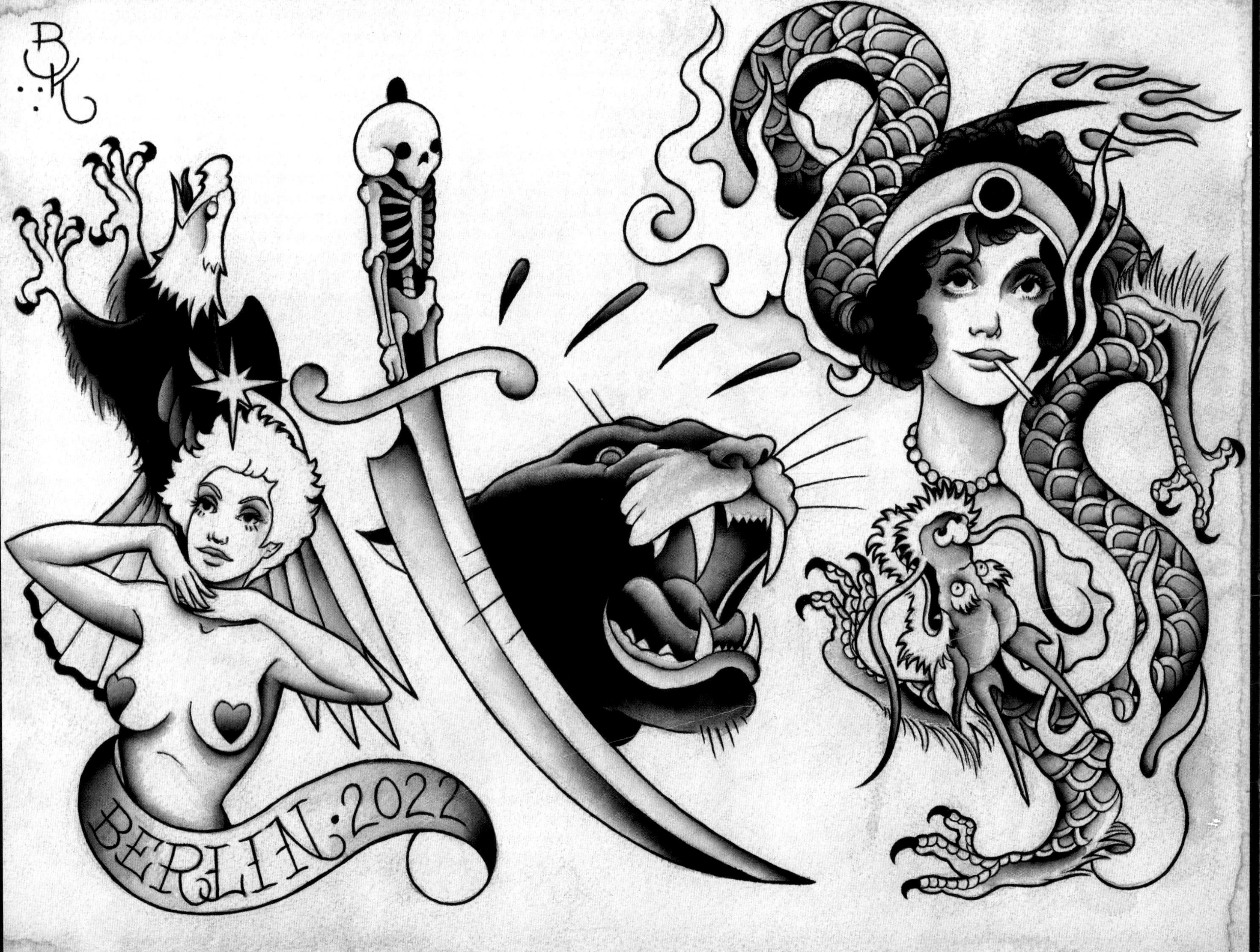
BK
BERLIN·2022

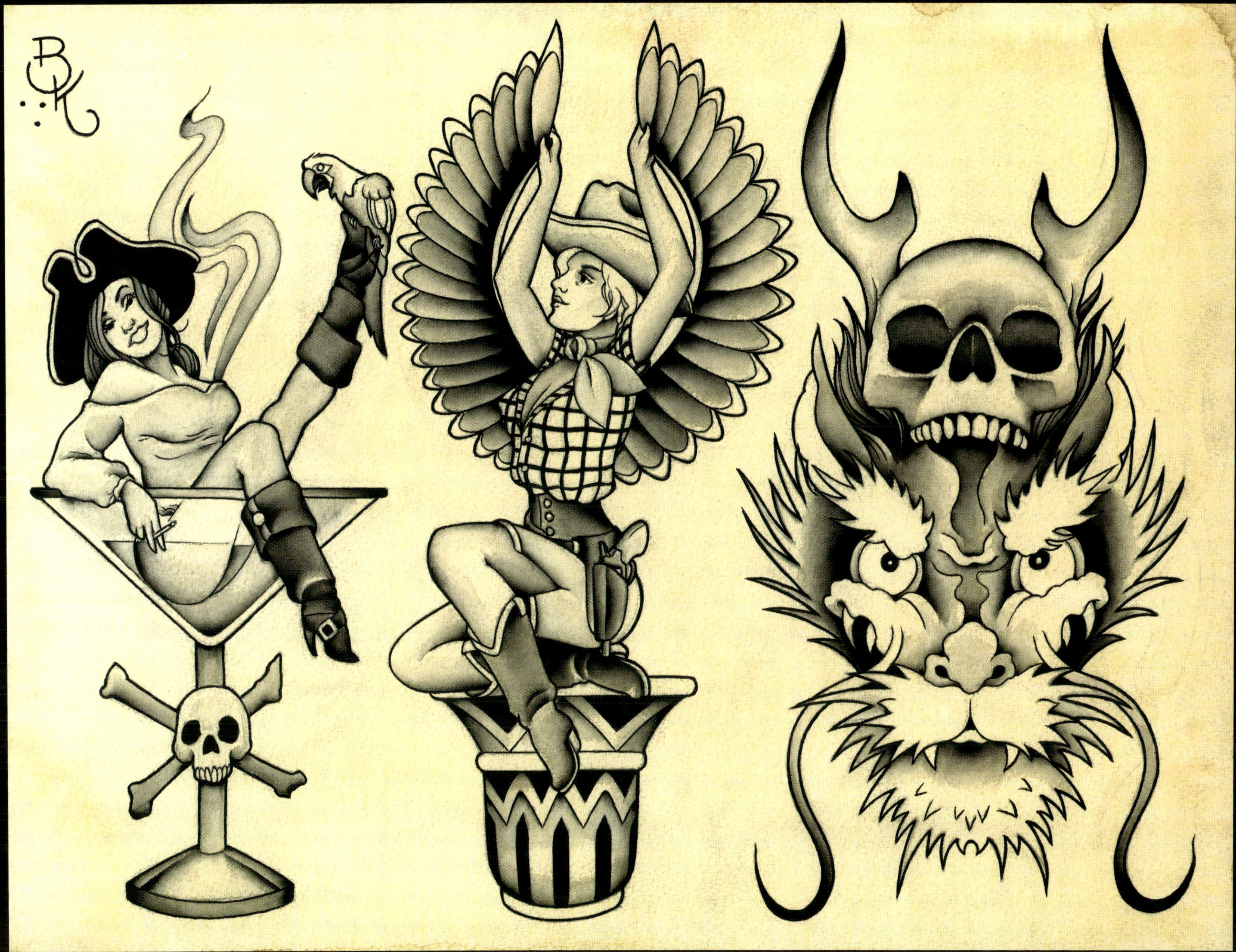

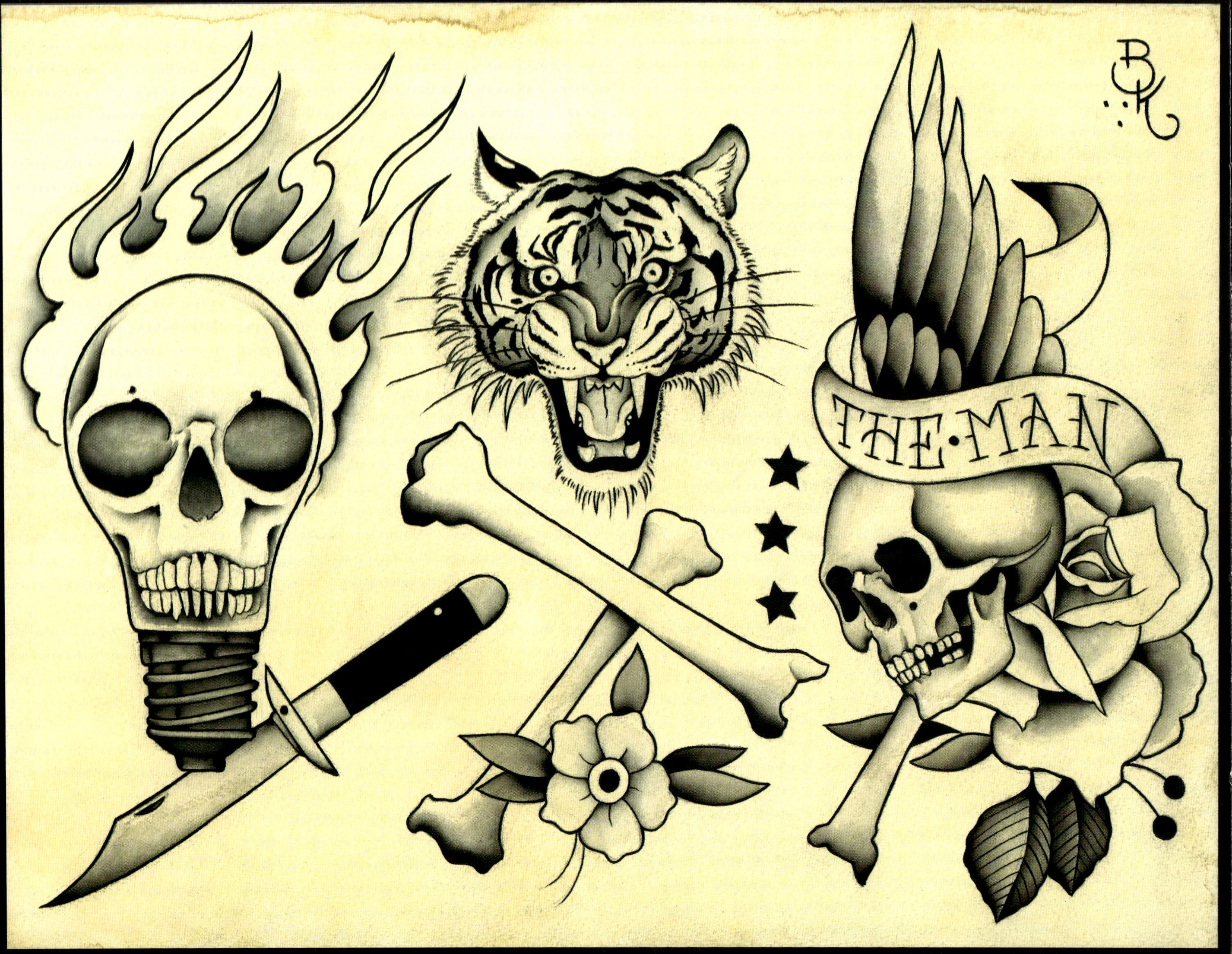
BK
THE·MAN

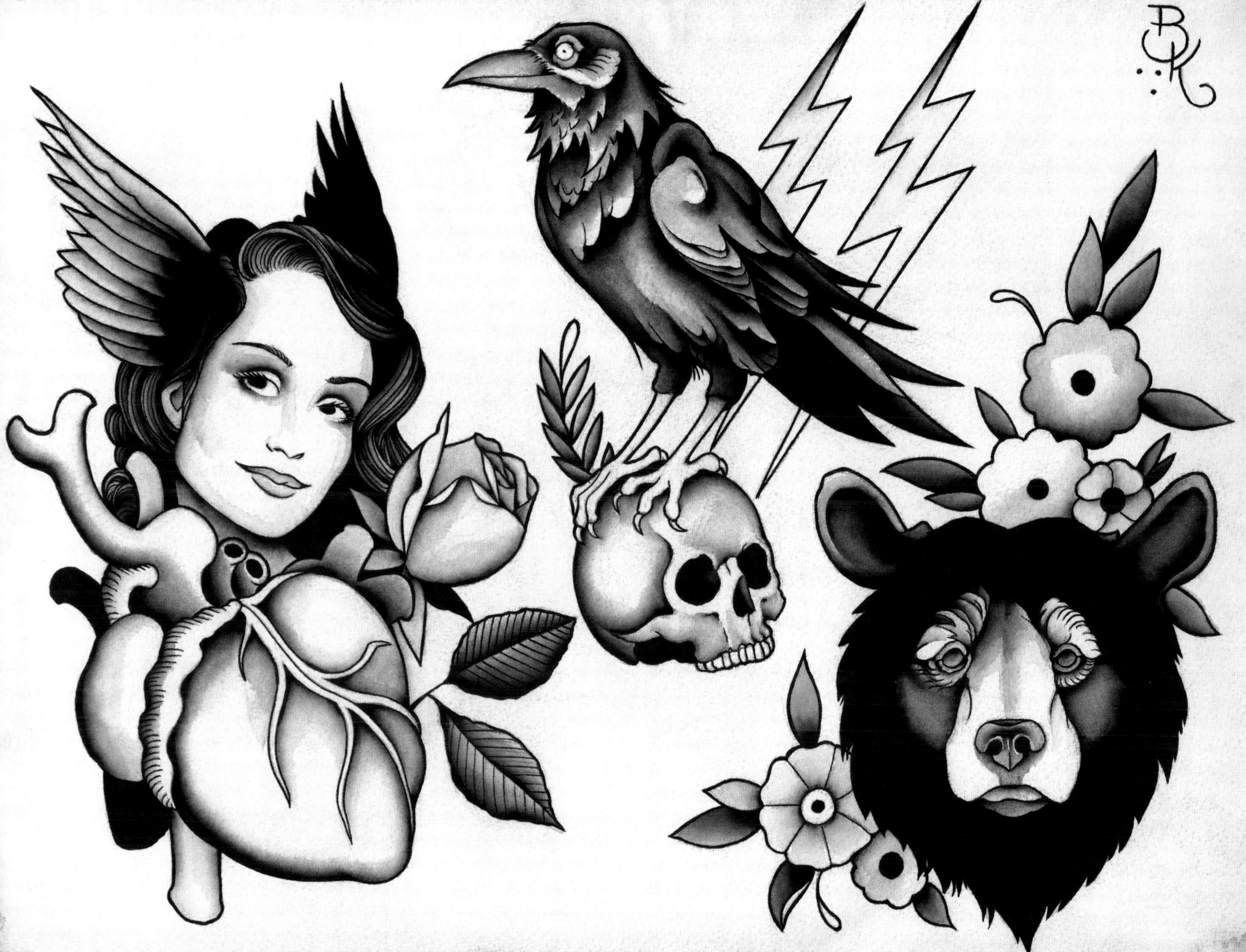
BK

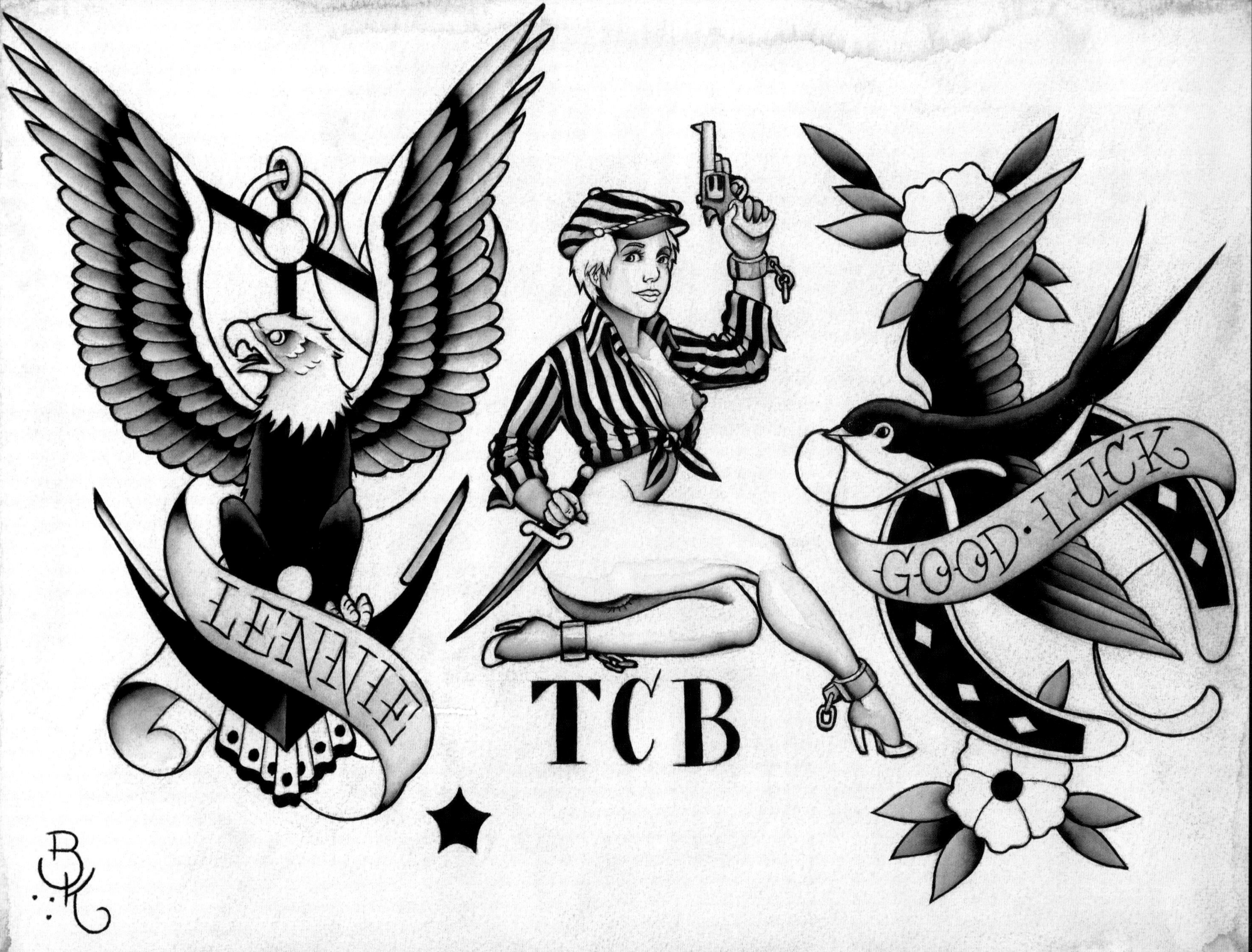
LENNIE
TCB
GOOD·LUCK

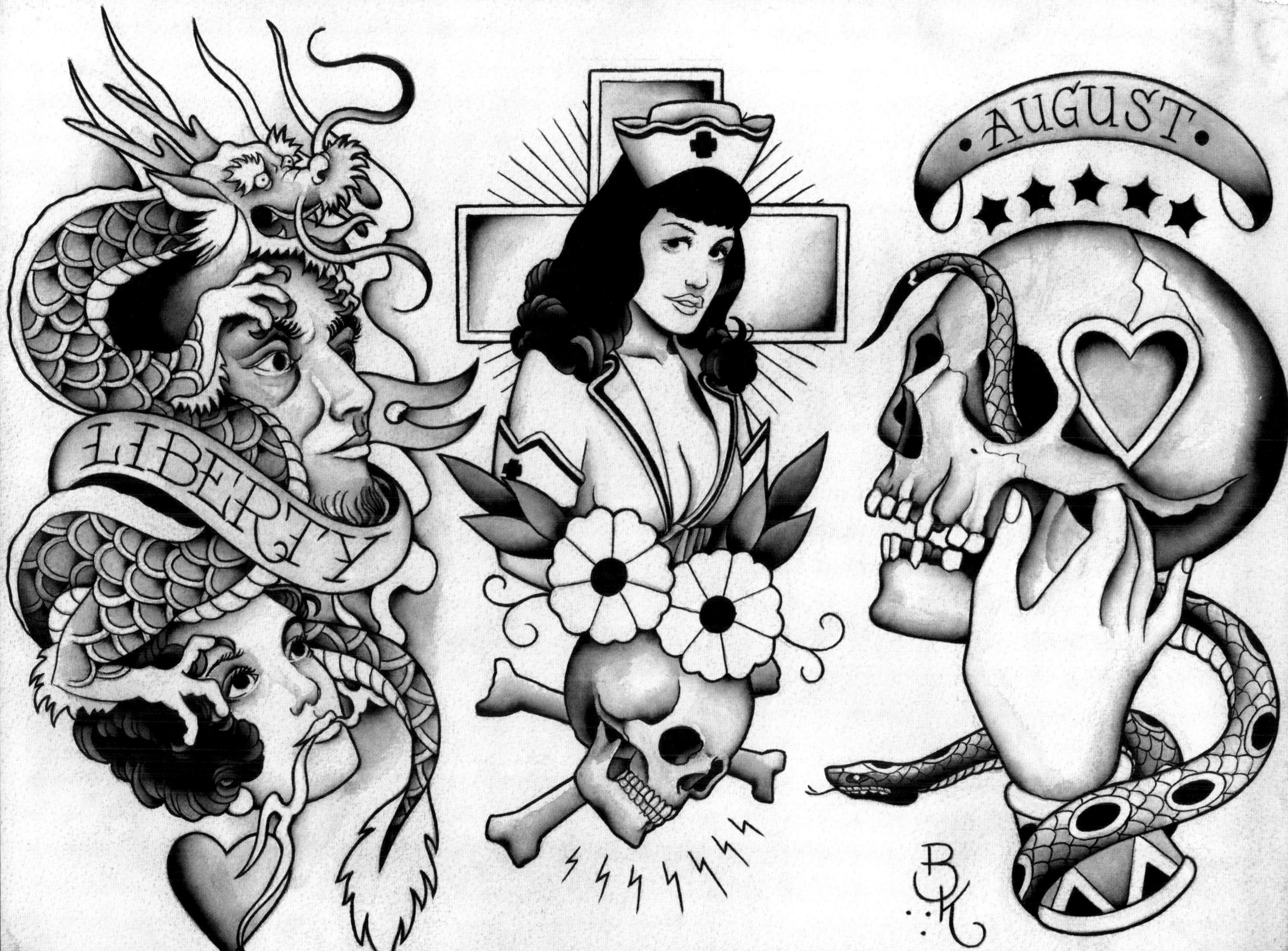
LIBERTY
AUGUST

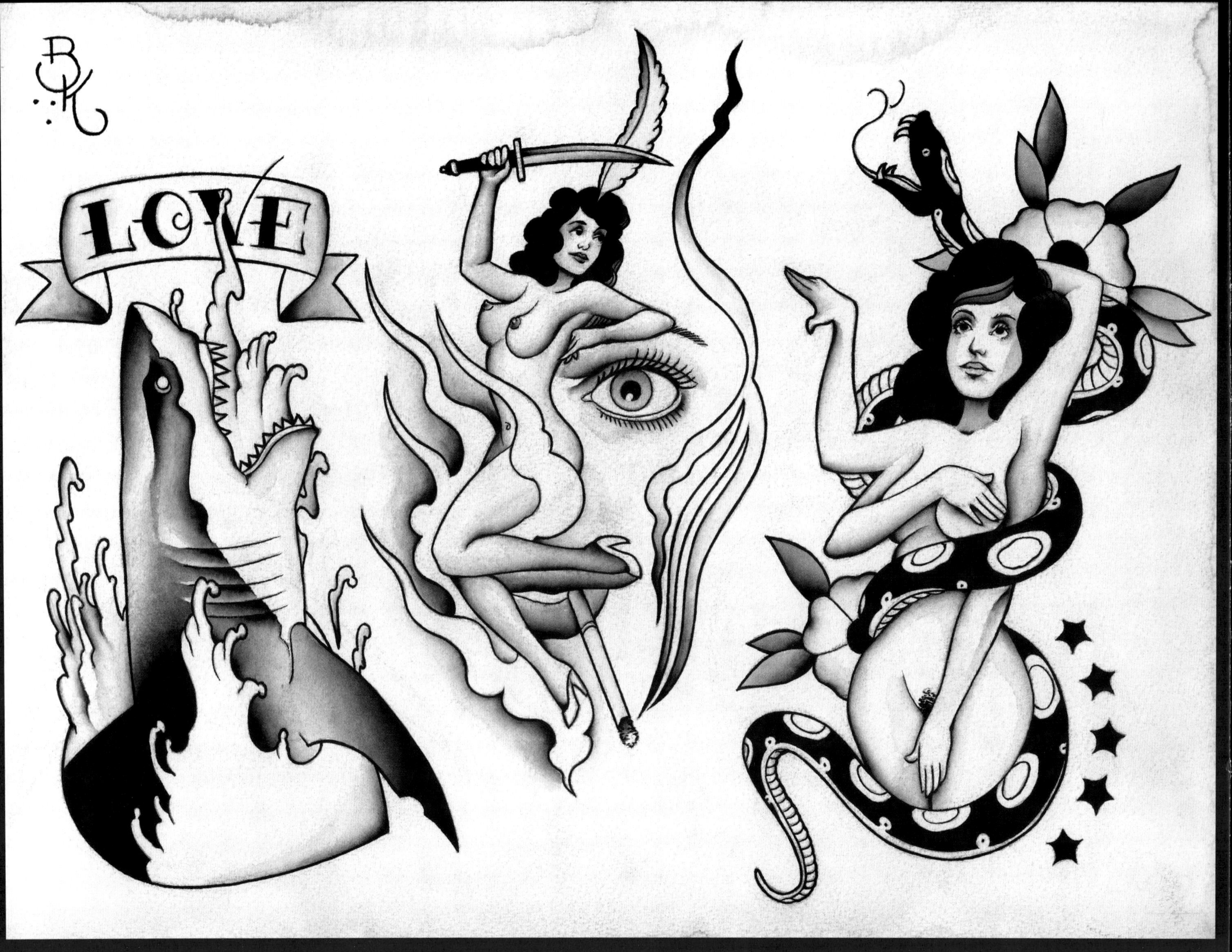
LOVE

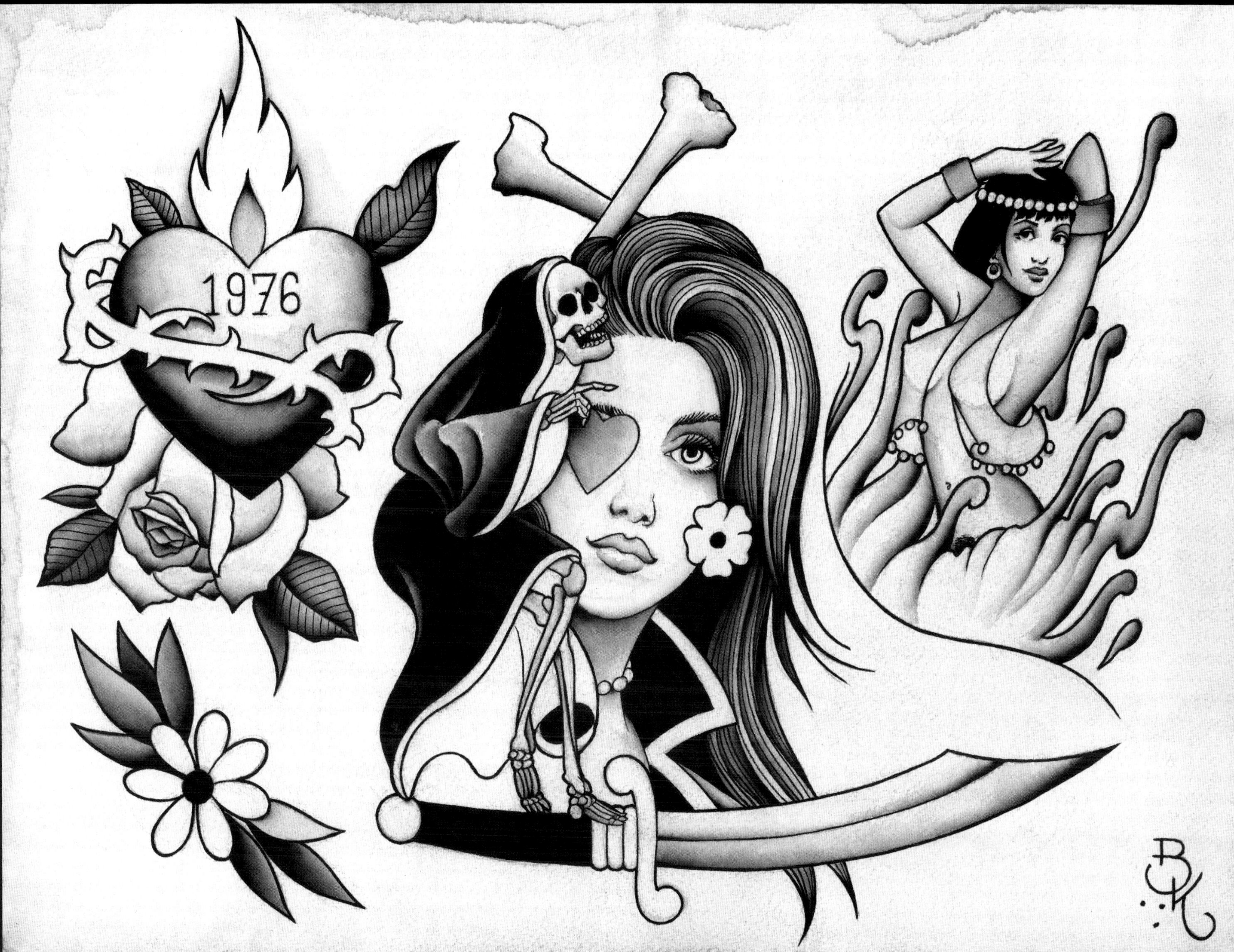
1976
BK

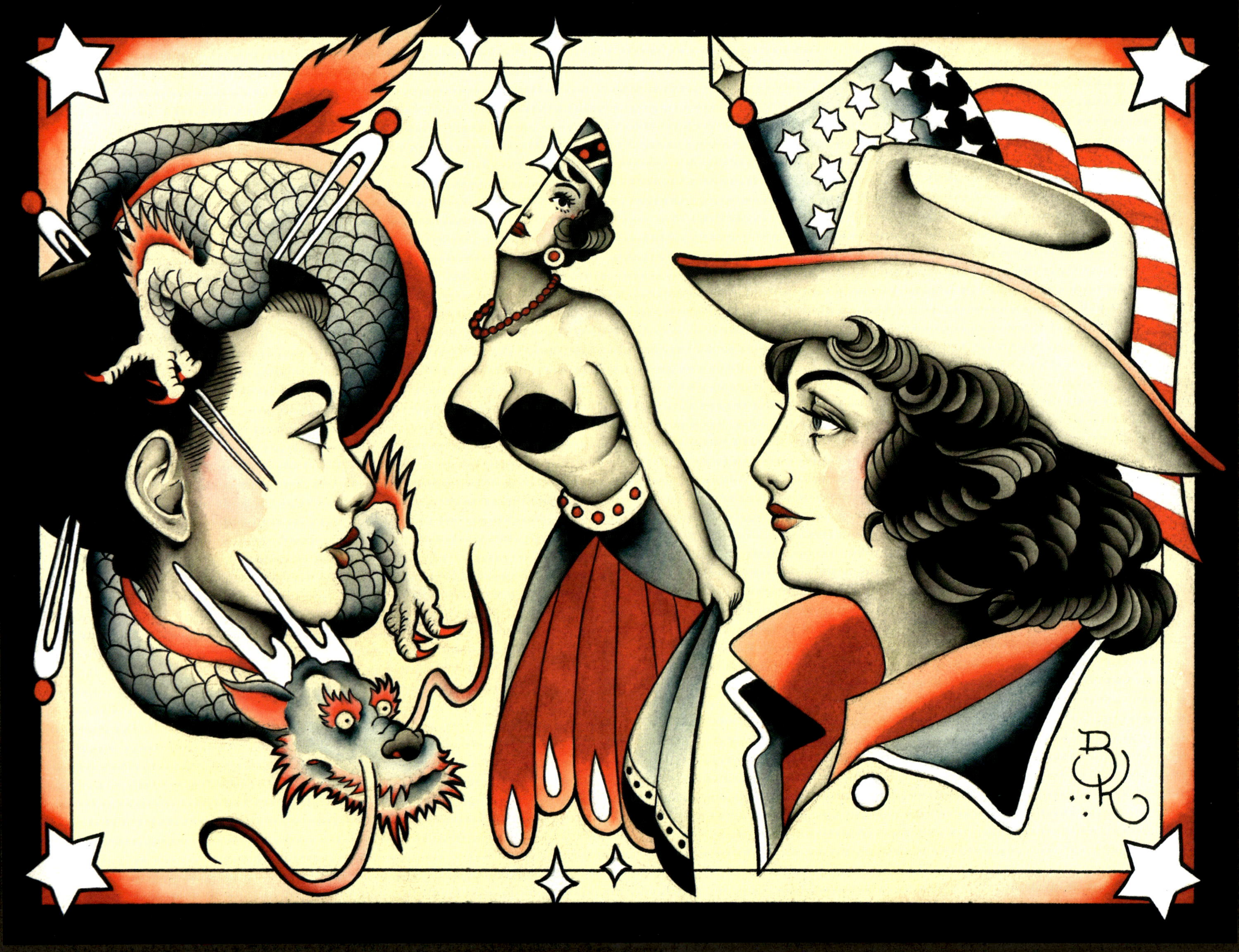

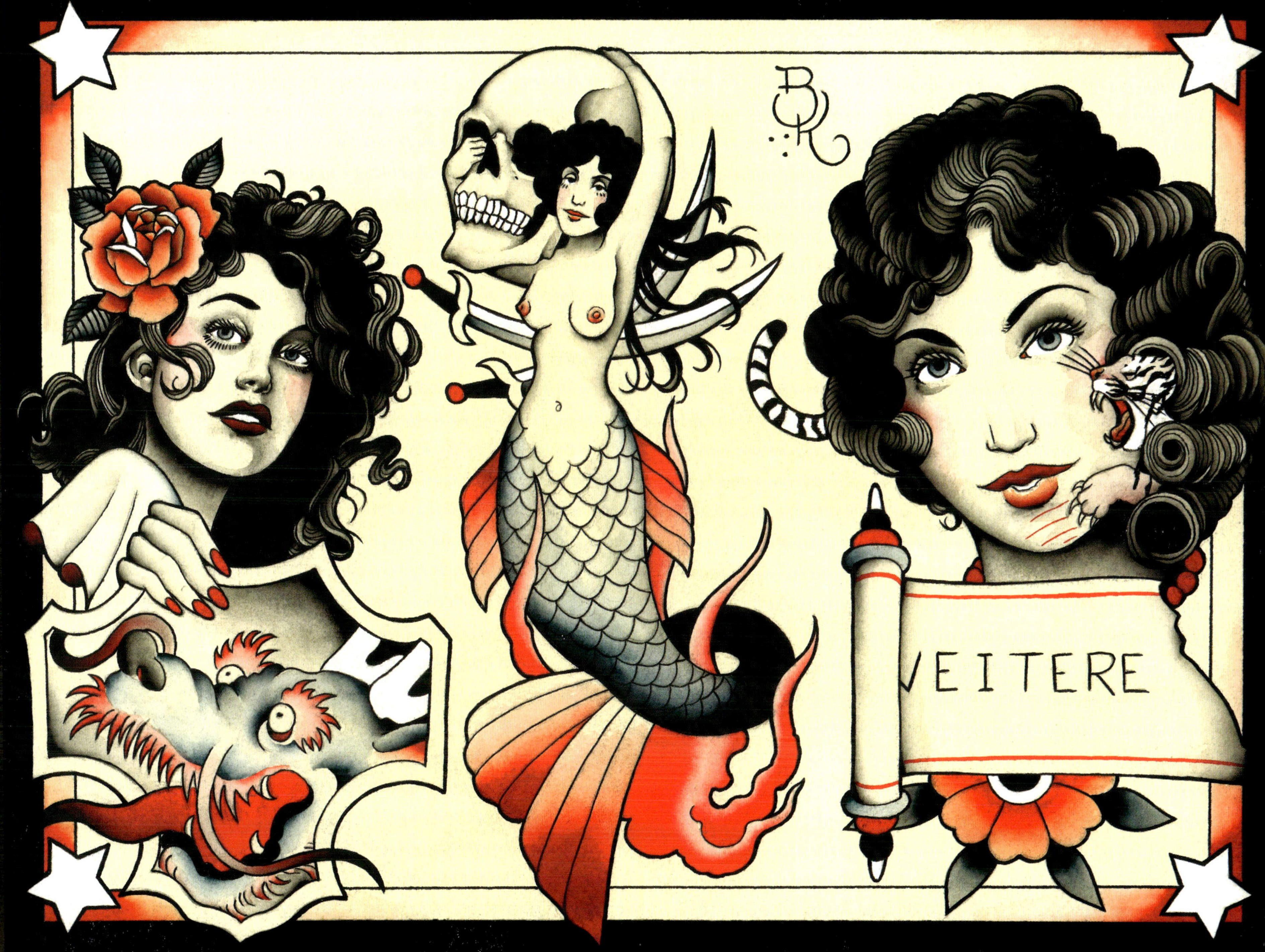
VEITERE

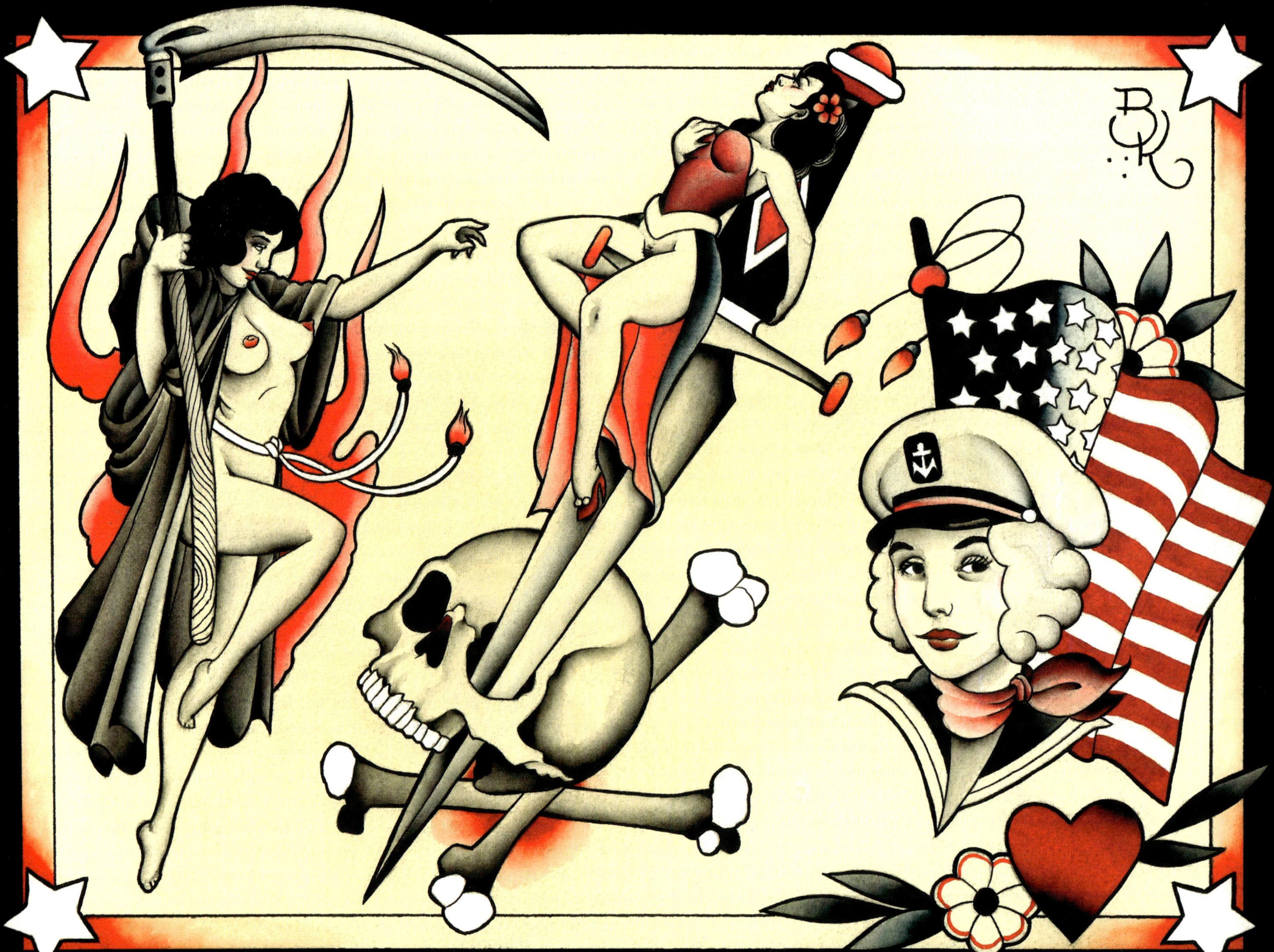

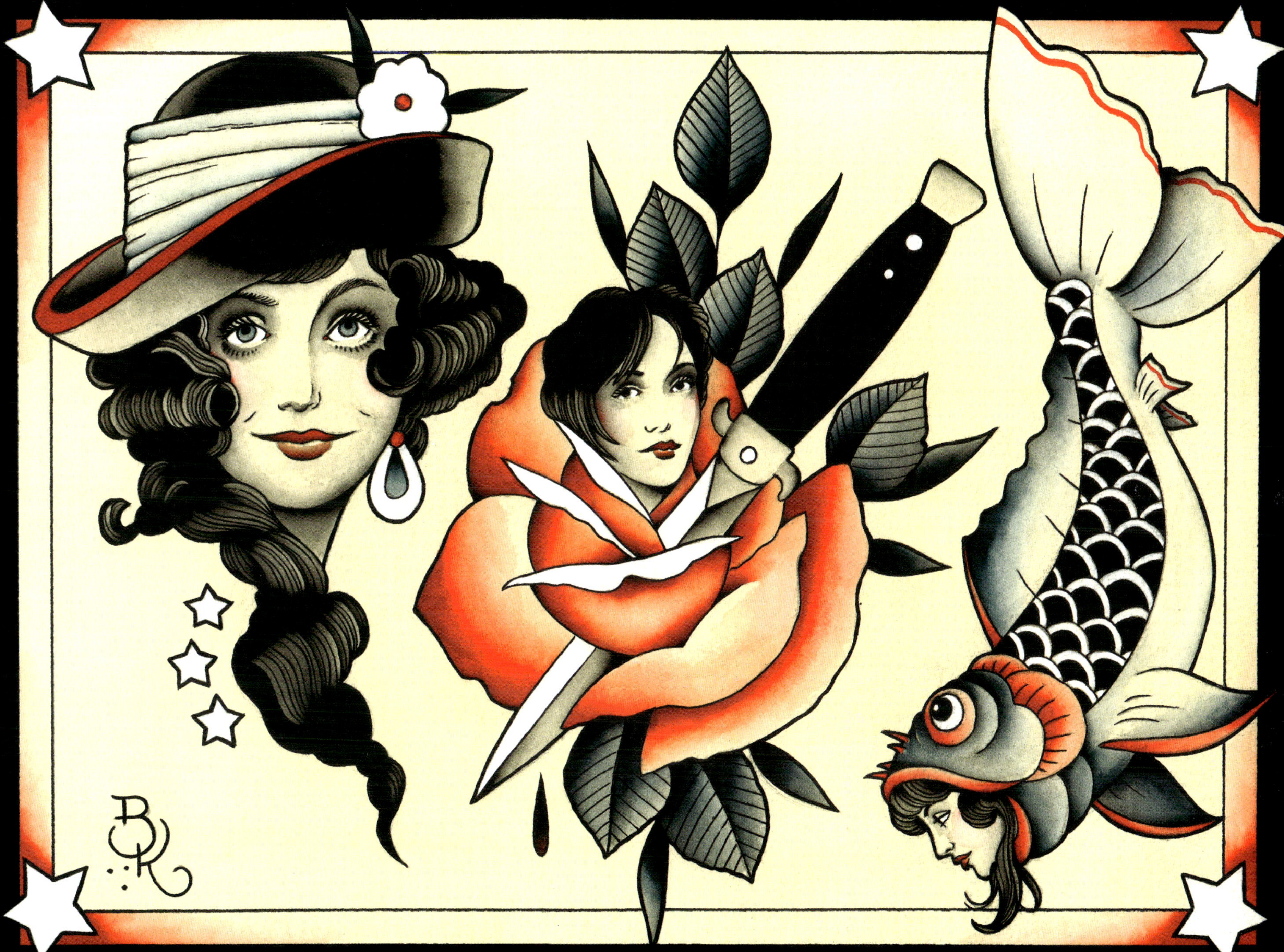

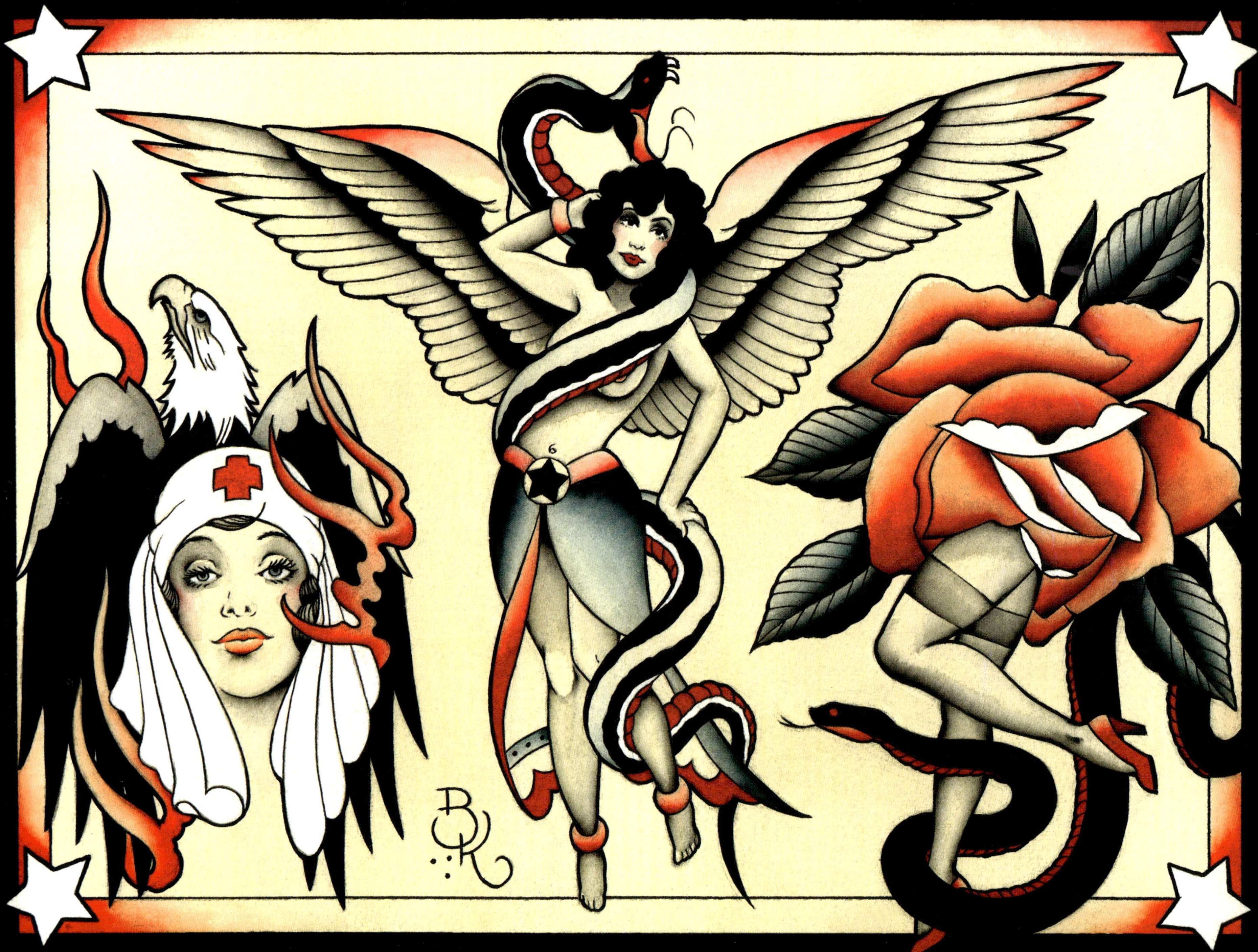

Acknowledgments

Thanks to all my tattoo customers and fans of my work. I love painting flash, and I love designing tattoos for you.

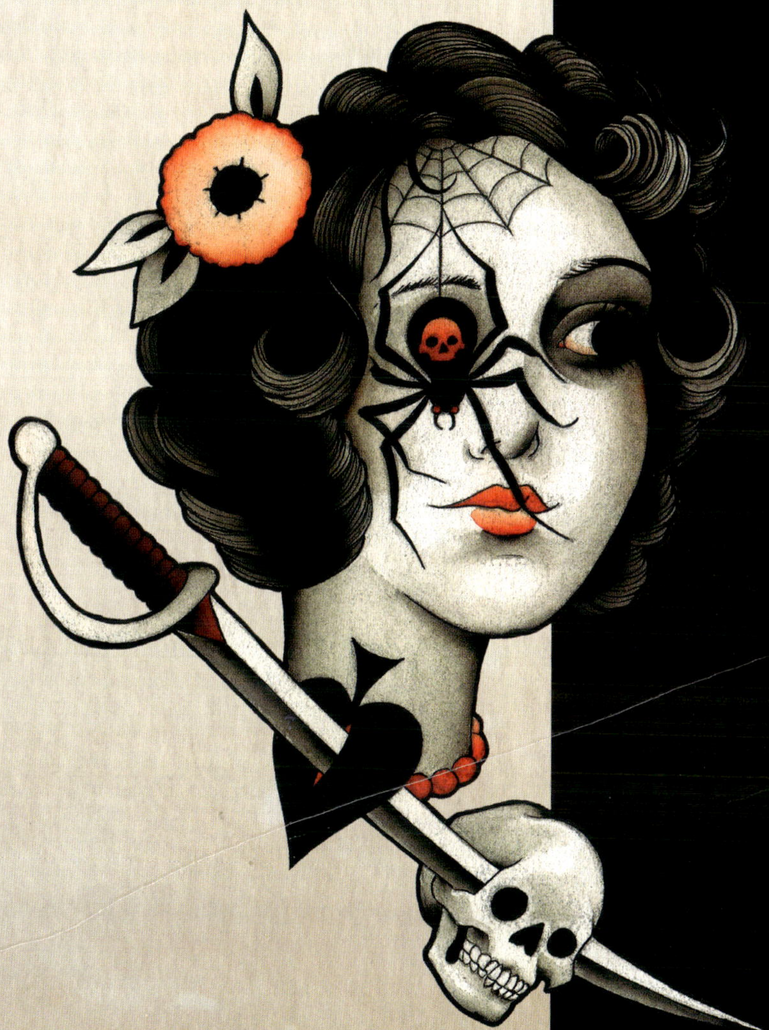

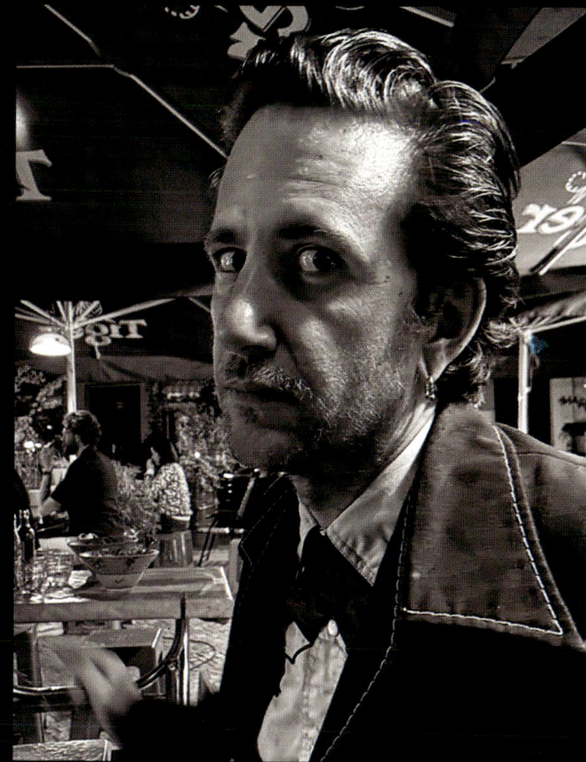

Brian Kelly has been tattooing since 2002, founding the Brian Kelly Army in the same year. He holds a BFA from the Minneapolis College of Art & Design and an MFA from the University of Galway in association with the Burren College of Art. With no direction home, Brian Kelly got lost and ended up in Berlin like everybody else. He now tattoos at Red Chapel Tattoo, by appointment only, in the lively artistic district of Friedrichshain in former East Berlin. He has lived in Berlin for the last decade, and somehow, his German is still not very good. This is Brian Kelly's second collection of tattoo flash. He is also a cartoonist and author of *Francis & The Vegas Tramps*.

www.briankellyarmy.com

@briankellyarmy